D1187519

Researching Western History

Researching Western History

Topics in the Twentieth Century

Edited by
Gerald D. Nash
and Richard W. Etulain

Foreword by Earl Pomeroy

University of New Mexico Press
Published in cooperation with the
University of New Mexico Center for the American West
Albuquerque

Library of Congress Cataloging-in-Publication Data

Researching western history : topics in the Twentieth Century / edited by Gerald D. Nash and Richard W. Etulain ; foreword by Earl Pomeroy. — 1st ed.
    p. cm.
  Includes index.
  Contents: Research opportunities in the economic history of the Twentieth-Century West / Gerald D. Nash — Research opportunities in Twentieth-Century western history : natural resources and environment / Thomas R. Cox — The impending western urban past : an essay on the Twentieth-Century West / Roger W. Lotchin — Research opportunities in Twentieth-Century western history : politics / Robert W. Cherny — Twentieth-Century western women : research issues and possibilities / Glenda Riley — Research opportunities in Twentieth-Century western cultural history / Richard W. Etulain — The enduring myth and the modern West / Fred Erisman — Research in a theater in the round / Gene M. Gressley.
  ISBN 0-8263-1758-8. — ISBN 0-8263-1759-6 (pbk.)
  1. West (U.S.) — History — 1890–1945 — Research. 2. West (U.S.)— History — 1945– —Research. 3. West (U.S.) — History — 1890–1945 — Historiography. 4. West (U.S.) — History — 1945– — Historiography. I. Nash, Gerald D. II. Etulain, Richard W.
  F595.R4 1997
  978′.0072—DC20
                                                                  96-9965
                                                                    CIP

Contents

Foreword

Earl Pomeroy

The published research cited in this volume recalls how much the concerns of historians of the American West have widened over the last half century. When Oscar O. Winther compiled the first edition of his bibliography of articles in periodicals on the history of the trans-Mississippi West, published in 1942, he drew on thirty-eight historical journals and four journals of political science, sociology, and general social science.[1] In second and third editions, published in 1961[2] and 1970,[3] historical journals increased to forty-three and forty-nine, while other journals, still the same four in 1961, increased to ten in 1970, adding coverage in economics, American Studies, literature, and folklore. Twenty-five years later, although the authors of these essays confine their citations to articles in periodicals to those that report significant research not represented in books, they draw also on serials in law, geography, ecology, urban studies, women's studies, ethnic studies, popular culture, the history of technology, urban history, and other fields.

The authors might have cast their nets still more widely. As studies that they cite indicate, readers who propose to go much beyond general surveys should look into work of legal historians, architects, urban planners, rural sociologists, demographers, anthropologists, and agricultural economists among members of other disciplines, and into publications of government agencies as well as of academically sponsored and recognized organizations. The published dictionary catalog of the Library of the Giannini Foundation of Agricultural Economics at Berkeley, for instance, conveniently indexes published materials on the social and economic history of the West, most fully on agriculture in California and its neighbors but extending over the entire country and including bulletins of the United States and state departments of agriculture and agricultural colleges as well as periodicals, books, and pamphlets.[4] When Frederick Jackson Turner prepared lists of references for his course on the history of the West, published 1911–22, he relied far more on general periodicals and government documents than on historical journals, especially for parts on the West after 1896.[5]

By 1922, two years before Turner retired from teaching, he took six of the fifty-three sections, as he called them, of his syllabus for the twentieth century, including a section on "The West in the World War and Reconstruction." Twenty of the topics that he suggested for theses emphasized or were confined to the 1890s and the twentieth century, including recent governors and other politicians, farmers' movements, and writers.[6] No substantial work on any of these topics appeared before he died in 1932. There are still no biographies of three of his twelve western writers or two of his three western governors, while work on several other figures still seems less than proportionate to the opportunities that they present. He also suggested topics that could have concerned the twentieth century at least as much as the nineteenth, including immigration of a foreign people, characteristics and influence of elements of different sectional and national origins, and the history of an Indian tribe. In view of the kinds of research he especially encouraged and applauded (as in the Wisconsin Domesday project, which Joseph Schafer developed at the State Historical Society in the 1920s), his disdain for approaches emphasizing exploration and combat, and his desire to substitute institutional analysis for antiquarian anecdote and to incorporate speculators along with homesteaders in accounts of occupation and settlement, we can imagine directions in which he might have guided his students as well as directions that would correspond more to concerns of later times.

The history of the twentieth-century West has become so active and fruitful a field of investigation that a review of condition and prospects has been long overdue. The trajectory of recent scholarship suggests that still another review will soon be in order. At once prompted and limited by contemporary concerns, we can only guess whether approaches to the past that we may propose will appeal to others and how long they may appeal even to ourselves. Meanwhile these essays should usefully inform both those who stop with reading the published product and those who go on to revise and add to it.

August 1996

Notes

1. Oscar O. Winther, ed., *The Trans-Mississippi West: A Guide to Its Periodical Literature (1811–1938)* (Bloomington: Indiana University Press, 1942).

2. Winther, *A Classified Bibliography of the Periodical Literature of the Trans-Mississippi West (1811–1957)* (Bloomington: Indiana University Press, 1961).

3. Winther and Richard A. Van Orman, *A Classified Bibliography of the Periodical Literature of the Trans-Mississippi West: A Supplement (1957–1967)* (Bloomington: Indiana University Press, 1970).

4. *Dictionary Catalog of the Giannini Foundation of Agricultural Economics Library, University of California, Berkeley* (12 vols.; Boston: G. K. Hall and Co., 1971). Although recently issued finding aids supplement the printed catalog for years since 1971, visiting the library should be rewarding for access to later entries as well as to holdings cataloged.

5. Frederick J. Turner and Frederick Merk, *List of References on the History of the West* (rev. ed.; Cambridge: Harvard University Press, 1922), 144–55.

6. Turner and Merk, *List of References,* 7–12.

Researching Western History

Introduction

Gerald D. Nash and Richard W. Etulain

Between 1960 and the waning years of the twentieth century the field of western American history underwent enormous expansion and profound changes. In 1960 most historians still wrote about the West as a frontier, and they restricted themselves to recording the years before 1890. But by the end of the century historians and social scientists were much more concerned with the West as a region and with its development in the one hundred years after 1890, the year Frederick Jackson Turner had designated as marking the demise of the frontier. In 1960 only a few scholars conceived of the West as a figment of the imagination, a West enshrined in myth, literature, art, music, and popular culture. A generation later a veritable small army labored to unravel the complexities of a West rooted in the perceptions of millions of people in the United States and around the world. In 1960 only a handful specialized in examining environmental themes in the West, for had not technology subordinated environmental influences to a secondary place? But a generation later environmental history occupied a central place within the broader spectrum of western studies. In 1960 the history of the West as it had been written dealt largely with the activities of men, usually of European backgrounds. By the 1990s awareness of gender and multicultural forces significantly broadened the field as historians wrote about the neglected roles of women, Hispanics, blacks, Asians, and other minorities, and reflected a much more positive appreciation of Native American cultures. And while in 1960 almost no one seriously delved into the development of cities in the West, by the end of the century a growing cadre of scholars had demonstrated that urban clusters rather than the frontier had defined much of western society and culture over a long span of years. By the end of the twentieth century, therefore, a new generation of scholars perceived the West in very different terms from their predecessors a few decades earlier.

What influences brought about these changes? The passage of time obviously had an impact—as in previous years. The general affluence of the 1950s imbued many Americans with a spirit of optimism that was very evident in writings about the West in 1960. But the succeeding generation lost much of that confidence, and an untainted faith in the idea of progress. By the end of the twentieth century self-doubts and pessimism had enveloped many who grew to maturity in this era, and this pervaded their perception of the nation's past. To them settlement of the West was not an unmitigated triumph. Rather, it was a sorry record of brutal exploitation of native peoples and minorities—even of genocidal proportions. It reflected the suppression of women, the despoliation of the environment, and the worst exploitative excesses of a capitalist system. Such strictures were fueled by the social criticisms of the New Left in the 1960s, and the deep disillusionment inspired by the Vietnam War among a broad spectrum of Americans. Their doubts were deepened further by the revelations of Watergate in the 1970s, and the crisis of the Nixon presidency. In the succeeding decade many younger academics were gripped by feelings of nihilism that gained academic respectability in the writings of Deconstructionists such as Paul De Man. By the last decade of the century a new generation of historians had come to view the West in very different terms from their predecessors just a few decades earlier.

No wonder, therefore, that many of those who wrote about the West after 1960 reflected a much greater concern with the West as a region rather than as a frontier. Such a perspective was much more viable near the end of the century than in 1960. Earlier, Americans looked back to more than a century of continental expansion characterized by a continually receding frontier line. But the enormous increase of population west of the Mississippi River—more than fivefold between 1900 and 1990—alerted historians to development of the area as a region, not a frontier. At the same time other historians increasingly devoted their energies to depicting the West as reflected in the realm of myth, art, literature, and music, as well as in television and moving pictures. A growing number of scholars came to focus on environmental influences in the shaping of the West, in marked contrast to the preceding generation, who had stressed the primacy of cultural factors. The changing roles of women and minorities in American society also left a deep impact on studies of the West as these approaches attracted a significant number of younger scholars. And urban historians provided new perspectives for an understanding of the West in the twentieth century as they stressed that it was primarily an area dominated by cities rather than rural or sparsely populated areas.

Although these varied approaches ranged over diverse spheres of the Western experience they also shared one common theme—an increasing emphasis on the West in the twentieth century. In 1960 only a few books or articles touched on the West after 1890. By the end of the century an increasing stream of such writings characterized the historiography of the West. In fact, in the last two decades, the twentieth-century West has rapidly emerged as a promising new frontier in the region's historiography. In the 1960s and 1970s an intrepid group of historians and journalists bridged the chasm of the 1890s and moved into the unfamiliar ground of the modern West. Supplying pioneer overviews of the new West, these writers have marked fresh trails for later arrivals to broaden and lengthen.

During the last generation, historians Earl Pomeroy and Gerald D. Nash furnished the most notable overviews of the modern West. Not only did Pomeroy's *The Pacific Slope* (1965) and Nash's *The American West in the Twentieth Century* (1973) provide valuable interpretive frameworks for studying the new West, they demonstrated how much historical research was still needed before other broad-based syntheses could be undertaken. Their pathbreaking works, along with a new crop of recent monographs, have proved particularly useful to such historians as Patricia Nelson Limerick, Richard White, Michael P. Malone, and Richard W. Etulain, authors of the latest overviews of western history.

Concurrently, journalists like Neil Morgan, Neal R. Peirce, and Peter Wiley and Robert Gottlieb produced readable and sometimes controversial introductions to the twentieth-century West. Utilizing both regional and state-by-state approaches characterized by lively narrative writing and useful analysis, Morgan and Peirce furnished still-useful glimpses of the post-1900 West, whereas Wiley and Gottlieb focused on the greater Southwest, its politicos, and power brokers, thereby producing a pessimistic revisionistic volume stressing clash and conflict.

The major purpose of this volume is to encourage additional study of the history of the twentieth-century West by providing specific research suggestions. We are under no illusions that our modest proposals are either all-embracing or complete. They are designed to be suggestive, not definitive; open-ended, not exclusive. Research agendas are never fixed, but in constant flux. Yet the final decade of the century seemed an appropriate time to urge a group of noted scholars to discuss research needs in their particular specialties. This volume contains the fruits of their endeavors.

The blueprints drawn here will undoubtedly influence work in the field for the next generation. Although contributors use previous publications as points of departure, they stress projects that need to be undertaken and suggest conceptions and interpretations central to carrying out these many research projects. During the next few years, we hope scholars and students will cite these essays as pivotal to their historical research and writing about the modern West.

At the same time, essayists have not been straitjacketed into a uniform format. They have been encouraged, while pointing out research needs in their respective fields, to adopt an organization that works well for their topic. Some authors have stressed a range of specific subjects and subtopics meriting new or additional research; others have utilized an overarching conception to structure their comments; and still others have combined specific and general commentaries in covering their topics. All writers, however, focus their essays on research opportunities their subjects offer.

The organization of the volume reflects still another planned diversity. Whereas some of the essays cover traditional topics such as economic, political, and cultural history, others discuss fresh trends in American and western American historiography such as those dealing with gender, environment, and the mythic West. Furthermore, readers will find that authors, although dealing with several requisite subtopics of their field, have been free to emphasize subjects within their areas that other specialists might have omitted. The diversity of topics and the variety of approaches clearly augment the value of the collection.

This volume also supplements the half-dozen or so other recent treatments of western historiography. Essayists in Michael P. Malone's *Historians and the American West* (1983) and Roger Nichols's *American Frontier and Western Issues* (1986), two indispensable guides for students and scholars of western history, summarize and frequently evaluate previous writings but do not plot out research needs in their discussions. Meanwhile, contributors to volumes edited by John R. Wunder (*Historians of the American Frontier: A Bio-Bibliographical Sourcebook*, 1988) and Richard W. Etulain (*Writing Western History: Essays on Major Western Historians*, 1991) treat individual frontier or western historians without suggesting research prospects in western historical writing. Finally, Gerald D. Nash, in *Creating the West: Historical Interpretations 1890–1990*, (1991) supplies a much-needed overview of the major trends in western historiography, but he too eschews providing a research agenda for the next generation. The present collection, then, is unique in furnishing a full discussion of the manifold research opportunities in twentieth-century western history.

The subject areas that have been included embrace a wide spectrum. Gerald D. Nash touches on selected topics related to economic development. Thomas R. Cox casts a wide net in his discussion of natural resources and environment, likely to be a major theme in the twenty-first century. Roger W. Lotchin skillfully explores the potentials of urban history facing scholars of the West. Robert W. Cherny uncovers the many opportunities that await scholars delving into the political history of the region after 1890. Glenda Riley provides a masterful discussion in the exciting field of western women's history. Richard W. Etulain provides new dimensions for those seeking to explore the varied facets of cultural development in the West during the last century. Fred Erisman skillfully initiates his readers into the complex domain of the West of the mind—the West of myth. Gene Gressley provides a delightful overview, in addition to providing his own insights into the dimensions of the subject. All of us engaged in this volume share a hope that it will achieve one of its prime objectives—to stimulate research and writing about a still underdeveloped area of western history, the twentieth-century West.

1

Research Opportunities in the Economic History of the Twentieth-Century West

Gerald D. Nash

Almost a century has passed since 1900, yet the economic history of the twentieth-century West remains still largely unwritten. This leaves a gap not only in the historical record, but creates a void for the makers of public policy. In the twenty-first century economic and environmental issues are bound to take the center stage in public discussion. By the 1990s Americans have come to realize that they lost the far-reaching competitive edge in the world economy they possessed a generation earlier. No longer is the American economy preeminent. The challenge for Americans in the twenty-first century is to regain the momentum that they demonstrated so effectively during the first six decades of the twentieth century. It was then that the economy of the American West was the newest—and often most dynamic—segment of American life. The experience of the West in those years is relevant not only to that of other underdeveloped countries around the world; it may also provide suggestive guidelines for economic dynamism and expansion such as will be needed in the future if the United States is to continue as a major competitive player in world markets. Thus, a more fully developed body of studies concerning the economic history of the West since 1890 can provide policymakers with possible directions for the future.

The closing decade of the twentieth century is thus an appropriate time for such stocktaking, for reviewing what has been done, for assessing gaps large and small, and for identifying those phases of the West's economic development that would benefit from further inquiry. Such an inventory can deal with broad general studies of the field as well as with works dealing with particular industries, whether agriculture, mining, business, finance, or manufacturing. Other categories include spheres of public policies affecting the economy at both the federal and the state levels. The history of institutions, corporations, or trade associations would be prime examples. Many aspects of the development of labor in the West are still obscure. And although the twentieth century was a corporate age, the role of individual entrepreneurs and managers cannot be wholly ignored. Thus, biographical studies are needed to illuminate that vital human element that, as Joseph Schumpeter demonstrated so well, plays an essential role in economic progress. The history of economic ideas, and approaches to economic growth, provides still another dimension to the subject, to an assessment of both successes and failures. Certainly this range of needed work is neither exhaustive nor complete, but it can indicate at least a portion of the territory that still needs to be explored.

Among the most obvious gaps are general surveys that cover the economic history of the West since 1890. Surprisingly, the last time that a historian made an initial effort toward such a synthesis was in 1911, when Katherine Coman published *Economic Beginnings of the Far West.*[1] Is it not time again to think of such a comprehensive general work that views one hundred years of western economic growth in its totality? We need a broad overview, with some conceptual framework that could suggest directions for more specialized scholars in the field. The twentieth century has been momentous for the economic development of the West—more so than any previous period. Such a volume might trace the far-ranging impact of technology—on transportation, agriculture, manufacturing, service, and electronics industries. It would assess the impact of America's wars on the West: the shock of World War I, the transforming influence of World War II, and the far-flung effects of the Korean and Vietnam embroglios. It would perhaps have some focus on entrepreneurship in the creation of new industries, on finance, on tourism, and on the burgeoning computer complexes that grew in many of the new western cities. It would pay attention to the rise of the urban centers of the West and their impact on the surrounding countryside. It would analyze a changing labor force as an increasing percentage of women, blacks, Asians, and Hispanics diversified what had been a largely Anglo homogeneous population at the beginning of the century. In short, broad overviews would provide a context and a perspective that are now missing in the field.

We are in need of historical studies of particular industries. One of those prominent in the nineteenth century was the mining industry, and historians wrote a goodly number of detailed works to illuminate its development. But for the twentieth century we have virtually none at the moment. Yet, throughout much of the 1890–1990 period, the West produced more than 90 percent of all the minerals in the United States. If mining no longer occupied as central a place in the American economy as before 1890, it was still a major source of income for many western states. The economies of Montana, Utah, Colorado, New Mexico, Arizona, and Nevada were heavily dependent on minerals production during these years. Copper, tin, molybdenum, and magnesium may not be as glamorous as gold and silver—but quantity production gave them considerable importance in the western economy.[2] Nor should petroleum be excluded from this category.

The activities of miners' associations that served as representative spokespersons and lobbyists for small- and medium-sized mining operators have received very little attention. In the twentieth century they reveal a great deal about the problems and issues facing small miners in a corporate economy. Thus, the Mining Association of the Southwest, headquartered in Los Angeles during World War II, lobbied desperately for federal aid for the construction of access roads to small mines eager to participate in war production. Small miners who banded together in the Western Mining Council protested vehemently against the World War II policies of the War Production Board, which they charged was dominated by large corporations in the industry. That agency also prohibited all gold mining during World War II, an experience that invites a detailed study by some younger up and coming historian. And the price ceilings enforced by the Office of Price Administration limited the operations of thousands of Western miners, some of whom channeled their complaints through the Arizona Small Mine Operators Association.[3] Activities of such groups at the grass roots reveal a great deal about the nature of the mining industry in an increasingly corporate America, yet at present, in the absence of detailed studies of their operations, their influence is largely obscure.

A major study is needed of federal policies in the western mining industry during the twentieth century. Throughout much of this period the federal government undertook a national stockpiling policy that had far-flung implications. Congress inaugurated this program in 1939 and expanded and modified it in ensuing decades. Essentially, public policymakers hoped to strike some balance between reliance on foreign imports, on the one hand, and domestic producers, on the other. This created bitter conflicts between large global multinational corporations in the industry and tens of thousands of small domestic miners. By and large, Congress listened more to the large corporate interests. They shaped national minerals policies not only on the basis of economic interests, but also in relation to considerations of national security and foreign policy.[4] This is a major subject requiring broadly gauged analysis.

After the Second World War, federal and state regulations increasingly affected western mining operations, especially with the growth of environmental consciousness. Along with Congress, state legislatures extended safety and environmental standards that directly affected operations in the industry. This was particularly true of strip mining of western coal after 1950, which enjoyed a revival after having declined in the 1880s. Detailed studies of these policies and the controversies they engendered in localities and states are needed. Federal, state, and corporate archives hold many of the records that would facilitate such research.[5]

One aspect of minerals exploitation in the West that has received some attention is petroleum. Despite a large literature on some aspects of the subject—such as international diplomacy—historians have devoted much less attention to examining its role in western development. The history of the industry in western states such as California and New Mexico, and Kansas after 1920, remains to be written. Gerald T. White analyzed the operations of the Standard Oil Company of California in great detail, but his volume only extends to 1919, and a historian is still needed to examine the role of petroleum thereafter, also in the much broader context of the state's economy. This would also include consideration of major independent producers and refiners, and the unique system of state regulation adopted by Californians. The impact of the oil industry on the southern part of the state needs to be detailed. Environmental historians are needed to study the pollution problems that arose as early as in the years from 1880 to 1914. These difficulties involved water contamination and seepage, both important public issues even in the early days of the industry. Similarly, the struggles between state and federal officials over off-shore drilling and the tidelands between 1914 and 1960 would reveal much about the nature of federalism in developing environmental policies.[6]

An excellent study of oil-shale development in Colorado appeared in 1989, but the long history of federal efforts to develop synthetic gasoline—at the Colorado School of Mines, at a pilot plant in Grand Forks, North Dakota, at facilities in Laramie, Wyoming, Rifle, Colorado, and elsewhere—remains buried in archives. Yet Congress appropriated funds for research on synthetic fuels for more than sixty years. As a source of energy that since 1914 provided Germany with a substantial percentage of its needs, it merits serious attention.[7]

Despite the fact that agriculture has been a mainstay of the western economy since the nineteenth century, it has not been an appealing subject for historians. No one has attempted a general history of agriculture in the West—such as is available for the North and South. The impact of mechanization on western farming in the years after 1920 is a story with many gaps. Little is known about agricultural trends on lands owned by Native Americans. What has been the impact of specialized training on Indian farmers? More studies of this nature would also be of practical use to policymakers and would clarify the relationships between modernization and traditionalism among Indian agriculturists. The impact of federal farm policies in western states awaits historical research. Nor have the policies of state departments of agriculture been subjected to serious scholarly scrutiny. One wonders how these affected large, medium-sized, and small operators. Is the image of western farming as a family-oriented enterprise accurate? The history of western agriculture in particular time periods is untouched. Paul W. Gates wrote a fine synthesis of the history of agriculture between 1815 and 1860, but no similar studies exist for any period within the twentieth century. Even the role of western agriculture during a major conflagration such as the Second World War has gone unnoticed.[8]

In the West no mention of agriculture can ignore the vital element of water. In the last two decades a growing number of scholars have devoted their attention to the subject and have done much to clarify major trends. Yet the subject has hardly been exhausted. Biographical studies of key individuals in the development of water policies would add a human dimension to the subject. Just as state engineer William Ham Hall was an important influence on water policies in California during the 1880s, so Stephen Reynolds in New Mexico, state engineer for more than three decades after 1945, had considerable impact, not only in his own state but throughout the Southwest. The influences of Spanish as well as Indian legal doctrines on water law in the Southwest beckons to discerning scholars seeking to examine the ethnic and cultural impact on water usage in the West.[9]

The history of business in the West during the twentieth century remains largely unexplored. That has not deterred various writers from making broad generalizations about business development in the region, however. Peter Wiley and Robert Gottlieb in *Empires in the Sun*, for example, have characterized the West as a colony of giant corporations that greedily exploit its resources for private profit. A similar theme pervades the indictment of Patricia Limerick in *The Legacy of Conquest* concerning the settlement of the West. But such strictures seem to be based not on a careful examination of evidence drawn from primary sources and on archives, but on a particular set of preconceptions, or "Weltanschauung."

Certainly, ideological perceptions can serve a useful purpose. A case in point is the experience of small business people in the West during World War II mobilization. Under the influence of the War Department, the armed forces awarded a very large percentage of new government contracts to large, rather than small, business firms. Western congressmen and senators as well as state legislators carried on a running battle with agencies in Washington to garner a larger share of government awards for small businesses in the West. Such efforts by the champions of small business have not yet been described in detail. They included the efforts of men like senators James E. Murray of Montana or Pat McCarran of Nevada. Both were major actors in the fight between small and large business. Nor has anyone so far studied the activities of the Smaller War Plants Corporation in its attempts to enlarge small business enterprises in the West. Its records are rather complete in the National Archives, awaiting the arrival of a diligent historian. And the personal papers of its dynamic

chairman, Maury Maverick—one of the most flamboyant western politicians of his day—are at the University of Texas. Scholarly analysis of particular phases of western business development can provide substantial
evidence on which to base broad generalizations about entrepreneurship
in the West.[10]

The impact of the military establishment on business—sometimes
identified as the military-industrial complex—has begun to attract the
attention it deserves. The influences of military bases and related installations on western communities have been a major factor in the region's
growth. Roger Lotchin has made a very impressive case for the significance to the West of the military in the development of California cities.
His study provides a model that others could follow in an analysis of
selected western cities. The impact on particular states in the West still
remains to be explored on a national level. Lotchin has analyzed the economic impact of military spending in World War I—indicating that fruitful studies with particular reference to individual western states would
clarify the subject. Other scholars are now engaged in assessing the military impact on the West as region—including federal contracts and science installations.[11]

Any study of business leads sooner or later to the field of finance,
another area requiring more intensive cultivation. The history of banking in the West was recently opened up by the fine general survey of Larry
Schweikart and Lynn Doti, which points to a whole range of topics requiring more intensive investigation. These include histories of banking
in particular states. Although Schweikart also published a survey for Arizona, and Smallwood for Oklahoma, other western states still await their
bank histories. The history of state banking regulation, of insurance companies, and of corporate securities is still largely untouched. Histories of
individual banks, such as Thomas Noel's study of the Colorado National
Bank, can be fruitful. Biographies of leading western bankers are far and
few between. Gerald D. Nash published a biography of A. P. Giannini,
founder of the Bank of America, but studies of other major figures are still
needed— men like Isaias Hellman and his family, or John Fugazi, one of
the most prominent Italian-American business entrepreneurs in the United
States and the man who founded the Columbus Savings and Loan Society
in San Francisco in 1893. Similarly, William H. Crocker, son of the Big
Four Southern Pacific railroad magnate, was president of San Francisco's
Crocker-Woolworth Bank and one of the state's most important finan-
ciers in the twentieth century. Other significant figures include Lewis
Douglas in Arizona and Marriner Eccles of Utah, who served as chair of
the Federal Reserve Board during the New Deal.[12]

Banking also provides an important perspective on the development
of ethnic groups in the West. Many banks were begun by immigrants who
found themselves stymied by well-established older bankers who viewed

them with mistrust. Giannini's Bank of Italy, for example, by 1928 established separate ethnic divisions, not only for Italians and Irish, but for Arabs, Russians and Chinese, Germans, French, and Japanese as well as Poles, Greeks, and Yugoslavs. In each case, Giannini required managers and staff to speak their particular language and to develop business policies of special relevance to them. The Bank of America archives contain many records bearing on this chapter of the immigrant experience, a chapter as significant in business as in ethnic history.[13]

Since much of the West was settled only after the initial stages of the Industrial Revolution had already affected the Northeast and Midwest during the nineteenth century, manufacturing in this new region never attained the importance it had acquired in the older sections. Indeed, before 1945 manufactures contributed less than 12 percent of the total income of most western states. Nevertheless, during the twentieth century westerners consistently hoped to increase manufactures. Historians have yet to provide detailed histories of these efforts. Between 1900 and 1940, for example, various entrepreneurs unsuccessfully attempted to develop a steel industry in the Pacific Northwest. Eastern capitalists built only relatively small facilities in Pueblo, Colorado, and Provo, Utah. But World War II gave a boost to these efforts as the federal government provided funds with which Henry Kaiser built a new plant in Fontana, California, and the U.S. Steel Company expanded the Geneva Works in Provo. Neither operation has received detailed coverage, nor has the opposition of eastern steel-company executives to the growth of a western steel industry.[14] In addition, the basing point system retarded western manufactures. While Earl Latham wrote a superb analysis of the impact of the basing point system with emphasis on the southern economy before 1950, no scholar has as yet written a similar study to assess the impact of basing points on the West.[15]

The history of particular industries in the twentieth-century West still remains to be written. Although aircraft and missile manufacturing has been a significant part of the western economy since World War I, we still do not have a comprehensive history of its development. Nor are histories of individual aircraft companies available. Even industry giants such as the Boeing Company of Seattle lacks a definitive history, although that company has done more to be aware of its historical record than the major companies of southern California.[16]

Similarly, it is puzzling that the shipbuilding industry on the Pacific Coast has not found a historian in the last generation. Before World War I, western shipyards produced mainly small vessels for the Pacific fishing and ocean trade. They boomed temporarily in wartime, and then became moribund between 1919 and 1939, with the exception of U.S. naval shipyards such as the one at Mare Island. Their dramatic expansion during World War II has not yet been detailed. Nor has the wartime shipbuilding activity of Denver found a careful scholar. Although half a century has elapsed since American entry into World War II, the history of the western shipbuilding industry is still unwritten.[17]

World War II brought expansion of many industries in the West, of which aluminum was among the more important. Before 1941 the West processed virtually no aluminum. But the wartime need for aircraft led the federal government to invest more than 100 million dollars in the industry, resulting in the construction of seven new plants west of the Mississippi River, most in the Pacific Northwest where electric power was cheap. In 1945 the Defense Plant Corporation sold these plants at a fraction of their original cost to private enterprises, including the Aluminum Company of America, Henry J. Kaiser, and Reynolds Metals Company.[18] Just what their impact was on the western economy between 1945 and 1990 is not clear since that development in these years has been ignored by historians.

In addition, in 1942 the war prompted federal construction of the world's largest magnesium plant at Henderson, Nevada, just outside the sleepy little community of Las Vegas. Employing fourteen thousand people, the facility gave birth to a new nearby town (Henderson) that in succeeding years became a suburb of Greater Las Vegas. Although the federal government closed Basic Magnesium in 1944, during the next half-century various chemical and manufacturing enterprises utilized the plant. Extensive archives relating to the history of Basic Magnesium are stored in the National Archives, while state and local historical depositories contain rich holdings that would allow an enterprising scholar to do justice to the subject.[19]

But as every student of the western economy knows, the twentieth century was characterized not so much by the expansion of basic manufacturing industries as by the growth of the service sector. That included not only financial or health services, but tourism and the increasingly important military-industrial complex. Although tourism has been a major source of income for most western states, historians have not given it much attention. When Earl Pomeroy pioneered with his book on nineteenth-century tourism in 1957, his colleagues in the profession largely ignored it for nearly three decades. Only in the 1980s did scholars begin to take the subject seriously. John Findlay published his history of gambling and approached Disneyland and Sun City, Arizona, not only as cultural icons, but as beacons for tourism.[20] Environmental historians who have written about the natural wonders of the West, and its national parks, invariably have to deal with tourism. Yet much of the story dealing with the economic dimension of tourism remains to be told, such as the activities of local boosters—whether in Colorado Springs or numerous other western communities. Successive generations of hotel operators, resort developers, and publicists developed images of the West for Americans.

They also provided facilities for all strata of the population, from rich to poor, and facilitated temporary realization of their dreams. If Hollywood served as America's dream factory, the West served as America's playland, not only because of its scenic wonders, but because boosters persuaded Americans that it allowed them a realization of their fantasies.

The history of health industries has been fragmentary. Several studies have explored the attractions of the West for health seekers and an older population. A few studies of major hospitals have appeared. Still, not only southern California, but Denver, Phoenix, Tucson, and El Paso, as well as scores of smaller communities, became magnets for health seekers after 1914. The economic impact of hospitals and medical establishments, in major centers such as Denver and San Francisco, as significant parts of western service industries invites attention.[21]

During much of the twentieth century westerners were heavily dependent on military expenditures for sustained economic growth in the region. Already by 1900 the volume of such expenditures was significant. As Roger Lotchin has demonstrated persuasively, the growth of western cities such as San Diego, Los Angeles, San Francisco, and Seattle was profoundly influenced by their function as naval bases. Through large-scale construction and maintenance of large annual payrolls, the U.S. Navy affected a myriad of people and business establishments in these communities. Although the United States was involved in the First World War for only eighteen months, the expansion of army training camps gave a decided boost to the economy of the West. The records of this experience have remained largely unused in the National Archives and offer exciting opportunities for research. Examinations of other western cities in subsequent years are likely to result in fruitful findings as well.[22]

Any discussion of manufacturing and service industries invariably underscores the importance of government at all levels in the economic development of the West. Despite the image of many westerners that they have been exemplars of rugged individualism, the historical record reveals otherwise. Just as the West in the nineteenth century was to a large extent the creation of the federal government, so in the twentieth century Congress continued to be a major investor in the region. Whether through direct grants to the states, extensive irrigation, reclamation, and water development programs, or through establishment of scientific laboratories and scores of military installations, government poured millions of dollars annually into the western economy. In many spheres this huge investment dwarfed the efforts of private enterprisers. Needed, therefore, are more detailed studies of large corporate enterprises in the West.[23]

While western historians have written extensively about the development of transportation in the region during the nineteenth century, the literature on this subject is much sparser for the last one hundred years. No general survey—such as that written by George Rogers Taylor for the years from 1815 to 1860—exists. Has a preoccupation with race, class, and gender between 1970 and 1990 drawn attention away from other fundamental subjects relating to economic development? Fortunately, environmental historians have been more sensitive to the relation of ecology to transportation—which provides themes for exploring aspects of transportation history.

If the twentieth century was not a period of growth for western railroads, but one of contraction and consolidation, nevertheless historians should not fail to record these developments. Yet the history of western railroads after 1900 is mostly unwritten. For the nineteenth century it was clearly important to discern the economic impact of railroads on communities, as Robert Fogel did in his studies. But it is no less important to evaluate the results of the withdrawal of railway service during the second half of the twentieth century. This was a period of dominance of the automobile that significantly affected the spatial dimensions of most western communities. Declining railroads may not be as glamorous as those in the decades of expansion, but historians need to record not only growth, but decline as well.[24]

In recent years more historians have been attracted to study the influence of the automobile on western development, but air travel after 1930 has not yet received similar attention. The rapid growth of air carriers—of individual companies and their expansion—still needs to be recorded. The historical and economic impact of airport construction on western communities lies largely unexplored. Air travel changed the geographical and spatial position of many western cities. The once obscure and isolated town of Las Vegas in Nevada can serve as an example. Until 1940 it was merely a remote railroad stop, with very limited capacity for growth. But the development of jet travel after 1950 provided it with a totally different geographical identity. Like the spoke of a wheel, Las Vegas was now easily accessible to most large western cities—to Los Angeles, San Francisco, Seattle, Denver, Salt Lake City, Tucson, Phoenix, San Antonio, and El Paso. It was now in the center of the West's highly urbanized population.[25] It was hardly accidental, therefore, that western politicians were in the forefront of the movement to press for expansion of air travel in the region. One of the most vocal spokespersons for the industry after 1936 was Senator Pat McCarran of Nevada. He was also the author of the Civil Aeronautics Act of 1938 and other federal legislation affecting the industry. His role—and that of other politicians advocating regulation and deregulation of the airlines in the twentieth century—still awaits serious scholars.[26]

Much still needs to be done to clarify the history of workers and of labor in the West. Strikes have been most attractive to historians, whether in the Colorado or Arizona mining regions during the first three decades of the century. A few books have also recorded the travails of California farm workers during the Great Depression. But thereafter the literature becomes more sparse. The experiences of workers in the West during World War II remains largely unwritten. The efforts of women and blacks, for example, to secure full membership in the AFL Boilermaker's Union in California, Oregon, and Washington is still an obscure saga, although that union controlled most jobs in the Pacific Coast shipbuilding industry. Nor have the special problems of women in the California aircraft industry from 1940 to 1945 received attention, although females constituted half of the labor force. After 1950 the increase of Mexican workers added a distinctive element to wage earners in the West, but unlike social scientists, few historians have sought to describe the history of this movement and its effects.[27]

This brief inventory of selected topics in the economic history of the twentieth-century West is obviously highly selective and very incomplete. It is designed to be suggestive only, and in no way exhaustive. Historical fashions come and go, and interests change over time. Yet it is quite likely that the preoccupations of many historians in the last quarter-century will eventually be revised in the future. If historical experience of the Nazi, fascist, Stalinist, and communist eras since 1933 is any guide, soundly researched empirical studies are relevant to any period, and age more gracefully than strident calls to social action.

Notes

1. Katherine Coman, *Economic Beginnings of the Far West* (New York: Macmillan Company, 1911).

2. Russell R. Elliott, *Nevada's Twentieth-Century Mining Boom: Tonopah, Goldfield, Ely* (Reno: University of Nevada Press, 1966); Michael P. Malone, *The Battle for Butte: Mining and Politics on the Northern Frontier, 1864–1906* (Seattle: University of Washington Press, 1981); Ronald C. Brown, *Hard Rock Miners: The Intermountain West 1860–1920* (College Station: Texas A & M Press, 1979).

3. Duane A. Smith, *Mining America: The Industry and the Environment, 1800–1980* (Lawrence: University Press of Kansas, 1987). A brief account of western mining during the Second World War is in Gerald D. Nash, *World War II and the West: Reshaping the Economy* (Lincoln: University of Nebraska Press, 1990), 18–40.

4. A start for investigators into this topic can be made in the records of the War Production Board at the National Archives in Washington, D.C., and in manuscript collections of Donald Nelson at the Henry E. Huntington Library in San Marino, and the Harold Ickes Papers at the Library of Congress in Washington, D.C.

5. A fine broad study is by William S. Graebner, *Coal Mining Safety in the Progressive Period: The Political Economy of Reform* (Lexington: University of Kentucky Press, 1976). See also James Whiteside, *Regulating Danger: The Struggle for Mine Safety in the Rocky Mountain Coal Industry* (Lincoln: University of Nebraska

Press, 1990); Phyllis Smith, *Once a Coal Miner: The Story of Colorado's Northern Coal Field* (Boulder: Pruett Publishing, 1989), and Raye C. Ringholz, *Uranium Frenzy: Boom and Bust on the Colorado Plateau* (New York: W. W. Norton, 1989).

6. On literature before 1970, see Gerald D. Nash, "Oil in the West: Reflections on the Historiography of an Unexplored Field," *Pacific Historical Review* 39 (May 1970): 193–204; Gerald T. White, *Formative Years in the Far West: A History of Standard Oil Company of California and Predecessors through 1919* (New York: Appleton-Century-Crofts, 1962); Joe S. Bain, *The Economics of the Pacific Coast Petroleum Industry*, 3 vols. (Berkeley: University of California Press, 1944–1947). For a brief glimpse of Ickes's efforts on synthetic fuels, see U.S. Department of the Interior, *Annual Report* 1944 (Washington, D.C.: U.S.G.P.O, 1945), 73, 84.

7. On oil shale in Colorado, see Andrew Gulliford, *Boomtown Blues: Colorado Oil Shale, 1885–1985* (Niwot: University Press of Colorado, 1989).

8. Paul W. Gates, *The Farmer's Age: Agriculture 1815–1860* (New York: Holt, Rinehart and Winston, 1960). A few studies have touched on the years after 1910, including Leonard J. Arrington, "Western Agriculture and the New Deal," *Agricultural History* 44 (October 1970): 337–53; and James H. Shideler, ed., "Agriculture in the Development of the Far West: A Symposium," *Agricultural History* 49 (January 1975), a special 310-page issue. The Pueblo Cultural Resources Center, in Albuquerque, N.M., contains as yet unexploited manuscript and archival records that bear on the agricultural development of the Pueblo tribes. For a local study, see Richard G. Bremer, *Agricultural Change in an Urban Age: The Loup Country of Nebraska, 1910–1970* (Lincoln: University of Nebraska Press, 1976).

9. The literature of the last decade is extensive. A detailed bibliography is by Lawrence B. Lee, *Reclaiming the Arid West: An Historiography and Guide* (Santa Barbara: Clio Press, 1980). Harsh negative critiques include Marc Reisner, *Cadillac Desert: The American West and Its Disappearing Water* (New York: Viking Press, 1986); and Donald Worster, *Rivers of Empire: Water, Aridity and the Growth of the American West* (New York: Pantheon Books, 1986). A more balanced approach is Donald J. Pisani, *From the Family Farm to Agribusiness: The Irrigation Crusade in California and the West, 1850–1931* (Berkeley: University of California Press, 1984). See also Ira G. Clark, *Water in New Mexico: A History of Its Management and Use* (Albuquerque: University of New Mexico Press, 1987); and R. Douglas Hurt, *Indian Agriculture in America: Prehistory to the Present* (Lawrence: University Press of Kansas, 1987).

10. Nash, *World War II and the West*, 10–17, 178–88; Donald E. Spritzer, *The New Dealer from Montana: The Senate Career of James E. Murray* (New York: Garland Publishing, 1986).

11. Roger W. Lotchin, *Fortress California, 1910–1961: From Warfare to Welfare* (New York: Oxford University Press, 1992); Ronald Schaffer, *America in the Great War: The Rise of the War-Welfare State* (New York: Oxford University Press, 1991); Ann Markusen, Peter Hall, Sabina Deitrick, and Scott Campbell, *The Rise of the Gunbelt: The Military Remapping of Industrial America* (New York: Oxford University Press, 1991).

12. Lynne Pierson Doti and Larry Schweikart, *Banking in the American West* (Norman: University of Oklahoma Press, 1991); Schweikart, *A History of Banking*

in Arizona (Tucson: University of Arizona Press, 1982); James Smallwood, *An Oklahoma Adventure: Of Banks and Bankers* (Norman: University of Oklahoma Press, 1979); Robert Cleland and Frank Putnam, *Isaias W. Hellman and the Farmers and Merchants Bank* (San Marino, Calif.: Huntington Library, 1965); Sidney Hyman, *Marriner S. Eccles, Private Entrepreneur and Public Servant* (Stanford, Calif.: Graduate School of Business, Stanford University, 1976); Robert Browder and Thomas Smith, *Independent: A Biography of Lewis W. Douglas* (New York: Knopf, 1986).

13. The corporate archives of the Bank of America are located in San Francisco, California, and offer excellent insight into the operation of the bank.

14. Howard Lee Scamehorn, *Mill and Mine: The C F and I in the Twentieth Century* (Lincoln: University of Nebraska Press, 1992); Leonard J. Arrington and Anthony T. Cluff, *Federally Financed Industrial Plants Constructed in Utah during World War II* (Logan: Utah State University Press, 1965); Morris E. Garnsey, *America's New Frontier: The Mountain West* (New York: Alfred A. Knopf, 1950); Richard A. Lauderbaugh, *American Steelmakers and the Coming of the Second World War* (Ann Arbor: University of Michigan Research Press, 1980).

15. Fritz Machlup, *The Basing Point System* (Philadelphia: Blakiston, 1949). Earl Latham, *The Group Basis of Politics: A Study in Basing-Point Legislation* (Ithaca, N.Y.: Cornell University Press, 1952).

16. John B. Rae, *Climb to Greatness: The American Aircraft Industry, 1920–1960* (Cambridge, Mass.: MIT Press, 1968); Boeing Company, *Pedigree of Champions: Boeing since 1916*, 4th ed. (Seattle: Boeing Company, 1977); Joseph J. Corn, *The Winged Gospel: America's Romance with Aviation, 1900–1950* (New York: Oxford University Press, 1983).

17. Arnold S. Lott, *A Long Line of Ships* (Annapolis: United States Naval Institute, 1954); Wytze Gorter, *The Pacific Coast Maritime Shipping Industry, 1930–1948*, 2 vols. (Berkeley: University of California Press, 1952–1954). James H. Hitchman, *A Maritime History of the Pacific Coast, 1540–1980* (Lanham, Md.: University Press of America, 1990), is broad.

18. A brief account for the World War II era is in Nash, *World War II and the West*, 96–121; see also Charlotte F. Muller, *The Light Metals Monopoly* (New York: AMS Press, 1968).

19. See Russell R. Elliott, *History of Nevada*, 2d ed. (Lincoln: University of Nebraska Press, 1987), 307–10.

20. Earl Pomeroy, *In Search of the Golden West: The Tourist in Western America* (New York: Knopf, 1957); John M. Findlay, *People of Chance: Gambling in American Society from Jamestown to Las Vegas* (New York: Oxford University Press, 1986); Findlay, "Far Western Cityscapes and American Culture since 1940," *Western Historical Quarterly* 22 (February 1991): 19–43.

21. John E. Baur, *The Health Seekers of Southern California, 1870–1900* (San Marino, Calif.: Huntington Library, 1959); Billy M. Jones, *Health-Seekers in the Southwest, 1817–1900* (Norman: University of Oklahoma Press, 1967); Jake Spidle, *The Lovelace Medical Center: Pioneer in American Health Care* (Albuquerque: University of New Mexico Press, 1987).

22. Roger W. Lotchin, ed., *The Martial Cities* (New York: Praeger, 1984).

23. Peter Wiley and Robert Gottlieb, *Empires in the Sun: The Rise of the New American West* (New York: Putnam, 1982); see Michael P. Malone, "Beyond the Last Frontier: Toward a New Approach to Western American History," *Western Historical Quarterly* 20 (November 1989): 409–27, on the possible relevance of Braudel. The most recent study in this area is William G. Robbins, *Colony and Empire: The Capitalist Transformation of the American West* (Lawrence: University Press of Kansas, 1994).

24. George Rogers Taylor, *The Transportation Revolution, 1815–1860* (New York: Rinehart, 1951), and Oscar O. Winther, *The Transportation Frontier: Trans-Mississippi West, 1865–1890* (New York: Holt, Rinehart and Winston, 1964), survey the nineteenth century, but general works covering the last one hundred years have not yet been written. Robert W. Fogel, *The Union Pacific Railroad: A Case in Premature Enterprise* (Baltimore: Johns Hopkins Press, 1960); Don L. Hofsommer, *The Southern Pacific, 1901–1985* (College Station: Texas A & M Press, 1986); Keith L. Bryant, *History of the Atchison, Topeka and Santa Fe Railroad*[1] (New York: Macmillan, 1974); Albro Martin, *Railroads Triumphant: The Growth, Rejection, and Rebirth of a Vital American Force* (New York: Oxford University Press, 1992). The history of truck transportation, inland waterways, and Pacific ports since 1890 beckon to historians as unexplored topics. A special issue of *California History* on "Railroads in California and the Far West," 70 (Spring 1991): 2–113, 131–40, is helpful. See also Frederic L. Paxson, "The Highway Movement, 1916–1935," *American Historical Review* 51 (January 1946): 236–53.

25. Lee Scamehorn, "The Development of Air Transportation in the West," in *The American West: An Appraisal*, ed. Robert G. Ferris (Santa Fe: Museum of New Mexico Press, 1963). On the impact of automobiles, see Mark S. Foster, "The Western Response to Urban Transportation: A Tale of Three Cities, 1900–1945," in *The Urban West*, ed. Gerald D. Nash (Manhattan, Kan.: Sunflower University Press, 1979), 31–39, and Mark S. Foster, *From Streetcar to Superhighway: American City Planners and Urban Transportation, 1900–1940* (Philadelphia: Temple University Press, 1981).

26. Eugene P. Moehring, *Resort City in the Sunbelt: Las Vegas, 1930–1970* (Reno: University of Nevada Press, 1989); Nash, *The American West Transformed: The Impact of World War II* (Bloomington: Indiana University Press, 1985); McCarran's role needs to be delineated more fully. See Nash, *World War II and the West*.

27. The literature on the subject is far ranging; examples include Arthur P. Allen and Betty V. H. Schneider, *Industrial Relations in the California Aircraft Industry* (Berkeley: University of California Press, 1956); Vernon M. Briggs et al., *The Chicano Worker* (Austin: University of Texas Press, 1977); James W. Byrkit, *Forging the Copper Collar: Arizona's Labor-Management War of 1901–1921* (Tucson: University of Arizona Press, 1982); Daniel A,. Cornford, *Workers and Dissent in the Redwood Empire* (Philadelphia: Temple University Press, 1987); J. Craig Jenkins, *The Politics of Insurgency: The Farm Worker Movement in the 1960s* (New York: Columbia University Press, 1985). The Winter/Spring 1990 issue of *Labor History* contains a list of archival holdings concerning the history of labor in various western states, including California, Colorado, Texas, and Nevada; Philip Taft, *Labor Politics Ameri-*

can Style, The California State Federation of Labor (Cambridge, Mass.: Harvard University Press, 1968). Whiteside, *Regulating Danger*; Helen Zeese Papanikolas, *Louis Tikas and the Ludlow Massacre* (Lincoln: University of Nebraska Press, 1991). National Negro Congress, Los Angeles Council, *Jim Crow in National Defense* (Los Angeles: National Negro Congress, 1940); David F. Selvin, *A Place in the Sun: A History of California Labor* (San Francisco: Boyd and Fraser, 1981); Vicki L. Ruiz, *Cannery Women, Cannery Lives: Mexican Women, Unionization, and the California Food Processing Industry, 1930–1950* (Albuquerque: University of New Mexico Press, 1987).

2

Research Opportunities in Twentieth-Century Western History

Natural Resources and Environment

Thomas R. Cox

In the 1960s an ecological revolution swept across America. Suddenly environmentalism was a major force and ecology a household word. Rachel Carson's *Silent Spring*, published in 1962, was both a catalyst and a reflection of this sociopolitical movement, but its underlying causes were both older and more varied. There is no need to trace here the origins of the ecological revolution; that has been done elsewhere.[1] Suffice it to say, the movement occurred and changed, perhaps irrevocably, the way Americans in and out of government dealt with the natural environment. The effects were far reaching. Even the discipline of history, seemingly remote from all this, was affected. What were considered legitimate topics for historical investigation underwent major alteration, and practitioners of the emerging subdiscipline of environmental history soon found themselves drawing upon research techniques and a whole range of disciplines previously beyond the pale of historians.

Historians of the American West had, of course, long incorporated environmental considerations into their works. Frederick Jackson Turner's studies of the frontier proffered an essentially environmental interpretation of the shaping of American democracy.[2] Studies of land policy by Roy Robbins, Paul Gates, and John Ise were similarly environmental, although with a strong admixture of emphasis on class interests. Works by Walter Prescott Webb, Ernest S. Osgood, and Herbert E. Bolton were, in their own ways, environmental too.[3] Indeed, so pervasive had implicit environmental determinism become, and so effectively did it distance the West from older regions, that in 1955 Earl Pomeroy called for a reorientation that would emphasize the cultural continuities between East and West that post-Turnerian studies had too often ignored or blurred.[4]

But while Gene Gressley and others took up Pomeroy's challenge, they continued to frame their works in ways long familiar to the historian.[5] Studies of western land policy, economic development, and government activity in resource management drew upon sources and dealt with problems with which traditional modes of training had prepared them to cope.[6] There was, of course, plenty remaining to be done in this older realm. Long after new approaches to environmental history had emerged, valuable studies of the traditional sort continued to appear, and ample opportunity for additional work along such lines remained.

In due course, the forces set in motion by the environmental revolution led to new types of histories. In the vanguard was Richard White's *Land Use, Environment, and Social Change*, which focused on Island County, Washington (that is, Whidbey and Camano islands in northern Puget Sound), a place selected because nothing of great importance had ever happened there. As White explained, its "very absence of dramatic disasters . . . gives the county its significance." By studying such a place, one can come to understand the impact of humans on the land better than by selecting an area noted for some spectacular event or major change that was, in fact, atypical and that could cloud or distort normal patterns and developments.[7]

In tracing human impact on the two islands, White took a genuinely long-term view: his history encompassed the period from the last ice age to recent suburbanization. In addition to standard historical sources, White drew upon the contributions of geologists, anthropologists, ethnobotanists, practitioners in the new field of quaternary studies, foresters, sociologists, and others. His work was more thorough than and at least as pathbreaking as William Cronon's better-known and much-lauded study of New England, *Changes in the Land*—and White preceded Cronon into print by three years.[8]

White's approach, if not his chronological breadth of coverage, offers much to the student of the twentieth-century West. A great deal remains to be done if human impact on western lands is to be clearly understood. Because of accelerating population growth and the development that accompanied it, much of that impact has been within this century.

Studies of the West frequently touch upon such problems as overgrazing, destructive timber-harvesting practices, and stream pollution and degradation, but most focus on the political and economic battles that have accompanied—and shaped—these developments. Few trace the actual processes of degradation and restoration taking place on the land. Researchers for the Forest Service, National Park Service, Bureau of Land Management, and other government agencies responsible for managing natural resources have sometimes done so—as have geographers, ecologists, and natural historians—but few mainstream historians have followed their lead or, apparently, even been aware of their work.[9]

There is ample material on which to draw. Around the turn of the century the U.S. Geological Survey carried out extensive examinations of western forests, mapping, cataloging, and evaluating the nation's forest reserves (then under the administration of the General Land Office).[10] Its studies provide vital, but seldom-used material that—when combined with the work of pioneer naturalists, surveyors, and others—give a reliable, comprehensive picture of the state of vast tracts of western timberland on the eve of their being opened to major commercial exploitation. By comparing these benchmark studies with later surveys and present conditions, one can reconstruct the environmental history of an area and provide a solid basis for evaluating the effects thereon of various timber-harvest and forest-management policies.

Later surveys, and the maps and other records that accompany them, have been utilized even less often than those of the Geological Survey. For example, priceless studies of the forests near Bend, Oregon, one of the nation's leading lumber-producing centers through much of the first half of the twentieth century, lie untouched in the Federal Records Center in Seattle.[11] Surveys of many another forest, conducted at intervals from the twenties through the fifties, are also extant in various records centers. But the records in Seattle have gone unused, and historians have shown so little interest in them that it has not been clear to the records managers that these documents have lasting value and should be retained.

Like those of the Forest Service and Geological Survey, records of the Soil Conservation Service (now Natural Resources Conservation Service) and Bureau of Land Management, including the SCS's extensive mapping of soil types on America's farms during and after the 1930s, offer opportunities to trace changes on western lands with an exactitude not possible for earlier periods. Such precise knowledge would enable one to undertake evaluations of the effects of various land-use policies and practices that would be far superior to analyses rooted solely in traditional historical sources. But they would do more than that. They would provide a dynamic, long-term view that would show the land not simply being degraded by modern society's ill-advised initial patterns of use, but responding in a sequence of ways over time. In other words, they would make possible a less static—and much more accurate—view of natural environments, one that would encompass the ways in which lands respond to misuse and regain their health in addition to the ways they get degraded in the first place.

In 1941, Aldo Leopold wrote a brief but telling depiction of the destructive invasion of cheat grass into the grazing lands of the Great Basin. For those growing up during the 1940s and 1950s in the cheat-infested area he described, Leopold seemed to sum it up neatly: "the West has accepted cheat as a necessary evil, to be lived with until kingdom come."[12] But such conclusions were premature. Rabbitbrush and sagebrush pushed into the domain of cheat grass; junipers followed. Today, many a land manager worries more about the effects of thirsty junipers on the area under his control than he does about cheat grass. As the processes of ecological succession were played out, it became clear that the impact of overgrazing—which had opened the way for cheat in the first place—was far more complex than initial observations, even by so informed an observer as Leopold, would lead one to believe. Recent studies of the problems associated with the cheat grass–sagebrush–juniper succession point the way to a host of similar studies that would view living natural resources as dynamic elements, changing and evolving over time, rather than as something fixed and static and simply to be acted upon for better or for ill by humans.[13]

Photographic records also offer a rich resource, for they provide opportunities to view the changes that have taken place on a given tract with a precision written records seldom allow. Scholars have paired photographs of western sites taken during the late nineteenth century with recent photographs of the same scenes to demonstrate the changes in forest cover, range conditions, and the like over the intervening years.[14] Similarly, the late Kenneth Gordon, professor of zoology at Oregon State University, left the school his remarkable collection of photographs accumulated over several decades of studying what he called simply "the changing scene" of Oregon. Included are pictures of many of the same sites taken at intervals of some ten to twenty years.[15] They are untapped. Other photographic collections abound, especially in state and local historical societies. Utilized imaginatively, such collections could open new doors of understanding on changing land-use patterns and the effects thereof. To date, most have been little used, save for the pictures of individuals they provide. They offer far more than that.

Students of the twentieth-century West can gain fresh insights into the processes at work on the land by viewing them in the context of truly long-term change. In doing so, they would be following in White's footsteps. Those focusing on the desert Southwest would find stimulation in the works of Julio L. Betancourt and others who have reconstructed past climatic and botanical changes through such techniques as the analysis of materials collected over thousands of years in packrat middens (a technique that has yielded a remarkably detailed picture of the evolution of surrounding ecosystems).[16] Frederick Gehlbach's *Mountain Islands and Desert Seas* also offers a useful approach. By comparing the accounts of nineteenth-century boundary survey parties with conditions on the same sites today—and by drawing upon a host of related, area-specific studies by biologists, geographers, and others—Gehlbach provides insights into contemporary land-use problems that go far beyond what could be obtained by looking at twentieth-century developments alone.[17]

Much of the work on natural resources and the environment of the twentieth-century West has been unduly anthropocentric. It may be true that "the proper study of mankind is man," as Alexander Pope wrote, but the proper study of human impact on the land requires far more. Environmental history offers a chance to get people, great or small, off center stage and thereby to open the way for fresh understanding of the nature—humanity nexus. Mary Hunter Austin, Joseph Wood Krutch, and Charles Fletcher Lummis recognized the necessity of approaching the southwestern deserts on their own terms, and they recognized that the harsh environments of the region shaped and limited what could be done there, but historians, by continuing to emphasize human events—the activities and policies of people—have contributed to the anthropocentrism that leads Americans to persist in real estate development in southern California and Arizona when there are already too many people for the amount of water available and to view natural resources and the environment as something that, through technology, can be bent without limit to human will.

Environmental history offers a way out of this intellectual trap. By focusing on a place and how it has changed over time, rather than on the people who have inhabited it, one can take an additional step away from great-man history beyond the steps already taken by practitioners of the new social history and others who have restored the common people to a place of importance in the pages of the past. Such studies are rare, but Hugh Raup's "The View from John Sanderson's Farm" offers an approach that could be applied with value in the West.[18]

Species or groups of species also offer opportunities for escaping anthropocentrism. Biologist Kenneth Kingsley's work on irrigated pecan agriculture along Arizona's Santa Cruz River is a case in point. By focusing on the impact of this form of agriculture on animals native to the area, rather than on the contributions and problems it presents for humans, Kingsley has taken an approach that historians could emulate to their benefit, for it would provide them with a richer, fuller understanding of the effects of human activities, past and present, by keeping them from looking only at the impact of those actions on people.[19]

The desert fishes of the Southwest offer a further case in point. A number of native fishes, many of them relict species from the pluvial period of the late Pleistocene, inhabit scattered locations across the region. Several are on the federal endangered species list; some have already become extinct. Inconspicuous, valueless as game fish, and economically unimportant, they have been largely ignored except by a small coterie of biologists. They came into public view only briefly, when in the 1970s the case of the Devil's Hole Pupfish—a species found only in a single small body of water located in a detached segment of Death Valley National Monument—moved into the courts, pitting the National

Park Service against ranchers in Ash Meadows, Nevada, who by pumping water to irrigate their alfalfa fields were drawing down the water table and threatening the continued existence of the pupfish. This one incident aside, the desert fishes of the Southwest have been truly inconsequential to humans. Yet their history, a history of how they survived aeons only to become endangered or extinct in the twentieth century, can demonstrate the environmental forces at work and the place of humans in them without having humans loom disproportionately large in the story. The records of the Desert Fishes Council, an unstudied network of scientists and land managers concerned over the future of these rare life-forms, should offer historians a springboard from which to approach such a history.[20] Handled with imagination, the result would be a history far different from the usual anthropocentric studies that dominate the discipline—unfortunately, even in the field of environmental history.

Increasing interdisciplinary research and discouraging anthropocentrism have not been the only ways in which the ecological revolution has affected historians. As Donald Worster has noted, it is generating a history without borders.[21] Ecosystems seldom begin and end at political boundaries, but governmental policies do, a fact that provides environmental historians with numerous opportunities for evaluating the effects of differing policies and sociopolitical systems.

Alfred Runte has noted that the boundaries of Yellowstone National Park are ecologically meaningless and that this has resulted in problems for those charged with managing the resources therein, especially the elk and bison herds that migrate on and off the park oblivious to its manmade borders. Interagency friction has sometimes resulted. To Runte, this demonstrates how unconcerned the park's founders were with ecological considerations, how directed they were toward simply saving spectacular scenery.[22] Runte is correct, of course, but these facts also provide historians with a vehicle for comparative studies. By contrasting conditions in the same ecosystem, some located inside and some outside the park, one can gain concrete evidence of the efficacy of various public and private approaches to resource management over time.

Other opportunities for comparative study abound. The transformation of the tussock grasslands of New Zealand's South Island into grazing lands for sheep and the opening of areas in the American West to the cattle and sheep industries can, if carefully compared, help us to understand developments in both countries better. Similarly, the pine-oak forests on the peninsular ranges that stretch from Baja California into the United States beg for comparative analysis, for conditions in the forests have come to be quite different on the Mexican side of the border from those to the north of it. Foresters have suggested that the differing approaches to the control of wildfire in the two countries are primarily responsible. With fire-control policies currently the subject of considerable debate in the United States, studies of the contrast between conditions and policies in contiguous, ecologically similar forests in Mexico and in southern California would be especially timely.[23]

There are numerous other topics that might be approached comparatively. One could look at the public and private responses to the devastating Columbus Day storm of 1962, which blew down millions of board feet of timber across Oregon and Washington, and the responses to a very similar disaster that struck the forests of Japan's northern island of Hokkaido in the same period.[24] Such comparisons might tell much not only about the efficacy of vastly different forms of governmental organization, but also about that of sharply divergent environmental policies and systems of landownership and management. Similar insights could be gained by studying the work of George Chaffey, who helped bring irrigation to the San Gabriel and Imperial valleys in California and then to the Mildura area of Australia.[25]

The ecological revolution of the 1960s was as much a social as a scientific movement. Samuel P. Hays has traced the rise of citizen activism that was involved.[26] This activism led to frequent attacks on the decisions and policies of technocrats whose expertise had been largely unchallenged since the progressive era. Environmentalists now pitted their experts against those of the bureaucracy and brought on a wave of legal disputes that, some land managers complain, has resulted in their now spending more time in hearings and courtrooms than in the field.

The parameters of these contests have barely been traced; a number of major issues remain unstudied. Among them is the struggle that surrounded the opening of a major portion of the Three Sisters Wilderness Area to logging, a battle that led environmentalists to despair of the administrative protection for wild areas that the Forest Service provided and helped bring on their decade-long fight for the Wilderness Bill as a means of providing greater safety against inroads into the remaining wilderness.[27] The records of the Friends of the Three Sisters Wilderness, which trace this story, lie untapped in the University of Oregon library.

The citizen activism that Hays chronicled was especially evident in Oregon during the governorships of Tom McCall and Robert Straub (1967–1979). One product was Oregon's Land Conservation and Development Commission, established to regulate land use in the state. At first glance, the commission appears to have been an extension of the technocratic approach of the progressive and New Deal eras, but in fact it was quite different. The law mandated citizen involvement in decision making. Activist organizations seized the opportunities thus provided to stymie both government planners and private developers. The ways in which LCDC and any number of other agencies and laws were turned to such purposes remain largely unstudied, though such activities are central to the new environmentalism.[28]

Behind this citizen involvement in decision making lie basic shifts in western society. As Earl Pomeroy has demonstrated, much of the West was from the first highly urbanized;[29] nonetheless, the economies of the western states rested on agriculture and extractive industries, which encouraged an attitude that looked on the environment in terms of the natural resources that it could supply. This engendered a utilitarian approach to their management, if not always outright exploitation. But since World War II, much of the West has grown away from the land. Economies based on manufacturing and the service sector have become more common, and urban pressures have swelled. In the process, land has become less important for economic production, but increasingly valued for recreation, scenery, green belts, and ecological preserves.

Consider, for instance, Deschutes County, Oregon, the fastest-growing county in the state in recent years. During the first half of the twentieth century its economy rested on the twin pillars of agriculture and lumbering. Today, the major mills are closed, the woods more valued for recreation and tourism than for the logs they yield. Similarly, potato, alfalfa, and grain farming have virtually ceased. Although much of the population still lives on rural sites, the "farms" are now more often than not economically nonproductive, with subdivided tracts devoted to pasture for a few head of horses, cows, or even llamas. Bend, the major town, is a community much of whose population is made up of expatriate California urbanites, and its streets sport the boutiques, delicatessens, and antique shops that are hallmarks of the culture they brought with them—all of which has led some longtime residents to affix bumper stickers to their cars reading "Don't Californicate Oregon."[30]

Similar transitions are evident elsewhere: on Whidbey Island, Washington, which has become a retreat for Seattleites; in the mountains west of Denver, where Vail and many another community have become playgrounds for wealthy outsiders; and in Coeur d'Alene and McCall, Idaho, to which great numbers of southern Californians have flocked to escape the pressures of mass society. Social scientists have begun to analyze the forces involved in this transformation, and some who have done so sound more like urban advocates than scholars. When Frank and Deborah Popper spoke on "The Reinvention of the American Frontier," they predicted new patterns of western land use that would see vast parts of the region removed from agricultural, pastoral, and extractive uses and turned into wilderness, ecological preserves, and recreation grounds. According to historian Harry McDean, they were advocating turning the West into "a Yuppie playground."[31] A number of contests between economic and noneconomic uses of western lands—struggles surrounding the spotted owl or fish and game management, for example—could be viewed thus, most usefully by historians equipped to put the whole into the context of long-term social and economic change. So could the so-called Sagebrush Rebellion of the 1970s and 1980s, which, while echoing the antifederal rhetoric commonly heard in the Rocky Mountain–intermountain West during the early twentieth century, had a new, decidedly antiurban tone.[32]

But the Sagebrush Rebellion ought not to be viewed as representing the full scope of subregional thought. Out of its heartland came Governor Robert Smylie, the father of state parks in Idaho. Smylie sought practical alternatives to the outworn shibboleths of state's rights and libertarianism. As an advisor to Dwight D. Eisenhower on western affairs and then during three terms as governor, he pushed for citizen's advisory committees that would bridge the gap between the people on and near the land and government resource management agencies too often grown aloof and bureaucratic. Idaho's senator Frank Church, author of the Wild and Scenic Rivers Bill, also sought to address both local concerns and the need for governmental action. His ability to do so effectively lay behind Church's success in getting the Wild and Scenic Rivers Bill through Congress quickly, unlike the Wilderness Bill that languished for years in hearings and debate. Much of the work of such leaders has gone unstudied even though their papers are readily available.[33]

Within the world of parks and recreation, the concerns of the 1960s spawned a drive to make outdoor facilities more readily available to the urban public. This resulted in building state parks in or near various major cities as well as to the creation of the National Park Service's "Parks to the People" program, which not only generated proposals for golf courses and other recreation facilities in older parks but also led to the diversion of funds from traditional parks to new urban ones, such as the Golden Gate National Urban Recreation Area in San Francisco. The movement created a deep schism among parks professionals, a division separating those holding to the old view of parks as natural beauty spots that should be preserved and a new group whose agenda was as much social as environmental, a group more concerned with educating and uplifting the urban populace than with protecting scenic beauty. Historians have only begun to probe the implications of this development.[34]

The struggle within the National Park Service was reflective of a larger disagreement over the purposes and uses of parks and outdoor scenic or recreational facilities. Divisions were sometimes clearly drawn along class lines.[35] The wilderness movement, in particular, was frequently attacked as a movement by and for an elite, a charge that wilderness advocates heatedly but unconvincingly denied. Analysis of the social bases of various environmental groups and of the beneficiaries of their programs invites the attention of historians. To date, few have chosen to address the issue, perhaps because the loyalties of so many environmental historians extend, on the one hand, to such things as the wilderness movement and, on the other hand, to the forces of egalitarianism. The uncomfortable intellectual dilemma in which such divided loyalties places them seems to have been solved largely by turning to other questions.[36]

Accompanying the postwar shift to urban-based concerns has been the creation of a new body of regulatory legislation. Through the nineteenth century, as James Willard Hurst has demonstrated, laws regarding forests and waterways were shaped to encourage economic development.[37] The same was true of legislation dealing with other resources. Since World War II, legislation has been increasingly aimed at restraining economic growth in order to protect natural resources and the environment. Some of these laws have been essentially utilitarian—and thus consistent with the approach of Gifford Pinchot who, during the early years of the century, advocated maximizing long-term output by restricting destructive, short-term exploitation—but much has been decidedly antidevelopment and preservationist in tone. Stephanie Pincetl and William McEvoy have taken steps toward an understanding of this shift, but much remains to be done.[38] Such legislation as the Endangered Species acts, the Highway Beautification Act, and the Air Quality and Water Pollution Control acts is a far cry from the system of laws chronicled by Hurst. The shift from the one sort of legislation to the other has been especially keenly felt in the West. That shift, the individual laws that reflect it, and the forces behind them all need to be analyzed if the place of the environment in the postwar West is to be appreciated fully.

The rise of urban environmental forces has not only created new pressures on those charged with land management, but also potential new allies for them. The nation's grasslands provide a case in point. Until recent years, the Forest Service and Bureau of Land Management dealt with users of public grazing lands essentially as adversaries or, some have charged, were co-opted to become their handmaidens.[39] However, as Paul J. Culhane has pointed out, the emergence during the postwar period of an environmental constituency interested in grasslands resulted in a new balance of power that forced grazing interests to accept less exploitative policies and practices advocated by land management agencies. A similar rebalancing of forces took place in the management of forests and various other natural resources. In California, where the struggle between farmers and the Los Angeles area's Metropolitan Water District over Owens River water had seemingly been settled for all time in favor of the latter, John Walton has shown how the appearance on the scene of environmentalists redressed the balance of power and changed the course of events.[40]

The implications of the emergence of environmentalists as a force in resource management decision making is as yet imperfectly understood; others need to follow the lead that Culhane and Walton have provided.

An examination of the Forest Service's multiple-use policy of land management, how it changed in the new climate of environmentalism, and what forces lay behind these changes would be an excellent place to start, as would the shift in power within that agency from its long-dominant utilitarian wing to environmentalists who challenged many of its traditional policies and assumptions.[41]

Increased attention to environmental questions and a broader range of individuals investigating them has led to the reexamination—and, on occasion, rejection—of various older "truths." Selective logging and sustained-yield timber management were long viewed by historians as wise practices whose adoption marked the progress of the lumber industry toward social responsibility and away from its extractive, frontier roots. Especially in the pine forests of the interior West, such practices seemed beyond reproach. The situation no longer appears so simple. In recent years a number of western sawmills that were originally expected to be permanent, and whose managers had adopted selective cutting to ensure a sustained yield, have closed, in the process bringing into question many accepted ideas about proper timber management. As an example, foresters of the Weyerhaeuser Company abandoned selective logging on the firm's extensive pine lands around Klamath Falls, Oregon, and instituted a system of even-aged management that incorporates periodic clear-cutting while keeping the basic concept of sustained yield. Some went even further. One forester declared bluntly that sustained yield was "a rather naive, elementary, oversimplified concept" that the profession had by the 1980s largely disavowed. Driven by economic realities, the Georgia-Pacific Corporation cut out its holdings on the Oregon coast and departed the region. Although their approaches differed, both firms recognized that land management must be attuned to the economic conditions of the times and that capital tied up in trees is a poor investment when inflation is outstripping any possible rate at which timber can grow. A comparison of the policies and practices of the two firms—or of others taking divergent approaches—would be most instructive.[42]

Nor should study be cast simply in terms of domestic factors. The West was from the first influenced by external economic forces;[43] in the twentieth century it has been increasingly so. As the internationalization of business has proceeded apace, so has interdependence. Developments in Canada, Japan, Southeast Asia, and elsewhere impact on decisions regarding western resources. The decisions themselves have come to be more and more frequently made overseas, and others do not necessarily view western resources as do Americans. To one used to prices in Japan, expensive American logs, ranches, and farms can seem a bargain, whereas resource management policies that seem appropriate to Americans can appear less so when seen from abroad. With growing cross-penetration of international businesses, decision making regarding western resources can no longer be understood without setting it in the context of the wider world where those resources will be used—and often owned.[44]

Devastating beetle infestations in the Blue Mountains of Oregon and Washington—and elsewhere—have been as effective as changing economic realities in bringing long-approved resource management practices into question. Indeed, investigators have concluded that these practices actually contributed to the outbreaks and that huge clear-cuts were the most feasible way of controlling them. Environmental groups, who initially objected, came to support this approach after the rationale behind it became clear, and they were assured it would be handled so that the needs of fish and wildlife would be addressed.[45] Although the old bugaboo of clear-cutting continued to have a considerable emotional impact in environmental circles, here and there a more sophisticated appreciation of the intricacies of forest management was emerging.

The science of fish and wildlife management has also made great strides. Susan Flader and James M. Glover approached this subject by analyzing key figures; Thomas Dunlap presented a less personalized view that considered the evolution and implementation of ideas; Keir Sterling traced the changes by taking an institutional approach.[46] All three methodologies are valuable, but none has offered the last word on the subject. Future researchers could usefully juxtapose William Hornaday's approach with that of Aldo Leopold, thereby illustrating the shift from negative, regulatory methods to an active approach emphasizing habitat restoration and improvement and other positive steps. Study of the controversy in midcentury over the shift in big-game management from the use of refuges to hunting regulations (including such things as legalizing the killing of does) could also illuminate the shift from passive to active management. Numerous agencies as yet unstudied also cry out for examination; in particular, state-level agencies, which have been largely ignored to date, beckon the researcher.[47]

So far, few historians have incorporated the new scientific understanding into their treatment of resource questions. In spite of the fact that the science of resource management is dynamic and growing, a field in which new insights are constantly emerging, most historians continue to approach such issues as if there were a fixed body of scientific truths that can serve as a yardstick to measure the social responsibility of resource users. Until such time as historians become more familiar with the technical developments in the relevant fields and stop writing their histories from intellectual positions determined in advance by their social and political allegiances, their studies will continue to reflect poorly the reality of what has transpired. Environmental activists have learned that to be effective they must rest their arguments on an understanding of relevant scientific knowledge. Historians must do so too if they are to deal

effectively with the tortured story of resource management in the twentieth-century West.

If new scientific knowledge has made only limited headway among
historians of the West, the same cannot be said of the new social history.
The concerns of the sixties spawned a host of studies focused on race,
gender, and ethnic relations and, at the same time, resurrected the interest of the thirties in questions of class and economic power. Environmental topics received a full measure of this attention, but opportunities
remain. Donald Worster and William G. Robbins have offered essentially
class-based interpretations of western resource utilization.[48] On the other
hand, land-use patterns have strong cultural roots, as a number of recent
studies—most focused on other regions—have demonstrated.[49] The extent to which cultural baggage has shaped and continues to shape western approaches to the land and the interrelationship between cultural
influences and those of class ought to be examined. Community studies
offer a useful vehicle for such comparisons, as the works of Patricia
Marchak, Jeremy Kilar, Robert MacCameron, and others who have analyzed resource-based local economies make clear.[50]

Extractive industries controlled from and exporting to locations outside the region have long led westerners to complain that theirs is a colonial economy. The recent boom in coal mining in the Rocky Mountain
states, the strip-mining techniques utilized in it, and the simultaneous
abandonment of older mining operations—such as those in Ely, Nevada—
have combined to reenergize the old complaints and give politicians such
as Governor Richard Lamm of Colorado a potent and heartfelt issue.[51]
This new version of the old lament deserves study. It could usefully be
approached by comparing the new complaint with the old.[52]

Greater recognition should also be given to intraregional relations. In
many a locale, complaints about dominance from San Francisco, Denver,
Salt Lake City, or Portland loom larger than complaints about the colonial dependency of West on East. For the Pacific Northwest, city–hinterland
relations and the transportation links that sustain them have been analyzed by Edward L. Ullman and Donald Meinig.[53] Elsewhere the record is
less impressive. Some studies, such as William H. Hutchinson's work on
San Francisco, are unduly impressionistic; such subjects cry out for rigorous quantitative analysis.[54] Regardless of approach, opportunities abound,
and although not all would involve analyses of issues related to natural
resources and the environment, many would, for the relations between a
metropolis and its hinterlands frequently revolve around ownership, control, and use of natural resources.

The new social history, a product of the activist sixties as surely as was
the ecological revolution, could be turned to comparative community
studies. Communities in the American West differ markedly one from
another even when quite similar in size. Differences in the distribution of

landownership and the degrees of economic equality help to shape differing community patterns. Towns dependent upon irrigation agriculture, and thus having a fragmented pattern of landownership in which holdings are more or less equal, could usefully be compared with towns in which landownership and economic power are concentrated in a few hands, such as lumber towns or communities dependent upon cattle ranching.[55] Company towns and noncompany towns dependent on the same types of business could also be compared.[56] Such analyses would not need to incorporate explicitly insights from the mainstream of environmental history, but they easily could, as Charles Peterson has made manifest through his work on the environmental impact of the Mormon pattern of smallholdings.[57] Such studies might also draw upon the work of Isaiah Bowman and his successors in the comparative study of frontiers.[58] In any case, comparative community studies would be fraught with implications for those seeking to understand the place of natural resources and environment in the history of the American West.

These examples fall far short of exhausting the list of questions the ecological revolution of the 1960s has opened to historians. Collectively, they point not just to a broadly based, interdisciplinary approach to the past, but also to a less anthropocentric orientation than that which dominated nearly all earlier histories. Such studies of westerners, their environment, and their use of natural resources could be pursued in such a way that they would not so much move humans off the stage of history as they would broaden and deepen understanding of the intricacies of the interaction of humans with their environment. Although this change might seem little more than a return to the environmentalism of Turner and his successors, it would be far more than that, for most such studies would focus on the postfrontier period and would draw upon works from a range of fields and with greater technical depth than those used heretofore.

Tackling studies such as those outlined above would mean catapulting oneself into intellectual areas unfamiliar to most historians and would frequently require intellectual retooling. But those unwilling to take on such a task need not despair; a host of more conventional topics are available. The impact of the automobile, and of attendant highway building, on parks and tourism and of the logging truck on the lumber industry could be investigated further.[59] So too could changes in scenic tastes that gradually led Americans to an appreciation of oceans, deserts, and grasslands and the rise of new forms of outdoor recreation, including the backpacking boom and the proliferation of off-road and four-wheel-drive vehicles, which brought great changes to resource utilization and management. Bureaucratic battles for control of resources could also be analyzed by using traditional methodologies and sources. Study of how the rivalry between the Forest Service and National Park Service led the former to eschew a purely utilitarian approach and begin developing recreational facilities on its holdings might be especially fruitful.[60]

Historians have given water resources and their utilization considerable attention in recent years. Still, opportunities remain. Additional studies of individual irrigation projects would be useful, especially if they focused on their social and environmental impacts. Much of the complex story of interagency rivalry and cooperation in watershed management, seen especially in the Colorado and Columbia drainages, remains to be sorted out, and the role of private interests in western irrigation has been poorly delineated.[61]

Water-rights controversies need attention too. Recent works on the Winter's Doctrine and on Hispanic water rights, which acquired standing in the Southwest through the Treaty of Guadalupe Hidalgo, have added new dimensions to discussions of water in the West. Other recent developments remain to be analyzed. Among these are the impact of the doctrine of implied reservation, articulated in the case that grew out of the pumping of groundwater near Devil's Hole, and the doctrine of public trust, extended to encompass the protection of waters for environmental or recreational purposes in order to protect Mono Lake from Los Angeles's insatiable thirst for water.[62] Also useful would be study of the impact of Arizona's recent success in gaining a greatly increased share of Colorado River water at California's expense and the effects of tapping the Ogallala and other nonrenewing aquifers.[63] Moreover, the recent drought in California and the resulting threat of a diversion of scarce water resources from agriculture to urban centers would make historical study of the impact of other droughts and of earlier rural–urban water controversies in the West extremely timely.[64] All of these studies would be instructive, especially if analyses were cast with an eye toward social and environmental effects as well as economic and political concerns.

Even so well established a subdiscipline as agricultural history offers a long list of opportunities. Although the history of the spread of traditional crops, especially grain, has been well chronicled, much remains unclear about newer, exotic, and minor crops. Potatoes, almonds, citrus, rice, avocados, dates, grass seed, cut flowers, and truck crops are all at least locally important in the West and deserve more attention than they have received.[65] The western wine industry, including its spread to new areas and the impact of the boutique winery phenomenon, needs historical analysis.[66] So too do the effects of the rise in agricultural exports from the West, especially to Japan, and the concomitant increase in agricultural imports from Chile, Mexico, New Zealand, and elsewhere.

Business history, like agricultural history, is an area that offers numerous opportunities. The Idaho Power Company, with its controversial dams in Hell's Canyon; Peter Kiewet Company, builder of the ill-fated Teton Dam and the oil terminal at Valdez, Alaska; J. R. Simplot, the privately held land and agricultural chemical giant; and even the activities of western supermarket chains, such as Safeway and Albertson's, could all be studied profitably by the researcher interested in the western environment.[67] Small firms too numerous to mention could be studied as well—and should be, for their importance, both individually and collectively, is all too often overlooked. In addition, the West Coast fishing industry and its activities need attention. The role of private interests in establishing salmon hatcheries is unstudied, and historians have done little on California's once important tuna fisheries.[68] By drawing upon the works of Alfred D. Chandler, Jr., and other key figures in business history, while at the same time incorporating insights from environmental studies, works on such subjects might become genuinely pathbreaking.

Even an area so well worked as the politics of conservation holds opportunities. California's governor George Pardee, a progressive forerunner of Hiram Johnson and an active champion of conservation, deserves a biography, as do Oregon's senator Charles L. McNary and Washington's senator Henry M. Jackson. McNary was a key figure concerned with natural resource issues from the 1920s to the 1940s, Jackson during Lyndon Johnson's presidency.[69]

The politics of conservation can be handled in other ways too. The differences among western states in their approaches to the conservation and management of natural resources have been analyzed by Elmo Richardson and Douglas H. Strong, among others, but the subject is far from exhausted.[70] Recent debates over the use of DDT and malathion, as well as over state regulation of timber-cutting practices on privately owned forestland, could also be investigated with profit.[71] Finally, although tax policies have clearly played a major role in shaping the utilization and management of natural resources, their impact is imperfectly understood. The forces involved in crafting them, the debates surrounding them, their eventual passage, and their implementation and modification over the years all deserve more attention than they have received.[72]

After all this, one thing at least is clear. Whether the modes of analysis are old or new, there is plenty to be done in studying the natural resources and environment of the twentieth-century West. Indeed, historians have done so little on the region after 1900 and environmental history as a field is so new that frustration over how much remains to be done will surely continue to be with us for a long time.

Notes

1. Donald Fleming, "Roots of the New Conservation Movement," *Perspectives in American History* 6 (1972): 7–91; Samuel P. Hays, "From Conservation to Environment: Environmental Politics in the United States since World War II," *Environmental Review* 6 (Fall 1982): 14–41; Robert Gottlieb, "Reconstructing Environmentalism: Complex Movements, Diverse Roots," *Environmental History Review* 17 (Winter 1993): 1–10.

2. The literature on Turner and his impact is almost without limit. Recent evaluations include William Cronon, "Revisiting the Vanishing Frontier: The Legacy of Frederick Jackson Turner," *Western Historical Quarterly* 18 (April 1987): 157–76; Martin Ridge, "Frederick Jackson Turner, Ray Allen Billington, and American Frontier History," *Western Historical Quarterly* 19 (January 1988): 5–20.

3. Among their more relevant works to this point are Roy M. Robbins, *Our Landed Heritage: The Public Domain, 1776–1970*, rev. ed. (Lincoln: University of Nebraska Press, 1976); Paul W. Gates, "The Homestead Law in an Incongruous Land System," *American Historical Review* 41 (July 1936): 652–81; Gates (with Robert W. Swenson), *History of Public Land Law Development* (Washington: Government Printing Office, 1968); John Ise, *United States Forest Policy* (New Haven, Conn.: Yale University Press, 1920); Walter Prescott Webb, *The Great Plains* (Boston: Ginn and Co., 1931); Ernest Staples Osgood, *The Day of the Cattleman* (Chicago: University of Chicago Press, 1929); Herbert E. Bolton, *The Spanish Borderlands: A Chronicle of Old Florida and the Southwest* (New Haven, Conn.: Yale University Press, 1921).

4. Earl Pomeroy, "Toward a Reorientation of Western History: Continuity and Environment," *Mississippi Valley Historical Review* 41 (March 1955): 579–600. See also Michael P. Malone, "Beyond the Last Frontier: Toward a New Approach to Western American History," *Western Historical Quarterly* 20 (November 1989): 409–28.

5. Gene M. Gressley, *Bankers and Cattlemen* (New York: Alfred A. Knopf, 1966); Gressley, ed., *The American West: A Reorientation* (Laramie: University of Wyoming, 1966).

6. My own *Mills and Markets: A History of the West Coast Lumber Industry to 1900* (Seattle: University of Washington Press, 1974), falls into this category.

7. Richard White, *Land Use, Environment, and Social Change: The Shaping of Island County, Washington* (Seattle: University of Washington Press, 1980). See also White, "The Altered Landscape: Social Change and the Land in the Pacific Northwest," in *Regionalism and the Pacific Northwest*, ed. William G. Robbins, Robert J. Frank, and Richard E. Ross (Corvallis: Oregon State University Press, 1983), 109–27. Compare Merle E. Curti et al., *Making of an American Community: Democracy in a Frontier County* (Stanford, Calif.: Stanford University Press, 1959), which is also locally focused, but in spite of its use of advanced quantitative methods, is so infused with the Turnerian view that it breaks little new ground.

8. William Cronon, *Changes in the Land: Indians, Colonists, and the Ecology of New England* (New York: Hill and Wang, 1983). A less satisfactory work of the same genre is Timothy Silver, *A New Face on the Countryside: Indians, Colonists, and*

Slaves in the South Atlantic Forests, 1500–1800 (Cambridge: Cambridge University Press, 1990). James C. Malin's work on the Great Plains was a forerunner of this approach, incorporating biological and other scientific insights into history long before the ecological revolution made such an approach timely. See, especially, Malin, *The Grassland of North America: Prolegomena to Its History* (Lawrence, Kan.: published by the author, 1947); and Malin, *History and Ecology: Studies of the Grassland*, ed. Robert P. Swieringa (Lincoln: University of Nebraska Press, 1984).

9. For examples, see Herbert G. Fisser, "Biology and Ecology of Sagebrush in Wyoming: II. Grazing, Sagebrush Control, and Forage Yield," in *Proceedings—Symposium on the Biology of Artemisia and Chrysothamnus*, comp. E. Durant McArthur and Bruce L. Wech, General Technical Report INT-200 (Ogden, Utah: Intermountain Research Station, 1986), 303–11; Richard H. Norwood, Charles S. Bull, and Ronald Quinn, *A Cultural Overview of the Eureka, Saline, Panamint, and Darwin Region, East Central California* (Riverside, Calif.: Bureau of Land Management, 1980); Linda Wedel Greene, *Yosemite, The Park and Its Resources: A History of the Discovery, Management, and Physical Development of Yosemite National Park, California* (Washington, D.C.: National Park Service, 1987); Arthur R. Kruckeberg, *The Natural History of the Puget Sound Country* (Seattle: University of Washington Press, 1991).

10. For examples, see Arthur Dodwell and Theodore Rixon, *Forest Conditions in the Olympic Forest Reserve, Washington*, United States Geological Survey, Professional Paper No. 7 (Washington: Government Printing Office, 1902); John Lieberg, *Forest Conditions in the Northern Sierra Nevada, California*, United States Geological Survey, Professional Paper No. 8 (Washington: Government Printing Office, 1902); H. D. Langille, et al., *Forest Conditions in the Cascade Range Forest Reserve, Oregon*, United States Geological Survey, Professional Paper No. 9 (Washington: Government Printing Office, 1903).

11. In addition to those in the records center, there are materials that have been designated for retention and transferred to the archives branch. Of the two, those in the records center seem the more promising. On Bend as a lumber center, see Philip Cogswell, Jr., "Deschutes Country Pine Logging," in *High and Mighty: Select Sketches about the Deschutes Country* (Portland: Oregon Historical Society, 1981), 235–59; Thomas R. Cox, "Closing the Lumberman's Frontier: The Far Western Pine Country." *Journal of the West* 33 (July 1994): 59–66. With the exception of developments in northern Idaho, lumbering in the pine country of the interior West has been inadequately studied.

12. Aldo Leopold, "Cheat Takes Over," *The Land* 1 (Autumn 1941): 310–13 (quotation on p. 312). See also: James A. Young and B. Abbott Sparks, *Cattle in the Cold Desert* (Logan: Utah State University Press, 1985), xix–xxi, 3–15. Leopold's essay was reprinted, in slightly altered form, in his *A Sand County Almanac and Sketches Here and There* (London: Oxford University Press, 1949), 154–58. Compare James A. Young, "Public Response to the Catastrophic Spread of Russian Thistle (1880) and Halogeton (1945)," *Agricultural History* 62 (Spring 1988): 122–30.

13. United States Department of Agriculture, Forest Service, *Proceedings of the Western Juniper Ecology and Management Workshop*, General Technical Report PNW-74 (Portland, Ore.: Pacific Northwest Forest and Range Experiment Station, 1978), esp. 3–7, 83–90, 163–67.

14. For examples, see Kendall L. Johnson, "Sagebrush over Time: A Photographic Study of Rangeland Change," in McArthur and Wech, *Proceedings—Symposium on Artemisia and Chrysothamnus*, 223–52; Charles R. Ames, "Along the Mexican Border—Then and Now," *Journal of Arizona History* 18 (Winter 1977): 431–46; S. Clark Martin and Raymond M. Turner, "Vegetative Change in the Sonoran Desert Region, Arizona and Sonora," *Journal of the Arizona Academy of Science* 12 (June 1977): 59–69; Conrad J. Bahre, *Legacy of Change: Historic Human Impact on Vegetation of the Arizona Borderlands* (Tucson: University of Arizona Press, 1991).

15. For the context of his photographs, see Kenneth L. Gordon, *The Natural Areas of Oregon* (Corvallis: Oregon State College, 1953).

16. Julio L. Betancourt, Thomas R. Van Devender, and Paul S. Martin, *Packrat Middens: The Last Forty Thousand Years of Biotic Change* (Tucson: University of Arizona Press, 1990). See also Paul S. Martin, *The Last Ten Thousand Years: A Fossil Pollen Record of the American Southwest* (Tucson: University of Arizona Press, 1963).

17. Frederick R. Gehlbach, *Mountain Islands and Desert Seas: A Natural History of the U.S.–Mexican Borderlands* (College Station: Texas A & M University Press, 1981). See also Ames, "Along the Mexican Border"; Conrad J. Bahre and David E. Bradbury, "Vegetation Change along the Arizona–Sonora Boundary," *Annals of the Association of American Geographers* 68 (1978): 145–65.

18. Hugh M. Raup, "The View from John Sanderson's Farm: A Perspective for the Use of the Land," *Forest History* 10 (April 1966): 2–11. Also suggestive are Herbert I. Winer, "History of the Great Mountain Forest, Litchfield County, Connecticut" (Ph.D. diss., Yale University, 1956); S. Clark Martin and Raymond M. Turner, "Vegetative Change in the Sonoran Desert Region," 59–69; Robert R. Humphrey, "The Desert Grassland: A History of Vegetational Change and an Analysis of Causes," *Botanical Review* 24 (April 1958): 193–252; Ronald U. Cooke and Richard W. Reeves, *Arroyos and Environmental Change in the American South-West* (Oxford: Clarendon Press, 1976).

19. Kenneth J. Kingsley, "Biological and Social Repercussions of Irrigated Pecan Agriculture in Southern Arizona," in *Special Biotic Relationships in the Arid Southwest*, ed. Justin O. Schmidt (Albuquerque: University of New Mexico Press, 1989), 131–50. For a similar approach, see Amadeo M. Rea, *Once a River: Bird Life and Habitat Changes on the Middle Gila* (Tucson: University of Arizona Press, 1983).

20. Robert Rush Miller, "Man and the Changing Fish Fauna of the American Southwest," *Papers of the Michigan Academy of Science, Arts, and Letters* 46 (1961): 365–404; W. L. Minckley, *Native Fishes of Arid Lands: A Dwindling Resource of the Desert Southwest*, General Technical Report RM-206 (Fort Collins, Colo.: Rocky Mountain Forest and Range Experiment Station, 1991); William W. Dudley, *Effects of Irrigation Pumping on Desert Pupfish Habitats in Ash Meadows, Nye County, Nevada*, United States Geological Survey, Professional Paper No. 947 (Washington, D.C.: Government Printing Office, 1976); Edwin Philip Pister, "The Desert Fishes Council: Catalyst for Change," in *Battle against Extinction: Native Fish Management in the American West*, ed. W. L. Minckley and James E. Deacon (Tucson: University of Arizona Press, 1991), 55–68; James E. Deacon and Cynthia Williams Deacon, "Ash Meadows and the Legacy of the Devils Hole Pupfish," in ibid., 69–91.

21. Donald Worster, "World without Borders: The Internationalization of Environmental History," in *Environmental History: Critical Issues in Comparative Perspective* (Lanham, Md.: University Press of America, 1985), 661–69.

22. Alfred Runte, *National Parks: The American Experience* (Lincoln: University of Nebraska Press, 1979), 108–10, 118–40.

23. Charles F. Cooper, personal communication with author, Nov. 20, 1989; Stephen J. Pyne, "Fire Policy and Fire Research in the U.S. Forest Service," *Journal of Forest History* 25 (April 1981): 64–77. On the forests of southern California, see Michael Sakarias, "The Cleveland National Forest: San Diego's Watershed," *Journal of San Diego History* 21 (Fall 1975): 54-65; Ronald F. Lockmann, *Guarding the Forests of Southern California: Evolving Attitudes toward Conservation of Watershed, Woodlands, and Wilderness* (Glendale, Calif.: Arthur H. Clark, 1981). Neither work touches on the transborder differences in the forests. Indeed, Lockmann overlooks the peninsular ranges and their forests altogether. The contrasting fire-control policies of the Forest Service and Bureau of Indian Affairs might also be compared. The papers of Harold Weaver, located at the Forest History Society in Durham, N.C., would be invaluable. See also Stephen J. Pyne, *Fire in America: A Cultural History of Wildland and Rural Fire* (Princeton, N.J.: Princeton University Press, 1982), esp 100–122.

24. For introductions, see Ted W. and Charlene P. Nelson, "Fire, Insects, Wind, Volcano: The History of Disaster Management by the Weyerhaeuser Company," in *History of Sustained Yield Forestry: A Symposium*, ed. Harold K. Steen (Santa Cruz, Calif.: Forest History Society, 1984), 21–30; Shigeru Shimotori, "Trends and Problems in National Forest Management in Hokkaido since 1950," in ibid., 284–88.

25. Chaffey's activities have been largely ignored by scholars. However, see J. A. Alexander, *The Life of George Chaffey: A Study of Irrigation Beginnings in California and Australia* (Melbourne: Macmillan, 1928); Ernestine Hill, *Water into Gold* (Melbourne: Robertson and Mullens, 1937).

26. Samuel P. Hays, *Beauty, Health, and Permanence: Environmental Politics in the United States, 1955–1985* (Cambridge: Cambridge University Press, 1987); Hays, "The Structure of Environmental Politics since World War II," *Journal of Social History* 14 (Summer 1981): 719–38. See also Will Sarvis, "The Mount Rogers National Recreation Area and the Rise of Public Involvement in Forest Service Planning," *Environmental History Review* 18 (Summer 1994): 41–65.

27. For the context of this issue, see Joel Gottlieb, "The Preservation of Wilderness Values: The Politics and Administration of Conservation Policy" (Ph.D. diss., University of California, Riverside, 1972), 169–84; Michael McCloskey, "The Wilderness Act of 1964: Its Background and Meaning," *Oregon Law Review* 45 (June 1966): 288–321. Most accounts of the drive for the Wilderness Bill emphasize the causative effects of the controversy over Echo Park Dam and downplay, when they do not ignore, those surrounding the Three Sisters and North Cascades wilderness areas, which were more directly relevant. See, for examples, Elmo Richardson, *Dams, Parks, and Politics: Resource Development and Preservation in the Truman-Eisenhower Era* (Lexington: University Press of Kentucky, 1973), 129–52; Roderick Nash, *Wilderness and the American Mind*, rev. ed. (New Haven, Conn.:

Yale University Press, 1973), 209–20; Mark W. T. Harvey, "Echo Park, Glen Canyon, and the Postwar Wilderness Movement," *Pacific Historical Review* 60 (February 1991): 43–67. On the North Cascades, see Alan R. Sommarstrom, "Wild Land Preservation Crisis: The North Cascades Controversy" (Ph.D. diss., University of Washington, 1970).

28. For an introduction to LCDC and its context, see Thomas R. Cox, *The Park Builders: A History of State Parks in the Pacific Northwest* (Seattle: University of Washington Press, 1988), 137–64.

29. Earl Pomeroy, *The Pacific Slope: A History of California, Oregon, Washington, Idaho, Utah, and Nevada* (New York: Alfred A. Knopf, 1965), 120–64.

30. A bare beginning toward analyzing these developments is provided by Robert Chandler, "Deschutes Country: Recent Times," in Vaughan, *High and Mighty*, 261–72. Shifting patterns of agriculture affect wildlife as well as social and economic patterns. For example, the displacement of grain crops by cotton, sugar beets, and alfalfa has had a major impact on migratory waterfowl (and on hunting) in California's San Joaquin and Imperial valleys. Such effects also deserve examination.

31. Frank J. and Deborah E. Popper, "The Reinvention of the American Frontier," paper presented to Western Historical Association (with comment by Harry McDean), Reno, Nevada, October 18, 1990. On both the Poppers' argument and McDean's reply, see *Christian Science Monitor*, December 18, 1990, 13. Revealingly, when the Poppers published their paper, they did so in the popular journal of the Natural Resources Defense Council. See *The Amicus Journal* 13 (Summer 1991): 4–7.

32. Morgan Sherwood, *Big Game in Alaska: A History of Wildlife and People* (New Haven, Conn.: Yale University Press, 1981); William L. Graf, *Wilderness Preservation and the Sagebrush Rebellions* (Totowa, N.J.: Rowman and Littlefield, 1990); R. McGreggor Cawley, *Federal Land, Western Anger: The Sagebrush Rebellion and Environmental Politics* (Lawrence: University Press of Kansas, 1993). Useful approaches are suggested by Lawrence Rakestraw, "The West, State's Rights, and Conservation: A Study of Six Public Land Conferences," *Pacific Northwest Quarterly* 48 (July 1957): 49–56; Richard W. Judd, "Reshaping Maine's Landscape: Rural Culture, Tourism, and Conservation," *Journal of Forest History* 32 (October 1988): 180–90.

33. On Smylie, see Cox, *Park Builders*, 104–20; on Church, see Terry DiMattio, "The Wild and Scenic Rivers Bill" (master's thesis, San Diego State University, 1976). Smylie's papers are at the Idaho State Historical Society, Boise; Church's at Boise State University. Church's papers were not yet open at the time DiMattio conducted his research. The American Heritage Center at the University of Wyoming holds a host of other collections that might be utilized in the study of key figures whose careers have dealt with the land and environmental questions.

34. J. William Futrell, "Parks to the People: New Directions for the National Park System," *Emory Law Journal* 25 (Spring 1976): 255–316; Joseph H. Engbeck, Jr., *State Parks of California from 1864 to the Present* (Portland, Ore.: Charles H. Belding, 1980), 121–27; John Hart, "Parks for the People: The National Debate,"

Sierra 64 (September–October 1979): 45–49; Thomas R. Cox, "From Hot Springs to Gateway: The Evolving Concept of Public Parks," *Environmental Review* 5 (Spring 1981): 14–26.

35. For parallels, see Galen Cranz, *The Politics of Park Design: A History of Urban Parks in America* (Cambridge, Mass.: Harvard University Press, 1982); Robert A. J. McDonald, "'Holy Retreat' or 'Practical Breathing Spot'?: Class Perceptions of Vancouver's Stanley Park, 1910–1913," *Canadian Historical Review* 65 (June 1984): 127–53.

36. This can be seen in works on the Wilderness Bill, which have tended to focus on the political aspects of the struggle for passage and the activities of various special interest groups that sought to influence the course of legislation or its implementation. See, for example Craig W. Allin, *The Politics of Wilderness Preservation* (Westport, Conn.: Greenwood Press, 1982). For a useful approach to the influence of class, see Susan Schrepfer, "Conflict in Preservation: The Sierra Club, Save-the-Redwoods League, and Redwood National Park," *Journal of Forest History* 24 (April 1980): 60–76.

37. James Willard Hurst, *Law and Economic Growth: The Legal History of the Lumber Industry in Wisconsin, 1836–1915* (Cambridge, Mass.: Belknap Press of Harvard University Press, 1964). See also Theodore Steinberg, *Nature Incorporated: Industrialization and the Waters of New England* (Cambridge: Cambridge University Press, 1991).

38. Stephanie Pincetl, "The Environmental Policies and Politics of the Brown Administration, 1975–1983" (Ph.D. diss., University of California, Los Angeles, 1985); Arthur F. McEvoy, *The Fisherman's Problem: Ecology and Law in California Fisheries, 1850–1980* (Cambridge: Cambridge University Press, 1986). See also Thomas More Hoban and Richard Oliver Brooks, *Green Justice: The Environment and the Courts* (Boulder, Colo.: Westview Press, 1987).

39. William Voigt, Jr., *Public Grazing Lands: Use and Misuse by Industry and Government* (New Brunswick, N.J.: Rutgers University Press, 1976). For more even-handed accounts, see R. Douglas Hurt, "The National Grasslands: Origin and Development in the Dust Bowl," *Agricultural History* 59 (April 1985): 246–59; Terry West, "USDA Forest Service Management of the National Grasslands," *Agricultural History* 64 (Spring 1990): 86–98.

40. Paul J. Culhane, *Public Lands Politics: Interest Group Influence on the Forest Service and Bureau of Land Management* (Baltimore: Johns Hopkins University Press, 1981); John Walton, *Western Times and Water Wars: State, Culture, and Rebellion in California* (Berkeley: University of California Press, 1992), 241–86. To appreciate fully the freshness of Walton's approach, compare Abraham Hoffman, *Vision or Villainy: Origins of the Owens Valley–Los Angeles Water Controversy* (College Station: Texas A & M University Press, 1981).

41. Harold K. Steen, *The U.S. Forest Service: A History* (Seattle: University of Washington Press, 1976), 278–323, is a good beginning. Steen focuses on controversies and decision making in Washington, D.C.; much study at the regional and local levels, where implementation takes place, remains to be done.

42. William G. Robbins, *Hard Times in Paradise: Coos Bay, Oregon, 1850–1986* (Seattle: University of Washington Press, 1988), 116–20, 132–37 (quotation on

136). Weyerhaeuser's Klamath Falls operations await thorough scholarly investigation. For introductions, see Ralph W. Hidy, Frank Ernest Hill, and Allan Nevins, *Timber and Men: The Weyerhaeuser Story* (New York: Macmillan, 1963), 403–6; Harry J. Drew, *Weyerhaeuser Company: A History of People, Land and Growth* (Klamath Falls, Ore.: Weyerhaeuser Co., Eastern Oregon Region, 1979), 48–54; Cox, "Closing the Lumberman's Frontier," 61, 64–66. The Weyerhaeuser Company archives in Tacoma, Washington, offer a wealth of materials on the firm's forest-management strategies.

43. Thomas R. Cox, "The Passage to India Revisited: Asian Trade and the Development of the Far West, 1850–1900," in *Reflections of Western Historians*, ed. John Alexander Carroll (Tucson: University of Arizona Press, 1969), 85–103; Cox, *Mills and Markets*, esp. 71–100, 199–226; Pomeroy, *Pacific Slope*, 83–119.

44. On the relationship between international trade and environmental concerns, see Seymour J. Rubin and Thomas R. Graham, eds., *Environment and Trade: The Relations of International Trade and Environmental Policy* (Totowa, N.J.: Allanheld, Osmun, 1982); John A. Zivnuska, *U.S. Timber Resources in a World Economy* (Washington: Resources for the Future, 1967); John Larsen, "Environmental Issues and Their Influence on World Wood Trade," in *World Trade in Forest Products*, ed. James S. Bethel (Seattle: University of Washington Press, 1983), 129–36. For an example of how these issues can be incorporated into an historical study, see my "The North American-Japan Timber Trade: A Survey of Its Social, Economic, and Environmental Impact," in *World Deforestation in the Twentieth Century*, ed. John F. Richards and Richard P. Tucker (Durham, N.C.: Duke University Press, 1988), 164–86.

45. For an introduction, see Jim Gladson, "Forest Health: A Shared Vision for Restored Forests," *Oregon Wildlife* 47 (September–October 1991): 4–6; Pat Wray, "The 'Around' Timber Sale," *Oregon Wildlife* 47 (September–October 1991): 7–8.

46. Susan Flader, *Thinking Like a Mountain: Aldo Leopold and the Evolution of an Ecological Attitude toward Deer, Wolves, and Forests* (Columbia: University of Missouri Press, 1974); James M. Glover, "Thinking Like a Wolverine: The Ecological Evolution of Olaus Murie," *Environmental Review* 13 (Fall–Winter 1989): 29–45; Thomas R. Dunlap, "'The Coyote Itself'—Ecologists and the Value of Predators," *Environmental Review* 7 (Spring 1983): 54–70; Dunlap, *Saving America's Wildlife: Ecology and the American Mind, 1850–1990* (Princeton, N.J.: Princeton University Press, 1988); Keir B. Sterling, "Builders of the U.S. Biological Survey," *Journal of Forest History* 33 (1989): 180–87.

47. On Hornaday, see Peter Wild, *Pioneer Conservationists of Eastern America* (Missoula, Mont.: Mountain Press, 1986), 95–105. On Leopold, see Flader, *Thinking Like a Mountain*; Douglas H. Strong, *Dreamers and Defenders: American Conservationists* (Lincoln: University of Nebraska Press, 1988), 134–51. Dunlap, *Saving America's Wildlife*, provides useful context, but fails to address the refuge vs. management controversy, while C. Raymond Clar's massive study of forestry in California, although uneven, demonstrates the great potential of in-depth studies of state environmental and natural resource management agencies. Clar, *California Government and Forestry from Spanish Days until the Creation of the Department of Natural Resources in 1927* (Sacramento: California Division of Forestry, 1959), and

California Government and Forestry, vol. 2, *During the Young and Rolph Administrations* (Sacramento: California Division of Forestry, 1969).

48. William G. Robbins, *Lumberjacks and Legislators: Political Economy of the U.S. Lumber Industry, 1890–1941* (College Station: Texas A & M University Press, 1982); Robbins, *Colony and Empire: The Capitalist Transformation of the American West* (Lawrence: University Press of Kansas, 1994); Donald Worster, *Dust Bowl: The Southern Plains in the 1930s* (New York: Oxford University Press, 1979); Worster, *Rivers of Empire: Water, Aridity, and the Growth of the American West* (New York: Pantheon Books, 1985). Implicitly or explicitly, considerations of economic class pervade much recent environmental history. In addition to the above, see Robert Bunting, "Abundance and the Forests of the Douglas-Fir Bioregion, 1840–1920," *Environmental History Review* 18 (Winter 1994): 14–62.

49. For examples, see Pyne, *Fire in America*, esp. 143–60; Grady McWhiney and Forrest McDonald, "The Celtic Origins of Southern Herding Practices," *Journal of Southern History* 51 (May 1985): 165–82. A broader study of cultural persistence is David Hackett Fisher, *Albion's Seed: Four British Folkways in America* (New York: Oxford University Press, 1989).

50. Patricia Marchak, *Green Gold: The Forest Industry in British Columbia* (Vancouver: University of British Columbia Press, 1983); Jeremy Kilar, *Michigan's Lumbertowns: Lumbermen and Laborers in Saginaw, Bay City, and Muskegon, 1870–1905* (Detroit: Wayne State University Press, 1990); Robert MacCameron, "Environmental Change in Colonial New Mexico," *Environmental History Review* 18 (Summer 1994): 117–39.

51. Gene Gressley, "Colonialism: A Western Complaint," *Pacific Northwest Quarterly* 54 (January 1963): 1–8; William G. Robbins, "The `Plundered Province' Thesis and Recent Historiography of the American West," *Pacific Historical Review* 55 (November 1986): 577–97; Richard D. Lamm and Michael McCarthy, *The Angry West: A Vulnerable Land and Its Future* (Boston: Houghton Mifflin, 1982). See also the series of articles "The American West as an Underdeveloped Region," *Journal of Economic History* 16 (December 1956). Gerald D. Nash states the argument simply: "During much of the first half of the twentieth century the American West constituted a colonial society in its relationship to the older areas of the United States." Nash, *The American West in the Twentieth Century: A Short History of an Urban Oasis* (Albuquerque: University of New Mexico Press, 1977), 6. However, as Earl Pomeroy notes: "If the Western economy sometimes seemed colonial, some of its greatest monopolies were home grown. Montgomery Street gave orders far more than it took them, even when San Francisco was young" (*Pacific Slope*, 85–86).

52. For an example of this approach, see Graf, *Wilderness Preservation and the Sagebrush Rebellions*.

53. Edward L. Ullman, "Rivers as Regional Bonds: The Columbia-Snake Example," *Geographical Review* 41 (April 1951): 210–25; D. W. Meinig, *The Great Columbia Plain: A Historical Geography, 1805–1910* (Seattle: University of Washington Press, 1968).

54. William H. Hutchinson, "California's Economic Imperialism: An Historical Iceberg," in Carroll, *Reflections of Western Historians*, 67–83.

55. For suggestive approaches, see Elvin Hatch, "Stratification in a Rural Cali-

fornia Community," *Agricultural History* 49 (January 1975): 21–38; Peter K. Simpson, *Community of Cattlemen: A Social History of the Cattle Industry in Southeastern Oregon, 1869–1912* (Moscow: University of Idaho Press, 1987); George Blackburn and Sherman L. Ricards, "The Timber Industry in Manistee County, Michigan: A Case History in Local Control," *Journal of Forest History* 18 (April 1974): 14–21.

56. James B. Allen offered a preliminary assessment, but few western historians have followed his lead. See Allen, *The Company Town in the American West* (Norman: University of Oklahoma Press, 1966); Allen, "The Company-Owned Mining Town in the West: Exploitation or Benevolent Paternalism?" in Carroll, *Reflections of Western Historians*, 177–97. For a useful exception, see Keith C. Peterson, *Company Town: Potlatch, Idaho, and the Potlatch Lumber Company* (Pullman: Washington State University Press; Moscow, Idaho: Latah County Historical Society, 1987).

57. Charles S. Peterson, "Small Holding Land Patterns in Utah and the Problem of Forest Watershed Management," *Forest History* 17 (July 1973): 4–13.

58. Isaiah Bowman, *The Pioneer Fringe* (New York: American Geographical Society, 1931); Jerome O. Steffen, *Comparative Frontiers: A Proposal for Studying the American West* (Norman: University of Oklahoma Press, 1980). For a number of years, Steffen and his associates put out a *Comparative Frontiers Newsletter*.

59. The starting point for the former ought to be Earl Pomeroy, *In Search of the Golden West: The Tourist in Western America* (New York: Alfred A. Knopf, 1957). For other useful approaches, see Robert E. Ankli and Alan L. Olmstead, "The Adoption of the Gasoline Tractor in California," *Agricultural History* 55 (July 1981): 213–30; Peter Berck, "A Note on the Real Cost of Tractors in the 1920s and 1930s," *Agricultural History* 59 (January 1985): 66–71; Kerwin L. Klein, "Frontier Products: Tourism, Consumerism, and the Southwestern Public Lands, 1890–1990," *Pacific Historical Review* 62 (February 1993): 39–71; Thomas R. Cox, "Before the Casino: James G. Scrugham, State Parks, and Nevada's Quest for Tourism," *Western Historical Quarterly* 24 (August 1993): 333–50. The struggle between Utah and Nevada over the routing of the Lincoln Highway is one topic needing further study. See Lincoln Highway Association, *The Lincoln Highway: The Story of a Crusade that Made Transportation History* (New York: Dodd, Mead, 1935).

60. The bureaucratic battles are well illustrated in Elmo Richardson, "Olympic National Park: Twenty Years of Controversy," *Forest History* 12 (April 1968): 6–15, but they can be seen in many another time and place.

61. Useful beginnings are provided by Norris Hundley, Jr., *Water and the West: The Colorado River Compact and the Politics of Water in the American West* (Berkeley: University of California Press, 1975); Richardson, *Dams, Parks, and Politics*; Dorothy Zeisler-Vralsted, "Reclaiming the Arid West: The Role of the Northern Pacific Railway in Irrigating Kennewick, Washington," *Pacific Northwest Quarterly* 84 (October 1993): 130–39; Hugh Lovin, "'New West' Dreams and Schemes: John H. Garrett and His Enterprises in Idaho and Montana," *Idaho Yesterdays* 34 (Spring 1990): 2–17; Lovin, "Water, Arid Land, and Visions of Advancement on the Snake River Plain," *Idaho Yesterdays* 35 (Spring 1991): 3–18; Lovin, "The Sunnyside Irrigation Debacle," *Idaho Yesterdays* 36 (Summer 1992): 24–33. See also Kenneth E. Hendrickson, Jr., *The Waters of the Brazos: A History of the Brazos River Authority,*

1929–1979 (Waco, Tex.: Texian Press and Brazos River Authority, 1981); John E. Thorson, *River of Promise, River of Peril: The Politics of Managing the Missouri River* (Lawrence: University Press of Kansas, 1994). Lawrence B. Lee, "Environmental Implications of Government Reclamation in California," *Agricultural History* 49 (January 1975): 223–29, provides a promising model, and Donald J. Pisani, *To Reclaim a Divided West: Water, Law, and Public Policy, 1848–1902* (Albuquerque: University of New Mexico Press, 1992), is richly suggestive. Less satisfactory, but useful for revealing how much remains to be done, is Paul Curtis Pitzer, "Visions, Plans, and Realities: The Columbia Basin Project" (Ph.D. diss., University of Oregon, 1990).

62. Mary Catherine Miller, *Flooding the Courtrooms: Law and Water in the Far West* (Lincoln: University of Nebraska Press, 1993); Lloyd Burton, *American Indian Water Rights and the Limits of Law* (Lawrence: University Press of Kansas, 1991); Michael C. Meyer, *Water in the Hispanic Southwest: A Social and Legal History, 1550–1850* (Tucson: University of Arizona Press, 1984); *Cappaert et al. v. United States*, 96 S. Ct. 2062 (1976); Antonio Rossman and Michael J. Steel, "Forging the New Water Law: Public Regulation of `Proprietary' Groundwater Rights," *Hastings Law Journal* 33 (March 1982): 903–57; Martha Guy, "The Public Trust Doctrine and California Water Law: *National Audubon Society* v. *Department of Water and Power*," *Hastings Law Journal* 33 (January 1982), 653–87; Cynthia Deacon Williams and James E. Deacon, "Ethics, Federal Legislation, and Litigation in the Battle against Extinction," in Minckley and Deacon, *Battle against Extinction*, 109–21; Walton, *Western Times and Water Wars*, 264–68.

63. Hundley, *Water and the West*; David E. Kromm and Stephen E. White, eds., *Groundwater Exploitation in the High Plains* (Lawrence: University of Kansas Press, 1992); John Opie, *Ogallala: Water for a Dry Land* (Lincoln: University of Nebraska Press, 1993); Marc Reisner, *Cadillac Desert: The American West and Its Disappearing Water* (New York: Viking, 1986), 452–73. Although journalistic, Reisner's work is a good introduction to the Ogallala aquifer and the problem of fossil water.

64. A provocative approach is offered by Al Richmond, Jr., and W. R. Baron, "Precipitation, Range Carrying Capacity, and Navajo Livestock Raising, 1870–1975," *Agricultural History* 63 (Spring 1989): 217–30.

65. For a useful example, see Glenna Matthews, "The Apricot War: A Study of the Changing Fruit Industry during the 1930s," *Agricultural History* 59 (January 1985): 25–39. Even such a much-studied phenomenon as wheat raising can still be viewed in fresh ways. See Dana G. Dalrymple, "Changes in Wheat Varieties and Yields in the United States, 1919–1984," *Agricultural History* 62 (Fall 1988): 20–36.

66. Like most historical studies of the wine industry in California, Vincent P. Carosso, *The California Wine Industry, 1830–1895* (Berkeley: University of California Press, 1951), concentrates on the premodern era. However, see Ray Cyril, *Robert Mondavi of the Napa Valley* (London: Heinemann, 1984); James Conaway, *Napa* (Boston: Houghton Mifflin, 1990). Although a popular history, Conaway's work is insightful and, indirectly, suggests many avenues for research.

67. Historical literature on these firms is not extensive. However, see Hollis J.

Limprecht, *The Kiewet Story: Remarkable Man, Remarkable Company* (Omaha, Nebr.: Omaha World-Herald Co., 1981). Leonard J. Arrington's work provides more useful examples of such studies. See, especially, his *David Eccles, Pioneer Western Industrialist* (Logan: Utah State University, 1975), and *Beet Sugar in the West: A History of the Utah-Idaho Sugar Company, 1891–1966* (Seattle: University of Washington Press, 1966).

68. A fresh approach to fisheries is offered in Patrick W. O'Bannon, "Technological Change in the Pacific Coast Canned Salmon Industry, 1900–1925: A Case Study," *Agricultural History* 56 (January 1982): 151–66. The William Kyle Papers, at the Lane County Historical Society in Oregon, contain unused materials on private efforts to establish salmon hatcheries during the turn-of-the-century period; the American Tunaboat Association Papers, equally unused, are at the Scripps Institution of Oceanography, University of California, San Diego.

69. On Pardee, see Edward F. Staniford, "Governor in the Middle: The Administration of George C. Pardee, Governor of California, 1903–1907" (Ph.D. diss., University of California, Berkeley, 1955); Clar, *California Government and Forestry . . . until . . . 1927*; Elmo Richardson, *The Politics of Conservation: Crusades and Controversies, 1897–1913* (Berkeley: University of California Press, 1962). McNary was an author of the McNary-Haugen plan for agriculture and the Clarke-McNary Act for forestry, proponent of federal aid to state parks, and champion of efforts to save roadside timber. No adequate study of either McNary's or Jackson's environmental record exists. In McNary's case, this is probably largely because his papers are divided between the Library of Congress and the University of Oregon. A recent, but not particularly pathbreaking study of another western leader is Gary E. Elliott, "Land, Water and Power: The Politics of Nevada Senator Alan Bible, 1934–1974" (Ph.D. diss., Northern Arizona University, 1990).

70. Richardson, *Politics of Conservation*; Douglas H. Strong, *Tahoe: An Environmental History* (Lincoln: University of Nebraska Press, 1984).

71. Pincetl, "Environmental Policies and Politics"; Lawrence S. Hamilton, "The Federal Forest Regulation Issue: A Recapitulation," *Forest History* 9 (April 1965): 2–11.

72. William A. Duerr and Henry J. Vaux, eds., *Research in the Economics of Forestry* (Washington, D.C.: Charles Lathrop Pack Forestry Foundation, 1953), esp. 11–13, 149–57, 242–54; Harold K. Steen, ed., "Capital Gains for Forest Lands: Origins of the 1944 Tax Legislation," *Journal of Forest History* 22 (July 1978): 146–53; Sanford Gaines and Richard A. Westin, *Taxation for Environmental Protection: A Multinational Legal Study* (Westport, Conn.: Quorum Books, 1991). See also John V. Krutilla and Anthony C. Fisher, *The Economics of Natural Environments: Studies in the Evaluation of Commodity and Amenity Resources* (Baltimore: Johns Hopkins University Press for Resources for the Future, 1975).

3

The Impending Urban Past

An Essay on
the Twentieth-Century West

Roger W. Lotchin

The new and the old collide with a vengeance in the American urban West. The city represents one of the most momentous continuities in human history. For example, economies have evolved through preindustrial, proto-industrial, industrial, and postindustrial phases only to be outlasted by their urban containers. An Atlantic age in economics has given way to a Pacific one. European colonialism has fallen to Third World independence. Money, the touchstone of modern capitalism, to which cities are supposedly subordinate, was invented by the Greeks only in 700 B.C., perhaps forty centuries later than cities themselves. Urbanism has outlasted all these things. Damascus, which in the tenth century attained a population of one million, has now reached the age of four thousand years. Urban places have not always been the same, but anyone reading Marco Polo on Chinese cities or the complaints of Babylonians about urban congestion, noise, and crowding will not be too handicapped by culture and the passage of time to comprehend. In short, urbanization and urbanism are among the most profound continuities in history, outlasting gods, empires, economies, regions, traditions, techniques, and tools.[1]

Settled mostly after 1840, the European-derived American dry West is obviously one of the newest American regions and represents anything but continuity. It has had an abbreviated, although eventful past; and it is the American region most attuned to the future, a place where rapid change occurs. This extraordinary encounter between old and new makes western cities remarkably interesting.

Cities are an appropriate western-history subject for other reasons as well. Although scholarly American urban history derives from the works of Bessie Pierce, Arthur Schlesinger, Louis Wirth, and Lewis Mumford in the thirties, the modern field was born on the frontier.[2] Several good books and articles appeared before 1959, but the vast majority of scholarly works emerged after the appearance in 1959 of Richard Wade's seminal book linking city and frontier.[3] So did most European urban historical works.[4] Moreover, portions of the West are the most urbanized in the United States. However, though highly urban, the West has never been typically urban. World urbanization stretches back for over sixty centuries; yet despite its origins in the Spanish borderlands, most western urban growth has happened since 1880.[5] Because of this recent origin, western cities have had a unique relationship with technology. Unlike Damascus, western cities came of age at a point in time of great technological sophistication. Finally, no other American region has the kind of dryland hinterlands that the West does, nor does any other region contain the kind of primate, or oasis, cities characteristic of the dry West. Due to their rush toward urbanization and their special kind of urbanization, dry-West cities are an eminently eligible subject.[6]

Among other things, urban history has traditionally been rent by a division of opinion over whether to advance the field by theory, method, or topical diversification. Yet it seems self-evident that each is appropriate to a field that is trying to uncover all, or some significant fraction of, the truth. Therefore, this essay will offer a research agenda for the urban West that endeavors to satisfy two of them. First, it will suggest topical gaps in the literature and, second, it will hypothesize an interpretation with which the voids might be filled and our current understanding refined. In doing so, I would like to escape the entirely too prevalent custom of borrowing historical interpretations from the field of politics. That custom has become very pronounced in recent western history with its insistence on the importance of race, class, and gender, but the tendency has existed since at least the 1840s. I would like to propose that, historically, major American cities have been geographically conservative and culturally dynamic.[7] That is to say, once an urban network is established, the spatial relationships of that intercity network remain relatively stable; yet at the same time within cities, rapid, powerful, and sometimes breathtaking change occurs.

Above all, the impending western urban past should be a complex vista, one sensitive to the contradictory, paradoxical, and ironic in history. And one of the most important paradoxes lurks in the relationship of urbanism to change. For better or worse, cities have been both conservative and revolutionary, settling and unsettling. European and American urbanists noticed early on that once a city network was established, it strenuously resisted change. The most important American cities were founded by the 1890s, and none has arisen since. Suburbanization rearranged the relative importance of center and periphery, but independent, freestanding, major new cities have not accompanied this shift. Moreover, "most of the major towns in contemporary Europe were founded before 1300." Thereafter, primacy vacillated between the Italian and the West European parts of the network, yet the network itself did not vacillate.[8] Similarly, dominance within the American system has swung from the Midwest–Northeast to the Sunbelt, but the principal cities remain in place. Whether they are winning or losing, the important players remain the same.

This geographically conservative effect has placed a premium on understanding the origins and networks of cities. Western urbanists have done better than their eastern counterparts at explaining networks. Gunther Barth, Carl Abbott, Lionel Frost, Bradford Luckingham, Robert Dykstra, Lawrence Larsen, Kenneth Wheeler, Duane Smith, Arthur Gómez, and Norbert MacDonald have written model studies of the process of urbanization in the West.[9] Timothy Mahoney, David Goldfield, Lawrence Larsen, and Don Harrison Doyle have produced the only comparable books on eastern systems.[10] Still, most twentieth-century western urban systems have not yet been exhaustively covered. Eugene Moehring has begun a study of the urbanization of the Pacific Slope, 1840–1885, that will substantially alleviate this problem. However, at present, all of the California cities, the cities of the Willamette Valley, Puget Sound, the Wasatch Oasis, the Colorado Piedmont, Montana, New Mexico, and Texas all need to be integrated into modern system studies. So does the overall western urban network.

Timothy Mahoney's investigation of nineteenth-century Illinois urban systems and Paul Hohenberg and Lynn H. Lees's comparable study of Europe, 1000–1950, are impressive prototypes for a larger western network study. According to the latter, one set of cities grew up as central place cities, largely dependent upon their own contiguous countryside, and a second arose as network cities dependent on other cities. Like Mahoney, the authors insist upon the importance of urban systems rather than individual entities. Gilbert Rozman employed the same tool to judge the general advancement of Chinese, Russian, and Japanese societies by measuring the overall maturity of their urban systems.[11]

Western cities can be viewed in any one of these perspectives. Despite the justly celebrated, pioneering work of Adna Ferrin Weber, American urbanists have avoided this problem of population. Yet what Jan de Vries calls demographic urbanization is one of the most striking features of western history.[12] The West has had its share of "instant cities," whether triggered by gold, silver, copper, agriculture, timber, health, atoms, or war.[13] The reduced circumstances of once muscular and uproarious Butte and the numerous ghost towns of the West reiterate the importance of both demographic urbanization and deurbanization. A western investigation of these processes might look at the extent of western demographic urbanization or deurbanization due to mining, agricultural mechanization, federal policy, the lure of the city, recreation, energy discoveries, health, aerospace, or lumber. One might envision several other kinds of statistical studies. Jean Gottmann's investigation of the metropolis stretching from Boston to Washington, Bos-Wash or Ton-Ton, should certainly be replicated for metropolitan southern California, hopefully by an urban historian. Gottman was optimistic about the massing of people in the eastern urban corridor, as is Kevin Starr about southern California. Still, no one has yet paid much attention to the numbers part of this problem.[14] Gerald Nash has provided a framework for such an investigation. His notion that the modern West is a series of oases is one of the more provocative generalizations about urbanization, but it has not yet been sufficiently explored. A comparison of these primate cities in the dry West with those in the Third World, or a comparison of eastern and western patterns, would also be useful.

The potential of demographic urbanization is also evident in population projections for the future. These forecast an urban shoreline and border belt, perhaps two hundred miles wide, running from Seattle around the country to southern Maine. Growth projections in this zone range from modest to violent, with less increase expected in the benighted interior, save in exceptional places like Las Vegas. This shift would be a notable realignment of power within a stable urban system. Futurist and presentist social-science studies of this trend are bound to multiply, and it would be comforting to have an accompanying larger historical perspective.

By the same token, it is important to understand the impact of hyperurbanization on the depopulated or unpopulated western countryside. Although this rural–urban relationship of love, hate, tension, cooperation, and interdependence is often remarked upon by scholars, it is not frequently enough investigated in the monographic literature. Don Kirschner's discussion of city and country tensions in the Midwest is a good example of how to begin, and so is the work of Earl Pomeroy on the Pacific Slope, which argues that city–country divisions were less important in the West.[15] The city–country relationship is relevant, both to the traditional Turnerian notion of the frontier as a safety valve for city population and the equally traditional urban-history thesis that cities are parasitic on the countryside. In reality, the relationship was reciprocal. Western cities may have been occasionally parasitic, but they also absorbed large southern and midwestern excess farm populations.[16]

These suggestions emphasize the importance of studying the process of urbanization instead of the history of individual cities. Quite a few historians have argued this necessity—Allan Pred, Jan de Vries, Paul Hohenberg, Lynn H. Lees, James Vance, and Gilbert Rozman. De Vries makes one of the most compelling arguments, one relevant for understanding the twentieth century. Many scholars and contemporary critics

have a pathological opinion of cities. Yet, as de Vries has shown, by concentrating on the long view and on the process of demographic urbanization, city growth is not always discouraging. For example, varying parts
of the European urban system had vastly different experiences. At one
point, large cities forged ahead and small ones stagnated, only to catch
up again during the Industrial Revolution. De Vries has also delineated
periods of urban creativity, which added new cities, and periods of urban
consolidation, which integrated the gains made in the earlier era without
creating fresh towns. Unlike the Thernstrom school, de Vries found that
urbanization and proletarianization were "alternative rather than associated phenomena." He also observed that in an age when most people live
in cities and towns, the creation of fresh urban communities must take
people from older ones. Unlike contemporary critics, he regarded this
process as creativity rather than decay. This cycle reiterates that the process of urbanization is dynamic and that it cannot be studied in isolation
from hinterlands, from the national state, and from other cities. As de
Vries commented about the Industrial Revolution:

> It is not the "city" that is industrializing or the "countryside"
> that is progressing. Rather it is a society, usually best viewed in
> a regional context, that is developing via the mobilization of its
> resources by individuals with access to an urban system.

Earl Pomeroy stressed this same regional context, in an even more urban
way. As the latter put it, "Economically and culturally, the most significant divisions were not state boundaries but the watersheds of urban allegiance and control." Bradford Luckingham found city leadership and
precedence as valid for the Southwest as for Wade's original urban frontier.[17]

Quantification among urban historians began with economic and
geographic mobility studies. Unfortunately, in their ardor to demonstrate
that the capitalist system had either failed or aided working people, these
investigators largely ignored the cities' fundamental numbers. Therefore,
we still, for the most part, lack the basic studies of the growth,
deurbanization, and reorganization of urban populations. Statistical inquiries were hailed as the "new urban history" from Stephan Thernstrom's
1964 investigation of Newburyport until the late 1970s. Although these
works were often more concerned with class than city, they nonetheless
turned up lots of important urban information. However, as Eric
Monkkonen has noted, the urban-history quantifiers became disillusioned
with their own studies and generally did not replicate them. Hopefully,
this renunciation of the world of numbers will itself be repudiated.

Western history did not participate fully in the original boom of the
"new urban history," but it did produce one study of middle-class economic mobility in San Francisco, 1850–1880. The quantifiers generally

discovered what they considered to be inadequate economic mobility alongside extraordinary geographic mobility. In any case, the twentieth-century West offers considerable opportunity for the study of both.[18]

Historians as diverse as Richard Wade, Jane Jacobs, Lewis Mumford, Robert Higgs, and Fernand Braudel have noted the dynamism of cities that strains against their geographic inertia. As Braudel put it, "Towns are like electric transformers: they increase tension, they precipitate change and keep men's lives in a state of permanent fermentation."[19] It is probably true, as Lawrence Larsen and Bradford Luckingham have argued, that western cities were initially imitative of eastern ones rather than innovative. Nonetheless, within the broader culture, cities were also innovative.[20]

Here again, the field is wide open. For example, computers, aerospace, nuclear physics, high dams, the automobile, and other technologies supposedly have uniquely shaped the American West, but without a proportionate outpouring of historical studies to help us understand them. And cities are an ideal focus for such technological inquiries.

As Harold Platt and Mark Rose have shown for Chicago, Kansas City, and Denver, only relatively great densities of people, department stores, skyscrapers, offices, media, theaters, apartments, elite residences, markets, and capital could support, finance, and popularize a new technology like electricity. Although social scientists and historians often stress the epochal importance of industrialization, electricity found its largest early market in the lowly urban streetcar. Industrialists took many more years to adopt this revolutionary technology fully. From center cities, electricity spread progressively to neighborhood shopping districts, neighborhoods themselves, suburbs, and small towns. Rural areas provided a poor market because of their low densities and because the process of urbanization lured millions of farmers to cities, simultaneously making urban markets better and rural ones worse. Not only did cities stimulate electrical innovations, but this challenge to older forms of power and illumination forced other technologies like gas technology to modernize in order to maintain their footholds in the urban market. Martin Melosi has discovered an equally fruitful interface between the city in all its complexity and the technological career of Thomas Alva Edison.[21]

Social scientists and historians have usually approached auto technology from the perspective of the car. Obviously, the car transformed cities, but, as Paul Barrett, Scott Bottles, and Eric Monkkonen have shown, the cities also influenced, perhaps decisively, automobile history. With the works of Bottles, David Brodsly, and John B. Rae, southern California in particular has generated an excellent base literature on the relationship between the automobile and the city; yet most of the remainder of the West has not received the same attention.[22]

The possibilities of these technological approaches for western urbanists are practically limitless. One study has gauged the impact of transit on southern California, but most cities lack transit histories. The impact of computers on cities has been touched on for Silicon Valley, but only lightly. Nuclear electricity plants sprouted all over the country to supply power and light to cities, even deindustrializing ones like Pittsburgh, where the first commercial reactor appeared. Nuclear science was also a spinoff of the various university and government laboratories of the West that provided marked benefits for giant construction companies like Bechtel, for scientists, and for working people like those in the Bay Area assembly plants.[23] If anything, the connection between commercial air transport and urbanization has been even tighter. Cities are often considered the dependent variable of technology; however, cities greatly antedated aircraft transportation by some sixty-odd centuries. They simply cannot be considered the effect and airplanes the cause. Each form of intercity transportation had different implications for its urban terminals. Stagecoaches and steamboats could easily stop almost anywhere en route. Thus, they did not give cities a great advantage. Railroads, because of the cost of stopping and starting, required a good excuse, like a town, to halt, whereas the automobile has been the most flexible transportation device, capable of stopping at towns, farms, crossroads, cities, and anywhere in between. By contrast, commercial planes sometimes do not even stop at places of fifty thousand, which was the minimum for inclusion in the interstate-highway system. In other words, commercial air travel is the least adaptable form and requires a dense population market for its operation. This necessity and the role of city boosters, like Fiorello La Guardia of New York and Carl Hinshaw of Pasadena, in creating the commercial air-transportation system, should have made air travel a target of urban historians long ago. Yet only a few, such as Paul Barrett, Betsy Braden, and Paul Hagan, have entered this conspicuously urban field.[24]

War has been one of the most dynamic elements in twentieth-century western history, and it is generally argued that it has added greatly to the dynamism of cities. Yet, as several studies have shown, western cities have also had a marked impact upon defense. Along with urbanization, war has been one of the other momentous continuities in history. However, apart from studies by myself, Carl Abbott, Martin Schiesl, Marilynn Johnson, Arthur Verge, Leonard Arrington, Gerald Nash, Ann Markusen, and Peter Hall, scholars have not concentrated upon this elemental western relationship.[25] And these scholars concentrate entirely on World War II rather than World War I and pay even less attention to cities during the Vietnam War. Historians have long admitted the important demographic, economic, social, racial, ethnic, and technological influences of war and defense, but they have yet to elaborate these ideas adequately in specialized historiographical studies, although Gerald Nash set out a guideline for such research at least twenty years ago.

The process of urbanization has also been unsettling to the environment. William Cronon has documented this urban reorganization of nature in one way, Stephen Fox in another. Concentrating on the development of Chicago and the West, Cronon has shown how cities have comprehensively interpenetrated nature to the extent of breaking down the dichotomy between the two and creating a symbiosis of them. Instead of living in city or country, most people now live in metropolitan areas tied together in myriad ways. Such a study for other western cities would help test Cronon's ideas and provide a realization of the Pomeroy thesis that city and hinterland are more important divisions of the West than states. Cities have sometimes played contradictory roles in this transformation of nature. Stephen Fox has demonstrated that urban areas have produced most of the notable twentieth-century environmentalists. Yet cities have also been gross polluters. Today, power plants as far away as Utah and Phoenix, which export electricity to Los Angeles, actually generate smog that drifts into the Grand Canyon. Cities have likewise engineered some of the earliest attempts to reorganize, and thus potentially threaten, western geography. William Kahrl has argued that Los Angeles's Owens Valley Project was the first great water engineering achievement in the West and the model for later engineers and boosters. And the Owens project, its Mono Lake addition, and Hoover Dam guaranteed the continued growth of the southern California megalopolis. Without outside water, Los Angeles was destined to a no-growth status.[26]

Kahrl, Vincent Ostrom, Norris Hundley, Abraham Hoffman, John Walton, and Margaret L. Davis have probably exhausted the field of Los Angeles water history.[27] However, despite the successful efforts of Hundley, Walton, Marc Reisner, Donald Worster, Turrentine Jackson, Donald Pisani, and Robert Kelley to put water on the historians' agenda, western urban historians have not generally taken this cue to write water histories of other western cities.[28] One might study individual urban areas, synthesize the water history of several cities, chronicle the cooperation between parched cities and countryside, or even look at water engineering as an urban technology.

Hopefully, these works would emphasize the political side of the story. Water has been an important tool in the struggles between cities, and cheap water is often an urban subsidy for agriculture. For example, in a pivotal state like California, agriculture consumes about 85 percent of developed water; yet in 1980, 92 percent of the population was metropolitan. The story of how politicians persuaded a largely urban electorate to support these projects is still largely unwritten. Still, it is a fascinating story that bears directly on the Turnerian notion that the West encouraged democracy and the more recent argument that great waterworks, historically, have created tyranny. One would welcome a test of this latter thesis, especially in California, where citizens vote on everything imaginable and often interminably.[29]

The idea that cities are geographically conservative and culturally dynamic can be tested in other realms as well. The most recent interpreters of the West have argued that the history of the region must be better informed by, and possibly even transformed by, a fuller exploration of race, class, and gender. Oddly enough, some of these subjects have already been better covered than supposed mainstream groups. For example, western historians often insist on the terms *Anglo, Caucasian,* and *white* to characterize one part of the population. Yet, to my knowledge, there is no study of the Anglos, *as an ethnic group,* in any western city. Given the added assumption that the Anglos were and are the molders of western destiny, this omission is curious. Jewish, Italian, Irish, Scotch, German, and Basque, westerners like Louis B. Mayer, A. P. Giannini, James D. Phelan, John Muir, Donald Douglas, Frederick Weyerhaeuser, or Paul Laxalt might have found the label amusing, and some of them would have found the implication of omnipotence laughable. The proper term should be *American* rather than *Anglo.* The English regularly pillory the American West, especially its most dynamic part, southern California, as "Lotus Land" and worse, and do not seem to recognize an Anglo kinship there. On the other hand, if terms like *Anglo, white,* and *Caucasian* are supposed to denote a mainstream, the much maligned melting pot must have largely succeeded.

This conclusion will doubtless scandalize the many able defenders of cultural pluralism in the field of immigration history. Nonetheless, the logic of the position is inescapable. The group currently labeled *Caucasian, white,* or *Anglo* initially came to the West as Jews, midwesterners, Germans, English, Canadians, Irish, Cornish, Irish, Serbs, and so forth. If they *have not* melted, that would indicate even more multicultural diversity in the West than the current multiculturalists and revisionists recognize. In the interest of multiculturalism itself, these ethnic groups deserve their own studies. On the other hand, if, as the terms *Anglo, Caucasian,* and *white* imply, these groups are no longer Jewish, midwestern, German, English, Canadian, Irish, Cornish, Basque, Canadian, Scots, and southerners, then the melting pot must have largely succeeded. One simply cannot have it both ways. In that case, we must explain how the ethnics got into that container and, more importantly, in what condition they came out.

This logic is in line with John Bodnar's recent synthesis of American immigration. He does not employ the odious terms *assimilation* or *melting pot,* but his immigrants, like those in Oscar Handlin's *Uprooted,* had to make their individual accommodations to American democracy, capitalism, and culture. Both, in turn, reflect what Louis Wirth called "individual pluralism," or what Zane L. Miller more recently described as the "shift from a focus on groups to individuals as the basic units of society."[30]

Since the West has often been so abundantly urban, such studies would concentrate heavily on western cities, where the ethnic groups have ended up. And although immigration historians regularly posit the persistence of ethnicity, cities just as frequently encourage people to mix and to adopt a common dress, cosmopolitan mainstream cuisine, similar architecture, suburban lifestyle, bureaucratic employment, unexceptional entertainment, political parties, and language—in short, to share a common culture. To a very marked extent, American ethnics, especially urban ones, have become both behaviorally and structurally assimilated. This process of forming a national identity is a critical transformation. It is one that can illuminate the current discussion of nation-state formation, which concentrates on the political and governmental dimension of statehood rather than on the cultural consensus which underlies it.[31] Somehow, the United States has created a common nationality, in part because of the dynamism of its cities.[32]

Kenneth Philp and Nancy Shoemaker have already begun to examine the role of the city in Indian assimilation. Indians adjusted positively to urban conditions and formed tribal and then pan-Indian groups. The western tribe was a loose cultural entity, but more importantly, the tribal reservation was an administrative convenience for whites. So contemporary pan-Indianism, an urban product, is the second level of cultural merging, comparable to the white ethnic experience in the triple melting pot, as various diverse tribes or individuals banded together to pursue their interests.[33]

Ironically, with the exception of women and Indians, there is actually more urban literature on some twentieth-century minorities than on the majority. Besides prostitutes and war workers, women have been badly neglected, and so have city children and elders, despite the prominence of seniors in the West and the stimulating articles and books of Elliott West on childhood in frontier towns. Yet there are many works on Hispanics and blacks, including very good studies by Richard Griswold del Castillo, Thomas R. Sheridan, Bradford Luckingham, Albert Broussard, Douglas Daniels, Quintard Taylor, Kevin Leonard, Ricardo Romo, Mario García, Richard A. Garcia, George Sánchez, and Lawrence de Graaf.[34] Among the European-derived Americans, there are whole or partial studies of the Italians in San Francisco, Irish in Butte, midwesterners in Los Angeles, Jews in a number of places, and precious little else. The Basques, Canadians, Germans, Irish, easterners, midwesterners, southerners, Slavs, Chinese, Indians, Filipinos, Scandinavians, and others have been relatively neglected. Even the urban Japanese have been studied so asymmetrically that most of their twentieth-century urban existence is still a blank to us. In 1942, the United States government incarcerated most of the Japanese-American population of the West, and yet in 1976 the electorate of California returned Samuel Hayakawa to the United States Senate. We are awash in literature about that first infamous and dreadful episode, but we know too little about how the urban Japanese-Americans recovered from it and arrived so quickly at the Hayakawa stage of their history. Something comparable to John Modell's work on the Japanese-Americans of Los Angeles, 1900–1942, or Quintard Taylor's on Seattle African-Americans, is in order for the postwar Japanese and the entire twentieth-century experience of the other urban ethnics.[35]

One might add that similar studies are especially needed for the World War II period. At least in California cities, all the ethnics supported the war, bought bonds, worked in industry, accepted the draft, and, in general, participated as both Americans and ethnics in the events of the era. Yet one would not know it from the ethnic literature of the war, which concentrates overwhelmingly on African-Americans and Japanese-Americans. Because of the scholarship of Scott Wong, Chinese-Americans are finally getting some coverage, but it is still amazing that in a time when historical multiculturalism is de rigueur, so many ethnic groups have been neglected.

Besides excluding so many ethnic groups from history, historians have also neglected their intergroup relations. Both western and American immigration history is replete with investigations of single ethnic groups and their often problematical relations with the "majority." Yet since most urban ethnics lived among other ethnics rather than in mainstream areas, we must broaden our attention from American versus ethnic to general intergroup relations. We know how the Japanese got along with whites, at least up to 1942, but how did they relate to the Chinese, Filipinos, Koreans, or blacks? Sometimes these groups lived in close proximity in areas like South Central Los Angeles, so there must be an important urban story there. Studies by Ronald Bayor, Charles Trout, and John Stack of 1930s and 1940s interethnic relations in New York City and Boston are models for western urban history as well. Bayor and Stack found "neighbors in conflict," but other literature suggests that ethnics eventually came to accept each other and win acceptance in the broader society as well, as Valerie Matsumoto has argued.[36]

Just as comparative urban ethnic history would serve us well, so would general comparative urban history. It would test cities' cultural dynamism and geographic conservatism as well as cover a gap in the literature. Jan de Vries, leaning heavily on Louis Wirth, stressed three kinds of urbanization—demographic, structural, and behavioral. The latter creates a different lifestyle, and urban ways spread progressively to others. Although cities contain the most vivid examples of cultural diversity, the assumption is that something common, which Gunther Barth called a "city culture," develops.

Others would agree. Norbert MacDonald found that urbanization explained what was similar about Seattle and Vancouver and nationality explained what was different. MacDonald's focus could also be extended southward from the restrained cities of the Northwest to the tumultuous California Southland, where the Mexican part of the Los Angeles-San Diego-Tijuana megalopolis is sometimes described as the fastest growing urban region in North America. This tri-national approach would involve a tripartite cultural contrast and a shared urban, maritime, and Pacific Rim experience. Or one might stretch MacDonald's comparison of Vancouver and Seattle southward and eastward to include Portland, Edmonton, Calgary, Butte, Great Falls, Billings, Missoula, Bismarck, and Spokane. Even more important would be a study of the Mexican–American border economic and urban system, stretching from Brownsville–Matamoros to Tijuana–San Diego. The interpenetration of cultures at and across a border is an event nearly unique in American urban history. The comparison could be between similar cities, as William H. Mullins has provided for four West Coast cities during the Great Depression, or it could test the notion of western exceptionalism by extending Lawrence Larsen's analysis to compare modern eastern and western cities. Finally, the comparison could be equally well tested *within* the twentieth-century West between Mormon Salt Lake City, Hispanic El Paso, polyglot Los Angeles, and European/American–derived Seattle and Portland.

These same geographic locales might be treated from a slightly different perspective, following urban or labor-urban historians who have studied culture and class in eastern cities. Christine Stansell found a working class and a well-defined female culture in New York City; Stuart Blumin discovered a middle-class culture in cities; and Gunther Barth described a distinctive city culture. It would be instructive to see if these cultural or subcultural cleavages were as much affected by nationality as MacDonald found.[37] John Findlay has woven city and culture together in a different way by comparing several modern urban forms: Disneyland, Stanford Industrial Park, the Seattle World's Fair, and Sun City, Arizona.[38]

There is already a considerable literature of urban biography upon which to base these comparisons. One of the negative achievements of the "new Urban Historians" has been to give urban biography an undeservedly bad reputation. Oscar Handlin was correct when he argued that the history of individual cities can be understood only by studying them in toto, investigating how each part fits into the whole urban mechanism evolving over significant periods of time. Nor can the history of urbanization capture the drama of lone cities as well as urban history or urban biography can. The experiences of individual cities and the work of particular leaders tend to become buried under numbers and the grand schema of urbanization. Urban biography, as the Lyle Dorsett series on the West shows, also creates an initial order in the history of cities, a narrative base from which subsequent studies of all kinds can and do build. It is not practical to expect comparative or system studies to unearth all of the rich details of urban history that urban biographies can. Topical studies like those of mobility are useful, but fragmenting and one-dimensional. Western cities have been very dramatic because they share with Los Angeles the characteristic of being highly "improbable." Salt Lake City was certainly that, as were boomtown San Francisco and Denver, but Las Vegas is undoubtedly the most preposterous. An unimportant town in an extremely uncongenial geographic spot as late as the end of World War II, by the 1990 census Las Vegas had climbed into the top fifteen U.S. cities. Were it not for Los Angeles, Chicago, and a few others, this growth might be considered an unprecedented feat of American demographic urbanization. Whatever else one may say about Las Vegas, it is a good story, one of the best in the country, and one that has just recently found its narrators in Eugene Moehring and John Findlay.[39] De Vries was too harsh in rejecting urban history—the histories of individual cities—and claiming that "the problem of the city in early modern Europe can be resolved only in the context of the history of urbanization."[40] This generalization is partly true, but it mistakes what is actually a division of labor for an antithesis.[41]

There are dozens of western cities that do not yet have comprehensive scholarly twentieth-century biographies. Not only do major cities like San Francisco, Los Angeles (after 1930), San José, Portland, San Diego, and Wichita lack *comprehensive* modern biographies; so do many secondary cities. Spokane, Butte, Pueblo, Colorado Springs, Sacramento, Stockton, Fresno, Bakersfield, Eugene, San Bernardino, Long Beach, Anaheim, Provo, Logan, Reno, Prescott, and many others are eligible subjects. They deserve the kind of treatment that Lyle Dorsett, Thomas Alexander, James Allen, Eugene P. Moehring, Bradford Luckingham, Lawrence Larsen, Barbara Cottrell, Edward Beechert, Carl Abbott, Stephen Leonard, Thomas Noel, and Roger Sale gave to Denver, Salt Lake City, Las Vegas, Phoenix, Omaha, Honolulu, Portland, and Seattle. Although Bradford Luckingham's profiles of the cities of the Southwest provide an excellent introduction to the histories of El Paso, Albuquerque, and Tucson, urban biographies could go into even more exhaustive detail about them.

Some of these cities have grown remarkably important in recent years. Even formerly obscure San Bernardino is now a metropolitan area of over two million. Finally, there are many western towns suitable for either biographies or community studies. Don H. Doyle and Ralph Mann have already provided model studies of frontier Jacksonville, Illinois, and Grass Valley and Nevada City, California, respectively, and their approach could be employed for twentieth-century subjects as well.

Crime and disorder have been at least as responsive to the dynamism of urbanism, and so has law enforcement. Yet with the exception of the works of David R. Johnson, Eric Monkkonen, and Robert Fogelson, urban police history has been largely confined to the nineteenth-century East.[42] The western frontier has generated many studies of law and order, ranging from gunman biographies to Kevin Mullen's investigation of criminal justice and Frank Prassel's history of law enforcement, but the twentieth century has not.[43] This subject is important for several reasons. Robert Dykstra's *Cattle Towns* disputes the assumption that frontier towns were peculiarly violent.[44] Despite that finding, some scholars assume that the lawless frontier heritage contributed to the making of U.S. organized crime. However, if a tumultuous frontier heritage carried over anywhere, it should have been in the dry West, and organized crime definitely did not originate there. Moreover, compared to a western city like San Diego, a place like Washington, D.C., is a garrison state, with four times as many police per capita. Either the frontier West was not so savage or that heritage did not extend beyond 1890. Whatever the outcome of that debate, westerners, like Berkeley police chief August Vollmer or academic chiefs like Orlando Wilson, often led the movement for order through police reform, which is another reason for studying them.[45]

Contemporary gang wars are lethal, and their flowering in Los Angeles has given added urgency to the theme of law and order. Unfortunately, Frederick Thrasher's *The Gang*, written in the 1920s, remains the classic work in the field. Except for Dan Monti, Scott Cummings, Humbert Nelli, and Jenna Joselit, neither history nor sociology is well represented today.[46] Conceding the field to presentists creates the impression that contemporary urban warfare is unprecedented and that it is a peculiarly black and Latino folkway. Yet neither is the case. Current gangs and Uzi firepower may be startling, but so were Al Capone and the Thompson submachine gun in the 1920s.

A twentieth-century investigation of western cities modeled on David Johnson's or Roger Lane's magnificent studies of counterfeiting and Philadelphia violence, respectively, would give us some badly needed perspective. Dynamic urban economies provided a stimulus to counterfeiting, which city police would not suppress. This failure eventuated in the creation of the U.S. Secret Service, which largely repressed counterfeiting and also forged a link between the exploding cities and the evolving modern nation state. We need more histories of the cops, too, whether one agrees with the view of Sidney Harring that the police are an instrument of bourgeois capital accumulation or with the majority view that they evolved to secure law and order (after all, Marxist states have or had plenty of them too). Kevin Mullen's forthcoming history of the San Francisco police and Martin Schiesl's essay on the L.A. police are a good start. Lawrence M. Friedman and Robert V. Percival suggest another approach to crime through their investigation of the criminal justice system in Alameda County, California. Preliminary sketches by Fred Viehe, John

Findlay, and Richard Whitehall of organized crime and gambling in twentieth-century Los Angeles and Las Vegas signal an equally fascinating opportunity. Particularly interesting is David Johnson's recent argument that American casino gambling developed from urban models south of the border in Juárez and Tijuana.[47]

If anything, the dynamism of urban economics was more profound and has been more slighted than the search for order. Perhaps that vacuum has occurred in part because American urban historians have been loath to insist on the importance of urbanism and urbanization to economic development, although their European counterparts have suffered from no such diffidence. A book by Arthur Verge looks at the impact of World War II on Los Angeles, and several studies examine the economic experience of women and African Americans or of other ethnics in western cities. Yet the economics of urbanization cannot be understood simply by exploring the richly documented job discrimination against women and minorities.

As economic historians from the early 1960s pointed out, city building itself is a dynamic process, which generates heavy demands for goods and services. That is especially true of cities like contemporary Las Vegas or 1920s Los Angeles, which doubled from 576,000 to 1,200,000. To put the matter differently, Angelenos in the 1920s had to construct in ten years another city as large as the one with which they entered the decade. In addition to this city-building thrust, urbanization created a great stimulus in other economic realms. As the boosters knew, an urban boom is a real estate bonanza, as Marc Weiss and Patricia Limerick have emphasized for Los Angeles and the wider West.[48] A city is also a device for capital accumulation and for the redistribution of that money once it is amassed. John D. Haeger and Jeffrey Adler have shown how New York and Boston capitalists made frontier Chicago into a classic boomtown. And Luckingham, Larry Schweikart, and Lynne Pierson Doti have noted a similar process for twentieth-century southwestern cities.[49]

By the same token, the dynamics of demographic urbanization are tantamount to the gathering of a labor pool, an obvious necessity for manufacturing. Cities collect other assets that entrepreneurs, especially smaller ones, can draw upon to begin a manufacturing or other business. These external economies, or externalities, allow small firms to start up before they are able to afford a full complement of lawyers, designers, architects, engineers, accountants, and so forth. Once in business, these thousands of small firms, like the aerospace and defense subcontractors in southern California, further increase the competitiveness of larger firms that draw on them. Nor did these assets always create lawful businesses, as David R. Johnson documents in melancholy detail. Like any other business, counterfeiting also required certain external economies, such as a skilled labor force of printers, numerous printing establishments, ample supplies of paper, a ready market, underemployed or unemployed people, tolerant cops, and an urban wilderness in which to hide.[50]

The city is also a concentrated, accessible legitimate market. For example, Thomas R. Cox has shown that the coastal lumber industry sprang from demands of the Gold Rush, much of it from expanding cities like oft-burnt San Francisco and towns from Placerville to Hallelujah Junction. When the gold faltered, railroad building and the urbanization of Hawaii, China, Australia, and southern California took up the slack.[51] The lumber business and even faraway slate-mining Bethesda, Wales, still recall the golden age when the 1906 earthquake and fire forced the reconstruction of central San Francisco.

Urban dynamism exerted a similar impetus to agronomy. Although historians of preindustrial cities largely agree that an agricultural surplus is absolutely indispensable to urban development, they do not entirely discount Jane Jacobs's counterclaim that cities invented agriculture. It is clear that town growth often preceded and always stimulated farming. Michael Conzen, Geoffrey Rossano, Dino Cinel, Margaret L. Davis, and John Modell have documented this agrarian impetus. According to Modell, the exuberant Los Angeles urban market created a heavy demand for food, fiber, fish, and nursery products that Japanese Americans were uniquely suited by family traditions, work habits, and entrepreneurial style to provide. It was more advantageous to Southland realtors to rent the land while awaiting urbanization to raise its value than to let it lie idle. Thus, urban land speculation, city demand, and urban ethnic skills converged to create a thriving Japanese-American agrarian economy.[52] And cities actually provided water for western irrigation districts. Margaret Davis notes that Owens Valley water produced a bumper crop of San Fernando Valley suburbs and a harvest of agricultural products too.[53]

Yet, as the era of urban renewal proved, there is a limit beyond which urban concentration is economically stifling rather than stimulating. These problems appeared as early as the 1870s. As Christine Rosen has shown, the complexities of urban growth and the realities of the market inhibited large-scale environmental change that would have benefitted the center cities, and encouraged decentralization instead.[54]

There are two very different models for investigating these sometimes contradictory economic stimuli. Diane Lindstrom has looked at demand, intraregional specialization, industrialization, the rise of cities, and "change in agriculture, metals, mining and commerce" in the Philadelphia region. In other words, she examined "the changes in economic structure that ensured sustained growth." Burton Folsom investigated eastern Pennsylvania urban entrepreneurs who created the changes in metals, agriculture, intraregional specialization, commerce, and structure. One believes that larger forces determine the urban economy and the other believes that people, or human agency, create these transformations. Folsom's model is especially appealing to a region long accustomed to turning towns into megalopoli, as Joe Feagin's study of Houston and Luckingham's work indicate.[55]

Even in a stifling mode, cities create a dynamic of suburbanization that is ultimately stimulating. In order to escape the complexities of concentration, people, offices, factories, and stores flee. Soaring land prices, taxes, traffic, bureaucracy, and ethnocultural diversity all contribute to this flight. Although usually condemned by urbanists, this flight does allow the continual liberation of the urban economy. Anyone familiar with bygone center-city rents or house and land prices in places like San Francisco and Manhattan today is aware that the process of decentralization is mercifully deflationary. Small businesses, lower-paid home seekers, and large corporations alike benefit from being able to start over again, free of the economic and political constraints of the Central Business District (CBD). Yet they usually maintain their connection to the city by moving to suburbia, so that the local spatial reorganization does not alter the rooted urban network. The megalopolis effect may be new, but it is geographically anchored to the obsolescent location decisions of the city's founders.

With some exceptions, urban historians have neglected suburbanization as an economic process. And yet suburbia rearranges downtown land values, housing, tax bases, job opportunities, schools, industry, retailing, and populations, as Peter Muller has shown. Post–World War II Detroit has lost nearly a million persons, and even usually robust Chicago has surrendered 600,000. These economic consequences must be weighed against the liberating effects of suburban dynamism. So far, downtown decline has been studied, but not the overall economics of suburbanization.[56]

Beginning with Sam Warner's study of transit and growth, most of the historical studies of suburbanization have concentrated on the social, governmental, and spatial dimensions of that process. The genre became a growth industry in the 1980s, culminating in the publication of the superb *Crabgrass Frontier*. Kenneth T. Jackson argued that American urbanization is unique because its suburbanization is singular. American suburbs feature abnormally low density, uncommonly high home ownership, exceptionally high upper-class residence, and unusually long journeys to work. He argued that this extraordinary pattern derived from two "necessary conditions—the suburban ideal and population growth—and from two fundamental causes—racial prejudice and cheap housing."[57]

Others have both broadened and narrowed the inquiry. Henry Binford investigated the first American suburbs, especially their economic causation; Carol O'Connor traced the evolution of Scarsdale from the 1880s to the 1980s; and Zane Miller looked at planning in the pivotal Cincinnati suburb of Forest Park. Ann Keating studied suburban governments around nineteenth-century Chicago, and Robert Fishman stressed the evangelical and London capitalist origins of the British-style suburbs that eventually came to America. He found that continental aristocracies did not suburbanize because urban renewal, à la Paris and Vienna, provided superb center-city quarters for them. Los Angeles did not represent the culmination of either process, but rather the creation of a new species of city, Technoburb.[58]

In a fascinating and sweeping comparative history, Lionel Frost has attempted to reinterpret the suburb. Crowded cities arose in Europe, North America, New Zealand, and Australia, where capital was scarce and labor, plentiful. Where labor could not command high wages, investment went into industry instead of housing. Yet in the American West, parts of Australia, and New Zealand, where workers could bargain effectively, capital went into more congenial living arrangements for the masses.[59] In addition, Robert Fogelson, Robert Fishman, Fred Viehe, and Marc Weiss have surveyed Los Angeles as the prototype American suburban city, and Rob Kling, Spencer Olin, and Mark Poster have moved beyond that to postsuburban California. However, except for a few articles like Arnold Silverman's on suburbanization during World War II, other western works are lacking.[60]

This omission is doubly unfortunate because western suburbanization offers a different perspective on eastern-derived theory. Unlike eastern cities, most western ones grew rapidly only after the suburb was becoming the dominant form of residence. Moreover, suburban booms began in Seattle, San Francisco, Los Angeles, and San Diego long before people had significant urban racial problems to flee from. We tend to think of western suburbs as sprawling, but some western suburbs, like Huntington Park, actually had greater densities in 1980 than Rustbelt cities like Chicago. Furthermore, cities like San Francisco provided congenial neighborhoods, like Pacific Heights, Sea Cliff, and the Marina, that could accommodate an elite as well as Vienna and Paris. Finally, western suburbs often coalesced under different resource conditions—scarce water yet plentiful land.

More than suburbs, which were spatially tethered to their urban cores, the role of government and politics reflects the dynamism of cities. Terrence McDonald noted that the prevalent studies of boss and reform employed static models to show that either class or culture cemented the upper and middle class to reform and the working class and immigrants to the boss. This argument is an extension of the social-science debate over whether cities are governed by a privileged elite or pluralistically. Zane Miller's study of Cincinnati, which tied urban spatial growth to bossism, city services, and government, and the works of Melvin Holli, John Buenker, and William D. Miller also addressed the question of how cities were governed.[61] Still, for urban historians, the struggle for power and the question of *who* governed has been more important than *how* they governed.

Recently this preoccupation has broken down to reveal the relationship between dynamic city growth and evolving governmental and political forms. Following Miller's early lead, Terrence McDonald, William Issel, Robert Cherny, Amy Bridges, and Steven Erie have begun to link western city politics to policy. For example, McDonald examined San Francisco class and culture, ideology, tax rates, electoral rules, city and state relationships, budgets, education, and services. By asking *how* politicians governed, he neatly reversed our notions of politics. Bosses economized and reformers spent lavishly and changed the game toward its modern forms.[62]

Issel and Cherny stressed both who governed San Francisco and how. They concluded that businessmen consistently set the agenda of city politics and minimized working-class power, but Issel's more recent inquiries admit much more working-class influence. Amy Bridges concluded that city voters had "good reason to vote for" business reformers. They governed in the interests of the community and not just of capital. They alone could get outside capital without which the cities of the arid Southwest would stagnate. In a very complete historical study of elites, Frederick Jaher found that Los Angeles was run by a permeable elite, which also governed well.[63]

By emphasizing the limits of power, Christine Meisner Rosen has added a unique variant to the standard question by asking, "Who Doesn't Govern?" Fires leveled large portions of the downtowns of Chicago, Baltimore, and Boston; and this clearance should have allowed for extensive, rational redevelopment. However, the complexities of the city, urban democracy, including considerable working-class influence, and the market prevented this outcome. No one possessed the power to rationalize the Central Business Districts, and therefore policy stagnated. Ann Keating found that people coalesced around the service issue to secure water, sewer, paving, and lighting. She reinterpreted the origins of the famous Chicago machine, arguing that services, rather than political culture, provided the lead to neighborhood organization.

Finally, labor historians are beginning to find considerable working-class political influence over policy, and biographers are likewise pursuing the question of how cities are governed.[64] Joel Schwartz's revisionist study of urban renewal and Robert Moses in the Ohio State University Press *Urban Life and Landscape* series takes this same tack. Quite a number of western city politicians await a similar reward—Fletcher Bowron, Sam Yorty, and John Anson Ford of Los Angeles; Sunny Jim Rolph, Angelo Rossi, Roger Lapham, John Francis Neylan, and Jack Shelley of San Francisco; and district attorneys Earl Warren and Pat Brown of Alameda and

San Francisco counties. Treatments of the Knowland, DeYoung, and Hearst press-lord families along the lines of Robert Gottlieb and Irene Wolt's history of the *Los Angeles Times* are also needed. In addition, western urban history badly needs political biographies of several key congressional figures comparable to Jerome Edwards's work on Pat McCarran. These would include Ed Izak of San Diego; Chet Hollifield, Norris Poulson, and Carl Hinshaw of Greater Los Angeles; and Jack Shelley, Franck Havenner, Julius and Florence Kahn, James D. McPhelan, and George P. Miller of the Bay Area. Most importantly, these studies should inquire into the use of federal power on behalf of urban interests, an inquiry that will relate these studies to both the emerging genre of nation-state literature and to the well-developed body of literature on intergovernmental relations. Cities are the most neglected and the most fundamental level of these governments. This does not belittle the previous emphases on elites, reform, bosses, elections, ethnicity, and efficiency. These works have been very useful, especially William Bullough's study of San Francisco's Chris Buckley and new ones by Roger Biles and Thomas Kessner on Chicago's Edward "Big Ed" Kelly and New York's Fiorello La Guardia, respectively. Still, an emphasis on policy is long overdue.[65]

Although they are not numerous, writers on urban government have consistently focused on policy. Kenneth Fox and Jon Teaford have revised the traditional progressive notion that city government was a colossal failure. Government met the challenge of urbanization with effective innovations, and the authors rated its performance very highly.[66] Several other authors have creatively documented this conclusion. City planning historians have not been as convinced. Carl Abbott, Judd Kahn, John Hancock, and Mansel Blackford have insisted that urban government missed important planning opportunities in Portland, San Francisco, San Diego, Oakland, Los Angeles, and Seattle.[67] Yet whether optimistic or gloomy, and whether their work emphasizes class, fiscal affairs, ideology, services, city planning and politics, elites, or pluralism, these authors demonstrate that the dynamism of urbanization forced varied and innovative responses from city governments.[68] Although Carl Abbott, Terrence McDonald, John Mollenkopf, Judd Kahn, Mansell Blackford, and Harold Platt have addressed phases of western urban government, the twentieth-century field remains wide open.

Thus, there is a promising future for the impending twentieth-century western urban past. There is much to be done, but that allows historians to shape a literature rather than struggle to reshape it. There is a pressing need for further topical diversification and a range of hypothetical challenges. This essay has offered one of these and reemphasized several others. While resisting geographic change, big cities produced fresh forms of government, novel styles of politics, additions to the modern bureaucratic state, reorganizations of nature, new professions like city planning, fresh suburbs, novel youth gangs, innovative police methods, unprecedented water engineering, staggering shifts of population from the countryside to town, novel class alignments, reconfigurations of the military, new products, several kinds of new cultures, fresh markets, new ethnic and nationality groups, original technologies, and even new casino-gambling concepts. This argument does not challenge reigning western hypotheses—the urban frontier, boosterism, quantitative methodology, power elites, western exceptionalism, urban oases, and imitation versus innovation. Nor is it antithetical to emerging notions of race, class, and gender. It offers a larger hypothesis around which to organize them. *Major* U.S. cities have been geographically conservative and culturally dynamic.

Notes

1. Kenneth T. Jackson, *Crabgrass Frontier: The Suburbanization of the United States* (New York: Oxford University Press, 1985), 12.

2. Arthur Meier Schlesinger, *The Rise of the City, 1878–1898* (New York: Macmillan, 1933); Bessie Louise Pierce, *A History of Chicago*, vol. I, *The Beginning of a City* (New York: A. A. Knopf, 1937); Lewis Mumford, *The Culture of Cities* (New York: Harcourt, Brace and Company, 1938).

3. Richard Wade, *The Urban Frontier: Pioneer Life in Early Pittsburgh, Cincinnati, Lexington, Louisville, and St. Louis* (Cambridge: Harvard University Press, 1959).

4. Paul Bairoch, "Urbanization and the Economy in Preindustrial Societies: The Findings of Two Decades of Research," *Journal of European Economic History* 18 (Fall 1989): 239–40.

5. Bairoch uses the date of 4,000 B.C., whereas De Vries argues an earlier origin. Bairoch, "Urbanization and the Economy," 241.

6. I am indebted to Gerald Nash for the phrase and concept of "oasis cities." Nash, *The American West in the Twentieth Century: A Short History of an Urban Oasis* (Albuquerque: University of New Mexico Press, 1977).

7. I would include under *culture, economics, technology, politics, government, ethnocultural relations, race,* and so forth. In other words, it seems that cities stay put geographically, but change everything else.

8. Paul M. Hohenberg and Lynn Hollen Lees, *The Making of Urban Europe, 1000–1950* (Cambridge: Harvard University Press, 1985), 1.

9. Gunther Barth, *Instant Cities: Urbanization and the Rise of San Francisco and Denver* (New York: Oxford University Press, 1975); Kenneth W. Wheeler, *To Wear a City's Crown: The Beginnings of Urban Growth in Texas, 1836–1865* (Cambridge: Harvard University Press, 1968); Carl Abbott, *The New Urban America: Growth and Politics in Sunbelt Cities* (Chapel Hill: University of North Carolina Press, 1981); Abbott, *The Metropolitan Frontier: Cities in the Modern West* (Tucson: University of Arizona Press, 1993); Norbert MacDonald, *Distant Neighbors: A Comparative History of Seattle and Vancouver* (Lincoln: University of Nebraska Press, 1987); Robert Dykstra, *The Cattle Towns* (New York: Alfred A. Knopf, 1968); Duane Smith, *Rocky*

Mountain Mining Camps: The Urban Frontier (Bloomington: Indiana University Press, 1967); Arthur R. Gómez, *Quest for the Golden Circle: The Four Corners and the Metropolitan West 1945–1970* (Albuquerque: University of New Mexico Press, 1994); Lawrence H. Larsen, *The Urban West at the End of the Frontier* (Lawrence: Regents Press of Kansas, 1978); Bradford Luckingham, *The Urban Southwest: A Profile History of Albuquerque, El Paso, Phoenix, Tucson* (El Paso: Texas Western Press, 1982).

10. Don H. Doyle, *New Men, New Cities, New South: Atlanta, Nashville, Charleston, Mobile, 1860–1910* (Chapel Hill: University of North Carolina Press, 1990); David Goldfield, *Cotton Fields and Skyscrapers: Southern City and Region, 1607–1980* (Baton Rouge: Louisiana State University Press, 1982); Lawrence H. Larsen, *The Rise of the Urban South* (Lexington: University Press of Kentucky, 1985).

11. Timothy R. Mahoney, "Urban History in a Regional Context: River Towns on the Upper Mississippi, 1840–1860," *Journal of American History* 72 (September 1975): 318–39; Hohenberg and Lees, *Making of Urban Europe*; Gilbert Rozman, *Urban Networks in Russia, 1750–1800, and Premodern Periodization* (Princeton, N.J.: Princeton University Press, 1976).

12. Jan de Vries, *European Urbanization, 1500–1800* (Cambridge: Harvard University Press, 1984), 101–13.

13. John M. Findlay, "Atomic Frontier Days: Richland, Washington, and the Modern American West," *Journal of the West* 34 (July 1995):32-41.

14. Kevin Starr, *Material Dreams: Southern California through the 1920s* (New York: Oxford University Press, 1990).

15. Don S. Kirschner, *City and Country: Rural Responses to Urbanization in the 1920s* (Westport, Conn.: Greenwood Press, 1970).

16. Bairoch, "Urbanization and the Economy," 262; Fred Shannon, *The Farmer's Last Frontier: Agriculture, 1860–1897* (New York: Farrar and Rinehart, 1964), 156–59.

17. Earl Pomeroy, *The Pacific Slope: A History of California, Oregon, Washington, Idaho, Utah, and Nevada* (New York: Alfred A. Knopf, 1965), 121–64.

18. Peter R. Decker, *Fortunes and Failures: White-Collar Mobility in Nineteenth-Century San Francisco* (Cambridge: Harvard University Press, 1978).

19. Fernand Braudel, *The Structures of Everyday Life: The Limits of the Possible,* vol. 1 of *Civilization and Capitalism, 15th to 18th Century,* 1992 ed. 3 vols. (Berkeley: University of California Press, 1992), 479.

20. Larsen, *Urban West*, 111–22.

21. Harold L. Platt, *The Electric City: Energy and the Growth of the Chicago Area, 1880–1930* (Chicago: University of Chicago Press, 1991); Mark Rose, "Urban Environment and Technological Innovation: Energy Choices in Denver and Kansas City, 1900–1940," *Technology and Culture: The International Quarterly of the Society for the History of Technology* 25 (July 1984): 503–39; Martin A. Melosi, *Thomas A. Edison and the Modernization of America* (New York: HarperCollins, 1990).

22. Eric H. Monkkonen, *America Becomes Urban: The Development of U.S. Cities and Towns, 1780–1980* (Berkeley: University of California Press, 1988); Scott Bottles, *Los Angeles and the Automobile: The Making of the Modern City* (Berkeley: University of California Press, 1987); David Brodsly, *L.A. Freeway: An Appreciative Essay* (Ber-

keley: University of California Press, 1981); Paul Barrett, *The Automobile and Urban Transit: The Formation of Public Policy in Chicago, 1900–1930* (Philadelphia: Temple University Press, 1983); John B. Rae, *The Road and the Car in American Life* (Cambridge: MIT Press, 1971).

23. William B. Friedricks, *Henry E. Huntington and the Creation of Southern California* (Columbus: Ohio State University Press, 1991). A University of Washington conference investigated the "Atomic West" in September 1992.

24. Thomas Kessner, *Fiorello H. La Guardia and the Making of Modern New York* (New York: McGraw-Hill, 1989), 432–38; Betsy Braden and Paul Hagan, *A Dream Takes Flight: Hartsfield Atlanta International Airport and Aviation in Atlanta* (Athens: University of Georgia Press, 1989); Rand McNally Corporation, *Rand McNally 1991 Commercial Atlas and Marketing Guide* (Chicago: Rand McNally, 1991), 22–23. Everett M. Rogers and Judith K. Larsen, *Silicon Valley Fever: Growth of High-Technology Culture* (New York: Basic Books, 1984).

25. Roger Lotchin, ed., "Fortress California at War: San Francisco, Los Angeles, Oakland, and San Diego, 1941–1945," *Pacific Historical Review* 63 (August 1994); Lotchin, *Fortress California, 1910–1961: From Warfare to Welfare* (New York: Oxford University Press, 1992); Lotchin, ed., *The Martial Metropolis: U.S. Cities in War and Peace* (New York: Praeger, 1984); Peter Hall, Ann Markusen, Sabina Dietrich, and Scott Campbell, *The Rise of the Gunbelt: The Military Remapping of Industrial America* (New York: Oxford University Press, 1991); Marilynn S. Johnson, *The Second Gold Rush: Oakland and the East Bay in World War II* (Berkeley: University of California Press, 1993); Arthur C. Verge, *Paradise Transformed: Los Angeles during the Second World War* (Dubuque, Iowa: Kendall/Hunt, 1993). See also Andrew Kirkby, ed., *The Pentagon and the Cities* (Newbury Park: SAGE Publications, 1992), which contains two chapters on western cities.

26. William L. Kahrl, *Water and Power: The Conflict over Los Angeles' Water Supply in the Owens Valley* (Berkeley: University of California Press, 1982). Kahrl's view overlooks both Roosevelt Dam in Arizona and Elephant Butte Dam in New Mexico, although both of these had important urban backing as well. Stephen Fox, *The American Conservation Movement: John Muir and His Legacy* (Madison: University of Wisconsin Press, 1985), 58; William Cronon, *Nature's Metropolis: Chicago and the Great West* (New York: W.W. Norton, 1991).

27. Vincent Ostrom, *Water and Politics: A Study of Water Policies and Administration in the Development of Los Angeles* (Los Angeles: Haynes Foundation, 1953); Nelson M. Blake, *Water for The Cities: A History of The Urban Water Supply Problem in the United States* (Syracuse, N.Y.: Syracuse University Press, 1956); Margaret Leslie Davis, *Rivers in the Desert: William Mulholland and the Inventing of Los Angeles* (New York: HarperCollins, 1993); Abraham Hoffman, *Vision or Villainy: The Origins of the Owens Valley-Los Angeles Water Controversy* (College Station: Texas A and M University Press, 1982); John Walton, *Western Times and Water Wars: State, Culture, and Rebellion in California* (Berkeley: University of California Press, 1992)

28. Norris Hundley, jr., *The Great Thirst: Californians and Water, 1770s–1990s* (Berkeley: University of California Press, 1992); Marc Reisner, *Cadillac Desert: The American West and Its Disappearing Water* (New York: Viking Penguin, 1986); John

Walton, *Western Times and Water Wars: State, Culture, and Rebellion in California* (Berkeley: University of California Press, 1992); Donald Worster, *Rivers of Empire: Water, Aridity, and the Growth of the American West* (New York: Pantheon Books, 1985); Robert Kelley, *Battling the Inland Sea: American Political Culture, Public Policy, and the Sacramento Valley, 1850–1986* (Berkeley: University of California Press, 1989); Donald Pisani, *To Reclaim a Divided West: Water, Law, and Public Policy, 1848–1902* (Albuquerque: University of New Mexico Press, 1992).

29. For hyperpluralism in San Francisco, see Fred Wirt, *Power in the City: Decision Making in San Francisco* (Berkeley: University of California Press, 1974). For the tyranny thesis, see Worster, *Rivers of Empire*.

30. John Bodnar, *The Transplanted: A History of Immigrants in Urban America* (Bloomington: Indiana University Press, 1985), 216; Oscar Handlin, *The Uprooted: The Epic Story of the Great Migrations that Made the American People* (Boston: Little, Brown, 1951); Zane L. Miller, "Urban History Society Presidential Address," Chicago Historical Society, at the annual meeting of the American Historical Association, December 27, 1991.

31. For a discussion of the American state, see Peter B. Evans, Dietrich Rueschemeyer, and Theda Skocpol, eds., *Bringing the State Back In* (Cambridge, England: Cambridge University Press, 1985); Alan Brinkley, "The New Deal and the Idea of the State," in *The Rise and Fall of the New Deal Order, 1930–1980*, ed. Steve Fraser and Gary Gerstle (Princeton, N.J.: Princeton University Press, 1989), 85–121.

32. For the formation of a common city culture, see Gunther Barth, *City People: The Rise of Modern City Culture in Nineteenth-Century America* (New York: Oxford University Press, 1980).

33. Nancy Shoemaker, "Urban Indians and Ethnic Choices: American Indian Organizations in Minneapolis, 1920–1950," *Western Historical Quarterly* 19 (November 1988): 431–48.

34. Douglas Henry Daniels, *Pioneer Urbanites: A Social and Cultural History of Black San Francisco* (Philadelphia: Temple University Press, 1980); Kevin A. Leonard, "Years of Hope, Days of Fear: The Impact of World War II on Race Relations in Los Angeles" (Ph.D. diss., University of California, Davis, 1993); Lawrence de Graaf, "The City of Black Angels: Emergence of the Los Angeles Ghetto, 1890–1930," *Pacific Historical Review* 39 (August 1970): 323–52; Philip M. Montesano, "The San Francisco Black Community, 1849–1890: The Quest for Equality before the Law" (Ph.D. diss., University of California, Santa Barbara, 1974); Bradford Luckingham, *Minorities in Phoenix: A Profile of Mexican American, Chinese American, and African American Communities, 1860–1992* (Tucson: University of Arizona Press, 1994); Ricardo Romo, *East Los Angeles: History of a Barrio* (Austin: University of Texas Press, 1983); Albert Camarillo, *Chicanos in a Changing Society: From Mexican Pueblos to American Barrios in Santa Barbara and Southern California, 1848–1890* (Cambridge: Harvard University Press, 1979); Mario García, *Desert Immigrants: The Mexicans of El Paso, 1880–1920* (New Haven: Yale University Press, 1981); Richard Griswold del Castillo, *The Los Angeles Barrio, 1850–1890: A Social History* (Berkeley: University of California Press, 1979), and *La Familia: Chicano Families in the Urban Southwest, 1848 to the Present* (South Bend: University of Notre Dame Press, 1984);

Arnoldo De Leon, *Ethnicity in the Sunbelt: A History of Mexican Americans in Houston* (Houston: University of Houston, Mexican American Studies Program, 1989); Thomas E. Sheridan, *Los Tucsonenses: The Mexican Community in Tucson, 1854–1941* (Tucson: University of Arizona Press, 1986, 1994); Jacqueline Baker Barnhart, *The Fair But Frail: Prostitution in San Francisco, 1849–1900* (Reno: University of Nevada Press, 1986); Amy Kesselman, *Fleeting Opportunities: Women Shipyard Workers in Portland and Vancouver during World War II and Reconversion* (Buffalo: State University of New York Press, 1990); Richard A. Garcia, *Rise of the Mexican American Middle Class: San Antonio, 1929–1941* (College Station: Texas A and M Press, 1991); George Sánchez, *Becoming Mexican American: Ethnicity, Culture, and Identity in Chicano Los Angeles, 1900-1945* (New York: Oxford University Press, 1993).

35. John Modell, *The Economics and Politics of Racial Accommodation: The Japanese of Los Angeles, 1900–1942* (Urbana: University of Illinois Press, 1977); Quintard Taylor, "Blacks and Asians in a White City: Japanese Americans and African Americans in Seattle, 1890–1940," *Western Historical Quarterly* 22 (November 1991): 401–29; Taylor, *The Forging of a Black Community: Seattle's Central District from 1870 through the Civil Rights Era* (Seattle: University of Washington Press, 1994); David M. Emmons, *The Butte Irish: Class and Ethnicity in an American Mining Town, 1875–1912* (Urbana: University of Illinois Press, 1989).

36. The latter comment is also based on my own study of California cities during the war. See also Charles H. Trout, *Boston, the Great Depression, and the New Deal* (New York: Oxford University Press, 1977); Ronald H. Bayor, *Neighbors in Conflict: The Irish, Germans, Jews, and Italians of New York City, 1929–1941* (Baltimore: Johns Hopkins University Press, 1978); John Stack, *International Conflict in an American City: Boston's Irish, Italians, and Jews, 1935–1944* (Westport, Conn.: Greenwood Press, 1979); Valerie Matsumoto, "Japanese American Women during World War II," *Frontiers* 8, no. 1 (1984): 6–14; Scott Wong, "Defending China, Claiming America: San Francisco Chinatown during World War II," paper read at the Western History Association meeting, October 20, 1994, 1–11.

37. Christine Stansell, *City of Women: Sex and Class in New York, 1789–1860* (Urbana: University of Illinois Press, 1987); Gunther Barth, *City People*; Stuart Blumin, "The Hypothesis of Middle-Class Formation in Nineteenth-Century America: A Critique and Some Proposals," *American Historical Review* 90 (April 1985): 299–338; William H. Mullins, *The Depression and the Urban West Coast, 1929–1933: Los Angeles, San Francisco, Seattle, and Portland* (Bloomington: Indiana University Press, 1991).

38. John M. Findlay, *Magic Lands: Western Cityscapes and American Culture after 1940* (Berkeley: University of California Press, 1992).

39. Eugene P. Moehring, *Resort City in the Sunbelt: Las Vegas, 1930–1970* (Reno: University of Nevada Press, 1989); John M. Findlay, *People of Chance: Gambling in American Society from Jamestown to Las Vegas* (New York: Oxford University Press, 1986).

40. De Vries, *European Urbanization*, 10.

41. Among the many good studies of twentieth-century cities, see Lyle W. Dorsett, *The Queen City: A History of Denver* (Boulder, Colo.: Pruett Publishing Company, 1977); Thomas G. Alexander and James B. Allen, *Mormons and Gentiles:*

A History of Salt Lake City (Boulder, Colo: Pruett Publishing Company, 1984); Roger Sale, *Seattle: Past To Present* (Seattle: University of Washington Press, 1976); David G. McComb, *Houston, the Bayou City* (Austin: University of Texas Press, 1969); Luckingham, *Phoenix: The History of a Southwestern Metropolis* (Tucson: University of Arizona Press, 1989); Stephan J. Leonard and Thomas J. Noel, *Denver: Mining Camp to Metropolis* (Niwot: University Press of Colorado, 1990).

42. David R. Johnson, *American Law Enforcement: A History* (St. Louis, Mo.: Forum Press, 1981).

43. Frank Richard Prassel, *The Western Peace Officer: A Legacy of Law and Order* (Norman: University of Oklahoma Press, 1972); Joseph G. Rosa, *They Called Him Wild Bill: The Life and Adventures of James Butler Hickok,* 2d ed. (Norman: University of Oklahoma Press, 1974); Rosa, *The Gunfighter: Man or Myth?* (Norman: University of Oklahoma Press, 1969); Kevin J. Mullen, *Let Justice Be Done: Crime and Politics in Early San Francisco* (Reno: University of Nevada Press, 1989).

44. Dykstra, *Cattle Towns,* 112–48.

45. Gene E. Carte and Elaine H. Carte, *Police Reform in the United States: The Era of August Vollmer, 1905–1932* (Berkeley: University of California Press, 1975).

46. See Jenna W. Joselit, *Our Gang: Jewish Crime and the New York Jewish Community, 1900–1940* (Bloomington: Indiana University Press, 1983); Humbert Nelli, *The Business of Crime* (New York: Oxford University Press, 1976); Frederic Thrasher, *The Gang: A Study of 1,313 Gangs in Chicago* (Chicago: University of Chicago Press, 1927); Daniel Monti, *The Origins and Impact of Contemporary Youth Gangs in the United States* (Albany: State University Press of New York, 1993).

47. Daniel Monti, "Gangs in More or Less Settled Communities," paper delivered to the Urban Affairs Association meeting, Vancouver, Canada, April 20, 1991, 2–18; Roger Lane, *Roots of Violence in Black Philadelphia, 1860–1900* (Cambridge: Harvard University Press, 1986); David R. Johnson, *Crime and Power: Counterfeiting, The Secret Service, and State-Building, 1863–1899,* forthcoming; Lawrence M. Friedman and Robert V. Percival, *The Roots of Justice: Crime and Punishment in Alameda County, California, 1870–1910* (Chapel Hill: University of North Carolina Press, 1981); Allen Steinberg, *The Transformation of Criminal Justice: Philadelphia, 1800–1880* (Chapel Hill: University of North Carolina Press, 1989); Findlay, *People of Chance;* Martin Schiesl, "Behind the Badge: The Police and Social Discontent in Los Angeles since 1950," in *Twentieth-Century Los Angeles: Power, Promotion, and Social Conflict,* ed. Norman M. Klein and Martin J. Schiesl (Claremont, Calif.: Regina Books, 1990), 153–94.

48. Marc A. Weiss, *The Rise of the Community Builders: The American Real Estate Industry and Urban Land Planning* (New York: Columbia University Press, 1987); Patricia Nelson Limerick, *The Legacy of Conquest: The Unbroken Past of the American West* (New York: W.W. Norton and Company, 1987), 55-77.

49. Larry Schweikart, "Financing the Urban Frontier: Entrepreneurial Creativity and Western Cities, 1945–1975," *Urban Studies* 26 (1989): 177–86; Lynne Pierson Doti and Schweikart, "Financing the Postwar Housing Boom in Phoenix and Los Angeles, 1945–1960," *Pacific Historical Review* 58 (May 1989): 173–94; John D. Haeger, *The Investment Frontier: New York Businessmen and the Economic Development of the Old Northwest* (Albany: State University of New York Press, 1981);

Jeffrey S. Adler, *Yankee Merchants and the Making of the Urban West: The Rise and Fall of Antebellum St. Louis* (Cambridge, England: Cambridge University Press, 1991).

50. Robert Rheinhold, "Test for Peace Dividend: Boom or Bust in California," *New York Times*, July 3, 1990, A7, 12; Mark Memmott, "The Price of Peace: Layoffs," *U.S.A. Today*, December 6, 1989, 1; Johnson, *Crime and Power*.

51. Thomas R. Cox, *Mills and Markets: A History of the Pacific Coast Lumber Industry to 1900* (Seattle: University of Washington Press, 1974).

52. Modell, *Economics and Politics*, 94–126; Geoffrey Rossano, "A Subtle Revolution: The Urban Transformation of Rural Life, New Gloucester, Maine, 1775–1930" (Ph.D. diss., University of North Carolina, 1980); Michael Conzen, *Frontier Farming in an Urban Shadow: The Influence of Madison's Proximity on the Agricultural Development of Blooming Grove, Wisconsin* (Madison: State Historical Society of Wisconsin, 1971) ; Dino Cinel, *From Italy to San Francisco: The Immigrant Experience* (Stanford, Calif.: Stanford University Press, 1982), 134–51, 213–14, 185.

53. Davis, *Rivers in the Desert*.

54. Christine Meisner Rosen, *The Limits of Power: Great Fires and the Process of Growth in America* (Cambridge, England: Cambridge University Press, 1986), 335–37.

55. Diane Lindstrom, *Economic Development in the Philadelphia Region, 1810-1850* (New York: Columbia University Press, 1977); Burton W. Folsom, Jr., *Urban Capitalists: Entrepreneurs and City Growth in the Lackawanna and Lehigh Regions, 1800–1920* (Baltimore: Johns Hopkins University Press, 1981); Joe R. Feagin, *Free Enterprise City: Houston in Political Economic Perspective* (New Brunswick, N.J.: Rutgers University Press, 1988); Mary A. DeCredico, *Patriotism for Profit: Georgia's Urban Entrepreneurs and the Confederate War Effort* (Chapel Hill: University of North Carolina Press, 1990).

56. Peter O. Muller, *Contemporary Suburban America* (Englewood Cliffs, N.J.: Prentice-Hall, 1981).

57. Jackson, *Crabgrass Frontier*; Sam B. Warner, Jr., *Streetcar Suburbs: The Process of Growth in Boston, 1870–1900* (Cambridge: Harvard University Press, 1962).

58. Henry C. Binford, *The First Suburbs: Residential Communities on the Boston Periphery, 1915–1860* (Chicago: University of Chicago Press, 1985); Robert Fishman, *Bourgeois Utopias: The Rise and Fall of Suburbia* (New York: Basic Books, 1987); Ann Durkin Keating, *Building Chicago: Suburban Developers and the Creation of a Divided Metropolis* (Columbus: Ohio State University Press, 1988); Carol A. O'Connor, *A Sort of Utopia, Scarsdale, 1891–1981* (Albany: State University Press of New York, 1983); Zane L. Miller, *Neighborhood and Community in Forest Park, Ohio, 1935–1976* (Knoxville: University of Tennessee Press, 1981).

59. Lionel Frost, *Urbanisation and City-Building in Australasia and the American West* (Kensington, NSW, Australia: New South Wales University Press, 1991), 154–64.

60. Robert M. Fogelson, *The Fragmented Metropolis: Los Angeles, 1850–1930* (Cambridge: Harvard University Press, 1967); Fred W. Viehe, "Black Gold Suburbs: The Influence of the Extractive Industry on the Suburbanization of Los Angeles, 1890–1930," *Journal of Urban History* 8 (November 1981), 3–26; Rob Kling,

Spencer Olin, and Mark Poster, eds., *Postsuburban California: The Transformation of Orange County since World War II* (Berkeley: University of California Press, 1990); Arnold R. Silverman, "Defense and Deconcentration: Defense Industrialization during World War II and the Development of Contemporary American Suburbs," in *Suburbia Re-Examined*, ed. Barbara M. Kelly (New York: Greenwood, 1989), 157–63.

61. Zane Miller, *Boss Cox's Cincinnati: Urban Politics in the Progressive Era* (New York: Oxford University Press, 1968); Melvin G. Holli, *Reform in Detroit: Hazen S. Pingree and Urban Politics* (New York: Oxford University Press, 1969); John D. Buenker, *Urban Liberalism and Progressive Reform* (New York: Scribner, 1973); William D. Miller, *Mr. Crump of Memphis* (Baton Rouge: Louisiana State University Press, 1964).

62. Terrence J. McDonald, *The Parameters of Urban Fiscal Policy: Socioeconomic Change and Political Culture in San Francisco, 1860–1906* (Berkeley: University of California Press, 1986).

63. William Issel and Robert W. Cherny, *San Francisco, 1865–1932: Politics, Power, and Urban Development* (Berkeley: University of California Press, 1986); Issel, "Liberalism and Urban Policy in San Francisco from the 1930s to the 1960s," *Western Historical Quarterly* 22 (November 1991): 431–50; Amy Bridges, "Winning the West to Municipal Reform," *Urban Affairs Quarterly* 27 (June 1992): 1–21.

64. George Leidenberger, "'The Public is the Labor Union': The Organizational and Political Action of Chicago Trade Unions in the Early Progressive Era" (master's thesis, University of North Carolina, Chapel Hill, 1991); Iver Bernstein, *The New York City Draft Riots: Their Significance for American Society and Politics in the Age of the Civil War* (New York: Oxford University Press, 1990); Keating, *Building Chicago*, 47–60; Rosen, *Limits of Power*, 325–37.

65. Martin J. Schiesl, *The Politics of Efficiency: Municipal Administration and Reform in America: 1880–1920* (Berkeley: University of California Press, 1977); Bernstein, *New York City Draft Riots*; Kessner, *Fiorello H. La Guardia*; Joel Schwartz, *The New York Approach: Robert Moses, Urban Liberals, and Redevelopment of the Inner City* (Columbus: Ohio State University Press, 1993); Deil S. Wright, *Understanding Intergovernmental Relations*, 2d ed. (Monterey, Calif: Brooks/Cole Publishing Company, 1982); Roger Biles, *Big City Boss in Depression and War: Mayor Edward J. Kelly of Chicago* (DeKalb: Northern Illinois University Press, 1984); William A. Bullough, *The Blind Boss and His City: Christopher Augustine Buckley and Nineteenth-Century San Francisco* (Berkeley: University of California Press, 1979); Stephen Skowronek, *Building a New American State: The Expansion of National Administrative Capacities, 1877–1920* (Cambridge, England: Cambridge University Press, 1977); Richard F. Bensel, *Yankee Leviathan: The Origins of Central State Authority in America, 1859–1877* (Cambridge, England: Cambridge University Press, 1990); Rhodri Jeffreys-Jones and Bruce Collins, eds., *The Growth of Federal Power in American History* (DeKalb: Northern Illinois University Press, 1985); Evans, Rueschemeyer, and Skocpol, *Bringing the State Back In*.

66. Bridges, "Winning the West," 1–21; Kenneth Fox, *Better City Government: Innovation in American Urban Politics, 1850–1937* (Philadelphia: Temple University Press, 1977); Jon Teaford, *The Unheralded Triumph: City Government in America,*

1870–1900 (Baltimore: Johns Hopkins University Press, 1984); Bernstein, *New York City Draft Riots*.

67. Mansel Blackford, *The Lost Dream: Businessmen and City Planning on the Pacific Coast, 1890-1920* (Columbus: Ohio State University Press, 1993); Carl Abbott, *Portland: Planning, Politics, and Growth in a Twentieth-Century City* (Lincoln: University of Nebraska Press, 1983); Judd Kahn, *Imperial San Francisco: Politics and Planning in an American City, 1897-1906* (Lincoln: University of Nebraska Press, 1979).

68. Estelle F. Feinstein, *Stamford in the Gilded Age: The Political Life of a Connecticut Town, 1868–1893* (Stamford, Conn.: Stamford Historical Society, 1973); Harold L. Platt, *City Building in the New South: The Growth of Public Services in Houston, Texas, 1830–1910* (Philadelphia: Temple University Press, 1983); Alan D. Anderson, *The Origin and Resolution of an Urban Crisis: Baltimore, 1900–1930* (Baltimore: Johns Hopkins University Press, 1977); J. Rogers and Ellen Jane Hollingsworth, *Dimensions in Urban History: Historical and Social Science Perspectives on Middle-Size American Cities* (Madison: University of Wisconsin Press, 1979); Terrence J. McDonald and Sally K. Ward, eds., *The Politics of Urban Fiscal Policy* (Beverly Hills: Sage Publications, 1984); David C. Hammack, *Power and Society: Greater New York at the Turn of the Century* (New York: Russell Sage Foundation, 1982); Robert Caro, *The Power Broker: Robert Moses and the Fall of New York* (New York: Knopf, 1974); John Mollenkopf, *The Contested City* (Princeton, N.J.: Princeton University Press, 1983); Carl V. Harris, *Political Power in Birmingham, 1871–1921* (Knoxville: University of Tennessee Press, 1977).

4

Research Opportunities in Twentieth-Century Western History

Politics

Robert W. Cherny

The twentieth century opened with the second presidential nomination of William Jennings Bryan, a self-conscious representative of the West, who promised to use federal power to rescue the producing classes from the maw of a voracious market economy. The twentieth century had run much of its course when Ronald Reagan, another self-conscious westerner, entered the presidency proclaiming his commitment to a virtually un-regulated market economy and to saving taxpayers from federal profli-gates—but left it with a multi-billion dollar disaster in the deregulated savings and loan industry (with much of the debacle centered in the West) and with a staggering increase in the federal debt (with much of it spent on defense in the West). The politics of the West in the twentieth century have to do in part with westerners' transition from seeing the federal government as Savior to seeing it as Satan. Central to that transition has been the pivotal role of government in the economic development of the West coupled with a long-term public debate over the nature and extent of governmental control.

The politics of the American West in the twentieth century have to do with much more as well. To explore the larger question of western political development in twentieth-century America, this essay first of-fers a definition of the West based on several unique characteristics that set it apart from the rest of the nation and then employs those character-istics to survey unique features of western politics and to suggest avenues for future research.

In this essay, the West includes the states that lie on or west of the ninety-eighth meridian,[1] the line marking the beginning of significantly reduced rainfall, running from eastern North Dakota through central Texas. By this definition, the West consists of nineteen states located partly or wholly within six major geographic regions: the Great Plains, the mountain and intermountain region, the Southwest, California, the Pacific Northwest (including Alaska), and Hawaii. Although this West contains significant diversity within it, nearly all of it also shares at least a majority of characteristics derived from environmental, economic, social, political, and chronological factors that establish the existence of a common identity as "the West."

Five factors distinguish this West: (1) an environment in which water is scarce; (2) an economy dominated by agriculture and the extraction of natural resources, and, more recently, tourism; (3) residential patterns, derived from the environment and economy, such that most of the West is sparsely settled and most of the population is concentrated in metropolitan areas; (4) ethnic and religious proportions significantly different from those of the rest of the nation, notably the presence of significant concentrations of Native Americans, Latinos, Asians, and members of the Mormon church;[2] and (5) relatively recent arrival as states—only three of the nineteen cast electoral votes in 1860, and twelve became states after 1888. Certain structural aspects of politics, notably nonpartisanship and a reliance on direct democracy, also set the West apart. These characteristics can define research opportunities in twentieth-century western political history when they are related to three central elements in political decision making: issues and policies, patterns of participation, and institutional structures.

Issues and Policies

Given patterns of environment, geography, economy, society, and chronology, the following categories—which sometimes overlap—represent significant sets of political issues: economic development, resource use, economic regulation, education and social services, and ethnic and cultural issues. All of these, of course, have existed throughout the nation, but all have unique western aspects.

Economic Development

Throughout most of the West's existence, first as territories and then as states, western politicians and entrepreneurs have looked to the state, especially the federal government, for assistance in promoting economic development. Vast distances and sparse population have always made efficient transportation facilities a priority for economic development. From the beginning, advocates of western growth looked to the federal government to provide improved transportation. Such efforts to generate federal assistance for improved transportation often sparked intense political conflict, from the Kansas-Nebraska Act (prompted in part by desires for a transcontinental railroad) to the Alaska pipeline. The land-grant railroads of the late nineteenth century and the interstate highway system of the middle of the twentieth century provide leading examples of the role of government regarding land transportation; proponents of the Panama Canal counted among their central objectives a more efficient transportation route between the Pacific and Atlantic coasts. In each instance, federal assistance prompted or required state and local contributions: city or state subsidies for railroads, city and state sharing of highway construction costs, and expansion of harbor and airport facilities through city, state, or federal funds. Such governmental expenditures often provoked intense political debate, but the debate usually focused on location rather than desirability. From 1854 to at least the 1960s, nearly all political participants agreed that the projects were desirable, but they wanted their own communities to reap the maximum benefits by capturing the railroad terminus, highway interchange, or harbor.[3]

Most political disagreement over economic development in the late nineteenth and early twentieth centuries arose from competition among potential beneficiaries of government development policies; the Raker Act in 1913 (the federal legislation authorizing the Hetch Hetchy project)[4] introduced a new perspective—those who opposed development in any form—and thereby forecast later struggles between proponents and opponents of development. After the 1960s, such conflicts became more and more frequent, ranging from the height of new commercial construction in San Francisco to the environmental impact of the Alaska pipeline, from logging practices in the Pacific Northwest to the location of electrical generating plants (especially nuclear-powered ones) and proposals for MX-missile trains in the Great Basin. While historians have described many of the earlier contests for federal largesse, they have been relatively slow to examine post–World War II environmental politics.

Resource Use

Resource use has often been closely tied to development issues. At the beginning of the twentieth century, many of the resources in the West were in the hands of the federal government. At the end of the twentieth century, federal lands in the western states still comprise more than 700 million acres, about a third of the total land area of the entire nation. In five western states, federal holdings (including Indian trust lands) account for more than half the land area. In five other states, federal land comprises between one-third and a half of the land area. In only five western states do federal holdings fall below a tenth of the total; among all the other thirty-one states, only in New Hampshire do federal holdings account for *more* than a tenth of the total land area.[5]

Thus, federal policies regarding lumbering, grazing, and mineral extraction, as well as policies on Indian lands, have been designed primarily for the West, and those policies have often produced bitter and long-running political battles. In 1959, Samuel P. Hays transformed historians' thinking about such policies when he described these political struggles as involving professional, federal resource managers and local resource users, and offered them as examples of the tendency of twentieth-century politics to pit centralizing and modernizing tendencies against decentralizing and traditional tendencies.[6] From the early twentieth century to the present, resource use has involved at least the two groups identified by Hays, and more recently has included both those committed to environmental concerns and the tourist industry—rather different kinds of resource users from those described by Hays.

Water

Water has been especially important in this regard. In the arid and semi-arid West, political power has not necessarily streamed to those who have water. Instead, those with power have made water flow to them. From the Owens Valley to the Grand Coulee, from Boulder Canyon to Gavins Point on the Missouri, from the Newlands Act of 1902 to the California Water Project bond issue of 1960, political power has created hydraulic power, and, in turn, access to water has directly or indirectly generated much of the built environment of the twentieth-century West.

The damming and rechanneling of western rivers has long attracted historians' attention.[7] The past two decades have witnessed a number of treatments that have opened new perspectives on the political dimensions of water projects, among them works by Norris Hundley, William L. Kahrl, Robert Kelley, Donald Pisani, Marc Reisner, Karen L. Smith, and Donald Worster.[8] Some of these pose clear implications for the very core of western politics. Worster, for example, describes the West's "hydraulic society" as "increasingly a coercive, monolithic, and hierarchical system, ruled by a power elite based on the ownership of capital and expertise."[9] In contrast, Hundley concludes that the politics of water in California present "a wide and often confused and crosscutting range of interest groups and bureaucrats, public and private, accomplishing what they do as a result of shifting alliances and despite frequent disputes among themselves."[10] Worster's power-elite paradigm and Hundley's pluralist model provide opposing possibilities for analyzing the politics of western water and should be explicitly addressed by the authors of future case studies of particular projects or states.

Western States and Economic Regulation

Given the significance of Populism and progressivism[11] in many western states, it is not surprising that most western states produced legislation to regulate aspects of economic activity, to protect certain economic classes, or even in a few instances to establish state ownership of important economic enterprises. Much of this state economic legislation from the first thirty or forty years of the century has been little studied or has been peripheral to other studies.

Public ownership reached a greater extent in some parts of the West than in other parts of the nation. North Dakota, under the Nonpartisan League, created a state-owned bank and a variety of other state-owned activities.[12] Paul Kleppner has demonstrated the extent to which Democrats used support for public power to redefine political alignments in Washington during the interwar years.[13] Nebraska, in the late 1930s and 1940s, built upon Rural Electrification Association cooperatives and WPA-funded hydroelectric projects to establish complete public ownership of the electrical power industry.[14]

Cities in a number of western states, notably Los Angeles, established public ownership of electrical power, but municipal ownership of electric utilities always centered in the Midwest. During the period 1934–1939, for example, 561 elections were held nationwide on the subject of municipal ownership, of which 306 were in favor; contrary to expectations,[15] comparing the seventeen western states with the rest of the nation indicates that the West was more likely to *oppose* public ownership. Rejection of public ownership was most pronounced in the Pacific Coast states (sixteen positive outcomes, forty-two negative); acceptance was most likely on the Great Plains (ninety positive and sixty-two negative, but Nebraska and Texas alone accounted for fifty-three positive and thirty negative outcomes).[16] Paul Kleppner has explored some of the politics of public power,[17] but there is much to be done on the politics of establishing and operating public power systems, with comparisons to other regions, before we shall be able to evaluate western political distinctiveness.

There are a number of other fields for research having to do with state legislation governing economic activity. State antitrust laws and exemptions from them for agricultural cooperatives, as well as other state legislation protecting and encouraging cooperatives, provide one example. The radical political implications of the cooperative movement play a central role in Lawrence Goodwyn's treatment of Populism,[18] but the development in the early twentieth century of state legislation protecting cooperatives and the spread of commodity marketing cooperatives seems to have generated no political upheaval of comparable moment. Much of the success of cooperatives in the early twentieth century came through the Farmers' Union (formed in Texas in 1902 and modeled on the Farmers' Alliance), which experienced its greatest growth on the central Plains and in the Northwest, and through commodity marketing associations in California and elsewhere on the Pacific Coast. All in all, historians have said surprisingly little about the politics of agricultural cooperatives in the twentieth century.[19]

A number of western states have approached regulation from a more populist perspective than either the federal government or other states, by requiring the popular election of the members of regulatory commissions or of the commissions that manage publicly owned industries. Nonetheless, there have been virtually no studies of the politics involved in elections for such commissions, nor comparisons between the behavior of elected and appointed commissions. Similarly, George Mowry described the law of 1911 that extensively revised California's public utilities commission as "one of the most comprehensive statutes regulating public utilities that have been passed by an American state," but little has been done on the politics of its creation, implementation, and operation.[20]

Education and Social Services

In considering what may be unique to the West with respect to education and social services, California casts a long shadow over the other western states, as a few examples will illustrate. Regarding social policy, the California Commission on Immigration and Housing, created in 1913, produced some of the first governmental investigations into conditions among migrant laborers and led to state legislation, in 1914, designed to regulate sanitation and housing in migrant labor camps. With regard to higher education, California passed state legislation in 1907 authorizing school boards to establish post–high school programs, and the state became the leader in the growth of community colleges. Many—perhaps most—states, both western and eastern, have imitated features of California's Higher Education Act of 1960, which enacted the California Master Plan, a tiered system for higher education intended to provide the widest possible access at the lowest possible cost to both the student and the state.

In K–12 education, the twentieth-century West has witnessed dramatic change through school consolidation, a process driven by the reality of ever-sparser rural population and the expense of technological advances in education. School consolidation often produced a high level of political conflict as it pitted local autonomy against claims of professional expertise. Between the early 1950s and the mid-1980s, the number of western school districts fell by more than half, with the reductions approaching 90 percent in Colorado (from 1,333 to 181) and Nevada (from 177 to 17).[21] Other sections of the nation also experienced school consolidation during those decades, and only comparative case studies will tell if the West was unique in the politics that accompanied it.

With regard to most post–New Deal social services, it is not clear that there is anything particularly unique about the West. All state governments, regardless of region, have had certain obligations imposed on them by federal legislation, and it is not clear that region is a significant variable in explaining the ways in which states have addressed those obligations.

Ethnic and Cultural Issues

Throughout the twentieth century, quite different political issues have revolved around ethnicity and culture. Running through many of the particular issues, however, has been a conflict between groups seeking to impose their cultural patterns on others and groups seeking to maintain their own cultural patterns in the face of such efforts.

In the early twentieth century, political conflict often swirled around moral reform, issues that often, if not always, had clear ethnocultural dimensions. In most places that have been studied, moral reforms drew their greatest support from middle-class, old-stock American Protestants, and from Swedish, Norwegian, Dutch, and British immigrants, all groups that tended to be Republicans; opposition came disproportionately from Catholics (including Irish, Italians, and Slavic immigrants) and from immigrants from Germany, who tended to vote Democratic.

Prohibition, the leading objective of moral reformers, divided citizens along an axis of ethnicity, religion, and culture. Between 1903 and 1918, the nation witnessed forty-eight state or territorial referenda on prohibition; twenty-five of them took place in the nineteen western states or territories, and twenty-three in the other thirty-one states. Contrary to stereotypes of hard-drinking frontiersmen, the results showed that westerners were more willing to drink water than their eastern counterparts: by 1919, only Hawaii and California stood as wet oases in the midst of a dry West. (For California, only the overwhelming vote of San Francisco and the wine-producing counties kept that state wet.) In contrast, only ten other states (mostly in the South and upper New England) had adopted prohibition by then.[22] Although there have been several state studies of prohibition, only a few have closely examined voting behavior to determine who supported the cold-water reform and who opposed, and even fewer have looked at the relation between prohibition sentiment and other aspects of voting behavior.[23]

Given the West's propensity for prohibition, many questions present themselves. James Timberlake, in 1963, suggested that the western states showed significant linkages from prohibition to woman suffrage, direct democracy, regulation of business, and social welfare reforms.[24] How did the West's attraction to prohibition relate both to other reform issues and to political patterns more generally? What happened to that impulse in subsequent years? How did this differ from patterns in other parts of the nation? What happened in Nevada between 1918, when voters closed the saloons, and 1931, when voters opened the casinos? Are there linkages between earlier moral-reform efforts and more recent ones? For example, much of the progressive-era women's movement supported prohibition and most Catholic voters opposed it; what does this historical pattern suggest, given current patterns of support and opposition for *Roe* v. *Wade*?

In terms of ethnicity and culture, the West differs from the rest of the nation partly through the prominence of certain religious groups. Midway through the twentieth century, five western states centered in the intermountain region (Utah, Nevada, Idaho, Wyoming, and Arizona) contained nearly four-fifths of American Mormons; in Idaho and Utah, Mormons constituted the largest religious group in the state. A sociopolitical coalition similar to the one favoring prohibition seems to have been behind efforts in the late nineteenth century to reduce the political influence of the Mormon church (which the Republican national platform in 1884 and 1888 labeled "a menace to free institutions") and to suppress plural marriage (which the Republicans described as "wickedness"). Although historians of Mormonism have noted the church's withdrawal from politics in the late nineteenth century and have provided examples of the pluralistic political behavior of Mormons in the twentieth century,[25] no one has systematically explored the influence of Mormon values and culture on the political development of the Great Basin.[26]

Other prominent ethnocultural issues in western political development have been related to American Indians, Asians, Latinos, and African Americans. Another set of cultural issues has had to do with gender. Each will be treated at more length in the section that follows, on political participants.

Participants

A narrow view of political participation limits consideration to voters, lobbyists, and government officials, and to the decision-making processes that take place within formal governmental institutions. Some historians, however, have defined political participants more broadly, in terms of groups defined by culture, ethnicity, race, economic interest, gender, or some other criterion or combination of elements. Political participation has also been considered more broadly, to include the process by which cultural groups define their own identity and thereby define their relation to the political process.

Race, Ethnicity, and Religion

Throughout the twentieth century, the West has displayed a distinctive profile with regard to ethnicity, religion, nativity, and race. The 1990 census reported that all the western states together accounted for 31.5 percent of the nation's total population, but 69.5 percent of all Native Americans, 65.6 percent of those of Hispanic origin,[27] and 61.2 percent of those of Asian or Pacific Islander descent, but only 17.6 percent of all African Americans.

Those ethnic and racial groups disproportionately concentrated *in* the West were also disproportionately concentrated *within* the western states. Five states (Arizona, California, Colorado, New Mexico, and Texas) claimed over three-fifths of the nation's total Hispanic population. Nine states (Alaska, Arizona, California, Oklahoma, Montana, New Mexico, South Dakota, Texas, and Washington) included three-fifths of all Native Americans. Seven western states (Arizona, California, Colorado, Hawaii, Oregon, Texas, and Washington) accounted for nearly three-fifths of all Americans of Asian or Pacific Islander descent. By contrast, nine western states are more than 90 percent white (compared to 80 percent for the nation as a whole), and the African American population in *every* western state is proportionately smaller than in the nation as a whole.[28]

At the dawn of the twentieth century, all four groups were effectively excluded from formal political participation. Most Native Americans and nearly all Asian immigrants were not citizens. In the nineteenth century, Latinos had participated in state and local politics at significant levels in both Texas and California, but had been almost completely marginalized by 1900. African Americans in Texas and Oklahoma experienced the disfranchisement that spread across the South between 1890 and 1910; in most other parts of the West, blacks lacked the numbers to form a significant political bloc. For each of these groups, much of the twentieth century witnessed a struggle both to maintain a sense of group identity and to establish meaningful participation in the formal structures and procedures of politics.

The presence of large numbers of Native Americans (and of the nation's largest reservations) in western states has affected western politics in many ways. Federal Indian policy has attracted many able historians, and much of that topic has been well covered, especially the transition from the assimilationist objectives of the Dawes Act to the cultural pluralism of John Collier. There are also a few studies on the evolution of federal policy since Collier, but little on the termination policies of the Truman and Eisenhower administrations and on the turn to self-determination under Kennedy, Johnson, and Nixon.[29] Recent years have seen some work on intratribal and reservation politics, the sovereignty movement, and the Indian political activism that emerged in the late 1960s; these topics deserve more attention, as does the role of American Indians in the politics of western states.[30]

There have been a relatively large number of studies of Latinos and politics, especially for those of Mexican birth or descent.[31] Two studies have recently surveyed much of that field since the mid-twentieth century: Mario García's study of the period from 1930 to 1960 and Juan Gómez-Quiñones's overview of Chicano politics from 1940 to 1990. Where García provides a series of essays, each focused on a particular person or organization, Gómez-Quiñones presents a broader survey.[32] Future work on Latino politics in the West must begin with these two works. At the same time, David Montejano's detailed study of south Texas provides an illuminating model that integrates social, economic, and political patterns for a region where a high proportion of the population is of Mexican descent.[33] There is nothing quite comparable to Montejano's work for other regions with large Latino populations, but several studies dealing with California (notably Los Angeles) and New Mexico permit some generalizations.[34]

Asians in the West in the early twentieth century experienced a continuation of late nineteenth-century political patterns, in which politicians, especially in California, vied with each other to demonstrate their commitment to Asian exclusion and to place restrictions on Asians already here.[35] Sucheng Chan and Ronald Takaki have recently produced works on the history of Asian communities, mostly in the West; important as studies of community development and development, they include only brief treatments of politics, either politics within those communities or group participation in the formal structures and processes of politics.[36] Yuji Ichioka's study of the Issei, by contrast, includes treatment both of politics within the Japanese immigrant community and of their efforts to affect the larger political process.[37] Some specific political topics fairly demand to be done: the internal politics of the Chinese community, especially San Francisco's Chinese Consolidated Benevolent Association (the Six Companies) and its relation to politics in the larger society; the politics involved in securing reparations for those Japanese Americans who suffered relocation; the political behavior of immigrants from the Philippines and South Asia[38]; and the political implications of the large-scale Asian and Pacific immigration since the mid-1960s.

Relatively few African Americans came west before World War II. To be certain, there were black communities throughout the West, especially in railroad centers and in the lower Plains states, but it was the demand for labor during the war that brought large numbers of African Americans to the Pacific Coast for the first time. In the 1890s and the early twentieth century, a few African-American Republicans won election to state office in Kansas and Nebraska. For the most part, however, significant black involvement in western politics came only after World War II, especially in California and Texas. However, there have been few efforts to chart the history of African Americans in western politics, separate from more general, national treatments.[39]

Examination of the political participation of Native Americans, Latinos, Asian Americans, and African Americans by no means exhausts the political significance of ethnicity. In a number of western states, especially in the early twentieth century, immigrants from Europe formed clear and important political blocs. In other instances, religious groupings have been and are important in defining political values and behavior; at the midpoint of the twentieth century, in addition to its distinctive concentration of Mormons, the West also included three of the four states with the largest proportions of Lutherans (Montana, North Dakota, and South Dakota) and three states where Catholics comprised a majority of those reporting a religious affiliation.[40] Similarly, the growth of fundamentalism has attracted some attention, but historians have yet to analyze the political implications of this movement in the West, especially in southern California.

Gender

Historians have treated many gender issues; few studies have suggested unique regional patterns. In research done to date, for example, western women seem to have responded to suffrage or to the left or to such issues as prostitution in much the same way as their eastern counterparts.

Nonetheless, there is a uniquely western aspect to woman suffrage: crucial early victories for suffrage all came in the West. Wyoming, the first territory to approve woman suffrage, became the first state with suffrage in 1890, and Colorado in 1893 became the first state to approve woman suffrage in a referendum by male voters. By 1919, when Congress voted to submit the suffrage amendment for ratification, *thirteen* of the seventeen western states had already adopted full suffrage (all but Nebraska, New Mexico, North Dakota, and Texas), as compared with only *two* of the other thirty-one. Although historians have studied suffrage campaigns in several states, no one has done a careful comparative analysis of eastern and western states to determine why suffrage was so disproportionately successful in the West.[41] Paul Kleppner has recently demonstrated at length the absence of meaningful political parties in much of the West; Paula Baker has recently suggested that it was no coincidence that woman suffrage succeeded only after the decline of political partisanship.[42] Together, these views present the possibility that woman suffrage succeeded earlier in the West because the weakness of western political parties seriously attenuated the most significant institution that defined politics as an exclusively masculine activity.

Following enactment of woman suffrage, western states also led in electing women to office: the first member of the House of Representatives (1916), the first governors (two, in 1924), first mayor of a large city (1926), and the first United States senator (in 1931). The West therefore presents the potential for studies of women in politics, including campaigns for office, performance as elected officials, efforts to influence state legislation, and (given western states' propensity to use direct democracy) activity in initiative and referendum campaigns.[43] Clearly, there is much more to be done in the way of state and local studies that may begin to indicate why the West led in opening the suffrage to women, and how women changed western politics by their participation.

Since World War II, gender issues also have included the emergence of gay and lesbian politics. Treatments of gay and lesbian politics have pointed to the relatively early date (the 1950s) of initial gay and lesbian political activity in Los Angeles and, especially, San Francisco, as compared with New York City and other eastern areas with significant gay and lesbian communities.[44] Whether there are uniquely western aspects to gay and lesbian politics awaits further studies.

Economic Groups

While studies of ethnic groups have sometimes included a class analysis, relatively few studies in western states have treated the political activities of economic groups, especially those who saw themselves as a class. William Domhoff's *The Bohemian Grove and Other Retreats* presented a view of the western elite,[45] but most have dealt with either Populism[46] or labor.

Most western labor histories have focused largely on unions and strikes and have left politics to the margins. Michael Kazin's study of the San Francisco building trades unions in the progressive era, *Barons of Labor*, is an impressive exception. It makes a crucial contribution to understanding that city's politics when the political power of labor reached its zenith there and, perhaps, its zenith in any large American city, ever. Kazin's book is a model local study that incorporates concerns of class and ethnicity, and gender in a limited way, into an analysis of economic and political decision making.[47] A recent study by Susan Englander, also focused on San Francisco, explores the intersection of gender, class, and politics by examining the role of women unionists in the California woman suffrage movement.[48] A few other studies have examined either the role of workers and workers' organizations in politics, or the role of the state in defining labor relations.[49]

For most of the West, however, the role of organized labor in regional, state, and local politics remains largely unexplored, as does the role of state and local governments in defining labor relations. Given the rapid expansion of both manufacturing and union membership—and especially CIO membership—on the Pacific Coast during World War II, we need studies that examine the lives of those workers, the nature of their organizations, and their political activities.[50] This is also the case for those workers in industries unique to the West—for example, migrant agricultural workers since 1941[51] or miners and oil workers in the middle and late twentieth century. In addition, historians should address the political role of western AFL and CIO central bodies during and immediately after World War II, their time of greatest proportionate strength in most of the West.[52]

Other Groups

Although the politics of race, class, and gender have often taken central place in the work of recent historians, other characteristics have also formed the basis for political definition and participation. For one example, in the 1930s, southern California provided the first striking demonstration of age as a political factor, when Dr. Francis Townsend mobilized what Arthur Schlesinger termed "the 'old folks' crusade."[53] For another example, since the 1960s the San Francisco Bay Area has been an important seedbed for the development of a political movement focused around issues of disability.

Prominent Decision Makers

In addition to political participation by organized interest groups, there are, of course, the individuals prominent in the day-to-day business of politics—the officeholders, lobbyists, and others prominently involved with the political process. Most major western electoral politicians have found an academic biographer, as have many of less prominent rank,[54] but many significant political figures have yet to find an academic biographer.[55] Political biography is not limited to those who held political office, however; biographies of, for example, Harry Bridges, Dolores Huerta, Carey McWilliams, Huey Newton, Floyd Dominy, Barbara Jordan, Howard Jarvis, Reies Tijerina, or Phoebe Apperson Hearst may reveal as much about the nature of western politics as an account of a senator successfully snagging federal funds to build one more dam. Students of California politics, especially, have at their disposal a rich body of source materials in the form of the oral histories collected by the Regional Oral History Office of the Bancroft Library.

Structures and Levels of Decision Making

With regard to structures and levels of political decision making, the two most uniquely western elements are undoubtedly the extent to which western states utilize direct democracy and limit political parties, and the nature of federal–state relations.

Direct Democracy and Nonpartisanship

Throughout the twentieth century, western states have usually taken the lead in adopting measures designed to extend direct democracy and to weaken the power of political parties. This has been accomplished through a variety of means, and most western states have embraced a range of devices: the direct primary, the initiative and referendum, recall, nonpartisan offices, and limits on political parties. Western states have also experimented with some of the more unusual antiparty or direct democracy devices in American politics, including the Oregon pledge law that preceded the direct election of United States senators, California's cross-filing law, and Nebraska's nonpartisan and unicameral legislature. In most cases, these laws date to the period from 1898 to World War I, and are linked to the influence of Populism or progressivism.[56] Both the adoption and operation of these measures provide fertile ground for further research.

The initiative and referendum seem especially western devices, endorsed by the first presidential nominating convention of the Populist Party in 1892. Of the nineteen states that adopted statutory initiative procedures between South Dakota in 1898 and Massachusetts in 1918, thirteen were in the West. Alaska entered the Union with such a provision in 1959, and Wyoming approved one in 1968. Among western states, only Hawaii, Kansas, New Mexico, and Texas now have no initiative procedure. Every western state that approved the initiative also adopted the referendum at the same time; New Mexico adopted only a referendum law in 1911.[57]

Western states have also proven more likely to *use* the initiative and referendum. Between 1898 and 1976, voters in twenty-three states considered a total of 1,224 initiative measures, both statutory and constitutional. (Recently, California voters may have felt that they faced nearly that number at every election.) During that seventy-eight-year period, fifteen western states constituted 65 percent of the states with the initiative but accounted for 81 percent of all measures submitted to the voters. California, Oregon, and Washington alone produced 36 percent; adding Arizona, North Dakota, and Colorado yields fully two-thirds of the total.[58]

In research on the adoption, use, and significance of the initiative and referendum, historians have to do a great deal of catching up; political scientists and public-opinion specialists have done the most work in this area. Only a few historians have used voting on initiatives and referenda as a part of voting studies, even though voting on such measures lends itself to use both as a dependent variable (to be explained by reference to other characteristics of the voters) and as an independent variable (a measure of voter attitude on an issue). A number of basic questions beg to be explored: Who has initiated measures? Why? How have voters responded? How have the initiative and referendum affected the structure of state politics? What has been the relationship between the initiative and referendum and political parties? How have all these changed over time? With several state and comparative studies, we may then begin to draw conclusions regarding the degree to which the western political experience with the initiative and referendum has been unique.

Federalism

The relation between the federal government and the states has been different in much of the West by reason of two major factors: (1) a high level of dependence on the federal treasury for the economic infrastructure, especially transportation, and (2) a high level of federal landownership, making federal land policies always central to much of the western economy. Even though westerners have embraced federal largesse, they have often chafed under the bit of federal land controls. Increasing resentment of federal restrictions prompted the "sagebrush rebellion" that began in 1979, when Nevada demanded control over nearly all federal lands within its boundaries, and other western states followed.[59] Irritation and anger at Washington has also fueled the rise of conservative Republicans, especially in the mountain West and Southwest, creating what Clive Thomas has described as the central paradox of contemporary western politics, epitomized by western politicians (Barry Goldwater was one of the first and most successful) who brag of their success in garnering large federal appropriations for their constituents at the same time that they denounce federal taxes, expenditures, and intervention.[60]

State and Local Politics

Most western states have found one or more students of state politics. California and Texas stand in contention for the largest number, but the full list is too long to include here. A few Texas studies stand out as models, especially Lewis L. Gould's study of Texas Democrats in the progressive era (1973) and Chandler Davidson's recent study of race and class in Texas politics (1990).[61] California state politics, especially since 1917, have attracted fewer historians.

Though Texas has seen more historical studies of state politics than California, both have seen a number of studies of urban politics. All the western states except the Dakotas were more than 50 percent urban at the time of the 1990 census, and some are among the most urban in the nation: above 90 percent for California (the most urban state in the nation), and above 80 percent for Arizona, Colorado, Hawaii, Nevada, and Utah. Indeed, Hawaii and Nevada are more urban than New York, Massa-

chusetts, and Illinois.[62] In the past ten years, western metropolitan politics has drawn the attention of a number of historians and political scientists and should attract more in the future. Some, especially Carl Abbott,
have focused on a regional approach to urban history, including urban
politics. [63]

Chronology

Issues and policies, participants, and formal structures all provide important windows on the nature of twentieth-century western politics. Historians are, of course, centrally concerned with the chronological dimension
as well. However, Gerald Nash and Richard Etulain have recently noted,
with surprise, that "the history of politics in the twentieth-century West
is still largely unwritten."[64] There are a few broad studies of the twentieth-
century West, or significant parts of the West, that include brief treatment of politics, and a few essays tackle some aspect of western politics,
but there has been little effort to treat the politics of the entire region
over time.[65]

As one starting point, western politics may be periodized by the same
critical-election/party-system paradigm employed by many political historians—notably by Walter Dean Burnham—for national politics. By this
approach, twentieth-century American politics fall into three major periods: from the mid-1890s to the early 1930s, from the early 1930s to the
late 1960s, and the period since the 1960s.[66]

Western Politics from Bryan to FDR

At a national level, the political realignment of the 1890s resulted in a
secure Republican majority, ending twenty years of close political balance and initiating an era of political change that included foreign policy,
domestic policy, and the role of the president. The Republicans won their
national majority partly in the well-established farming areas of the east
north central states, but primarily in the Manufacturing Belt that came
into existence during the previous generation, stretching west from Boston to Milwaukee, south to St. Louis, and back east to Baltimore. After the
depression that began in 1893, some of this region's voters moved into
GOP ranks and stayed there until the depression that began in 1929. Some
voters in the previously Democratic border states also moved toward the
Republicans (thereby making those states more competitive), but the South
moved in the opposite direction, becoming a monolithic Democratic bloc
with the disfranchisement of African Americans. Both the Northeast and
the South, therefore, became *less* competitive after the 1890s.[67]

In most western states, realignment began in 1890 with the emergence of Populism, not with the depression of 1893. In the West, only

Texas and the Pacific Coast states became less competitive; at least until World War I, the mountain states and Great Plains states became *more* competitive in presidential elections. In Montana, one of the most competitive states, the average margin between Republican and Democratic presidential candidates in 1900, 1904, and 1908 was only 2 percentage points. Perhaps most significantly, the West provided Wilson with the crucial margin for his extremely close victory in 1916, as he carried fifteen of the seventeen western states. Similar patterns can be seen in state elections. In Kansas, for example, before the 1890s Republican candidates for governor usually won by margins of 60 to 40; between 1898 and 1912 the Republican margin of victory for governor fell to less than 55 to 45.[68]

This increased competitiveness resulted from a compound of Populism, the silver issue, and the Bryan campaigns,[69] with the relative significance of each element varying from state to state. Studies of Arizona, Colorado, Idaho, Kansas, Montana, Nebraska, Nevada, New Mexico, Oklahoma, and Texas have demonstrated the importance of Populism or the silver issue in those states.[70] As Henry Fountain Ashurst of Arizona said to Henry Morgenthau, Jr., in 1933, "I was brought up from my mother's knee on silver and I can't discuss that any more with you than you can discuss your religion with me."[71] By contrast, for California[72] and the Pacific Northwest this period is better described as one created by McKinley than by Bryan.

The relation between Populism, silver, and Bryanism, on the one hand, and western progressivism, on the other, is less clear. In Nebraska, one result of the realignment of the 1890s was a permanent weakening of party loyalties and the creation of a body of voters who seem to have supported both Republican and Democratic progressives, including Bryan and George W. Norris.[73] Of the score or so of studies of Populism, the politics of silver, or progressivism in western states, however, only a few have crossed the divide between Populism in the 1890s and the progressive politics of the early twentieth century.[74]

More needs to be done in other western states to determine the electoral bases for western progressivism, especially the support for such leading progressives as William E. Borah, Hiram Johnson, George W. Norris, Miles Poindexter, William U'Ren, and Burton Wheeler. The activities of the Nonpartisan League and the various state Farmer-Labor parties across the northern tiers of western states also need more attention. From such studies may appear (1) confirmation that western progressivism was, in fact, more focused than its eastern counterpart on opposition to both monopoly and party; (2) confirmation that, and explanation why, many western progressives were more receptive to ideas of public ownership; and (3) clearer connections between western voters and western progressive officeholders.[75]

Western Politics, the New Deal, and World War II

Republicans dominated most elected offices in the West throughout the 1920s, except for Oklahoma and Texas; but they faced opposition both from the somewhat ragtag troops of the Democrats and, in the northern states, from the even less spiffy followers of the Nonpartisan League and state Farmer-Labor parties. In the 1924 presidential election, when Republican strength in some Manufacturing Belt cities began to show erosion, La Follette finished second in nine western states (in California and all the northern two tiers of states), but he seems to have drawn more votes from the Democrats than from the GOP.[76] Western states revealed little attraction to Al Smith in 1928; Herbert Hoover, after all, was a Californian and the first westerner since Bryan to have a chance at the White House. Hoover carried all the western states (including Texas and Oklahoma), some by margins larger even than Harding had received in 1920. We know little about western support for La Follette or about those western voters who contributed to Hoover's enormous margins.[77] To what extent did they overlap? Do they reflect western tensions between economic distress (La Follette voters) and religious antagonisms (anti-Smith voters)? Or was some other dynamic at work? Like most of the rest of the nation, the West embraced FDR and the New Deal, and Democrats swept into state and local offices all across the West.

Though general outlines are clear, there are not a half-dozen detailed studies in print of state politics during the interwar era: Montana during World War I and the Red Scare, Texas in the 1920s, Kansas in the early 1930s, California's "Little New Deal" in the late 1930s, and the New Deal era in Idaho.[78] Other state and local studies are needed, especially, to illuminate the regional dimension of the national political realignment of the early 1930s.[79] In the Manufacturing Belt, by the mid-1930s the realignment was paced by the growth of organized labor, especially the CIO unions. There is little evidence of a similar pattern in the West. In the Pacific Coast and the mountain states, before World War II, the major CIO unions (ILWU, IWA, and Mine-Mill) were closer to the Communist Party than most of their eastern CIO counterparts and less able to mobilize great numbers of voters than the CIO unions in, for example, New York, Michigan, Illinois, or Pennsylvania. Furthermore, much of the region's manufacturing developed only during World War II.

If the New Deal–Democratic coalition in the northeastern states achieved permanence and often majority status through coalition with industrial unionism, what was the nature of the New Deal–Democratic coalition in the West? It was built, in part it seems, on federal expenditures for resource development: the mountain states ranked first among the regions of the nation in New Deal expenditures per capita.[80] Richard Lowitt has given us a good overview of New Deal activities in the West, but did not address state politics or the local political dimensions of New Deal activities.[81]

Three dimensions of state and local politics in the Roosevelt era especially demand attention: changes in voting behavior, changes in state policies, and the impact of World War II. With regard to voting behavior, given the appeal of the New Deal–Democratic coalition at the national level, we want to know which groups of western voters changed parties and how long the change lasted. Michael Rogin and John Shover, for example, in their study of California politics, argue for a permanent change there that laid the basis for the administration of Edmund Brown, Sr., and for Democratic dominance of the legislature since the 1950s.[82]

The western states differed significantly in their adherence to the New Deal–Democratic coalition after 1936. From 1940 to 1958, the Great Plains states from Kansas north gave the Republicans some of their highest margins in the nation. In Nebraska, for example, the election of Democrats in the early 1930s was less the *beginning* of a new pattern of politics than the *culmination* of forty years of close competition;[83] Charles Bryan, brother of the Great Commoner, made his last pathetic bid for the governorship in 1942. The real change in Nebraska came after 1938, when Republicans swept state offices from top to bottom in a way they had not done since the 1880s, initiating two decades of almost unchallenged Republican control. A number of other western states also turned toward the Republicans after 1938, indicating that the Democratic victories of the early 1930s did not mark a realignment of the sort that occurred in California or in some eastern states.[84]

The second dimension that needs attention is state policy. Voting behavior and policymaking are not separate domains; one central element in Burnham's realignment model is that realignments produce changes in policy. Several states had some experience with "Little New Deals" during the 1930s, as the political upheaval of the era brought to power Democrats, some of them liberals, some of whom found allies among progressive Republicans.[85] Robert Burke explored California's late-blooming "Little New Deal," but other versions have yet to find their historians.[86] The Washington Commonwealth Federation seems an especially fruitful subject for study in this regard; it once prompted James Farley to refer to "the Soviet of Washington."[87] Its less successful counterpart in Oregon poses an interesting comparison.[88]

Studies of state politics in the 1930s must begin, however, with James T. Patterson's observation that nearly all the Little New Deals were failures and that most governors of the period were "yawn-inspiring men with legislative programs as pedestrian as they were unsuccessful."[89] Many western Democratic governors fit Patterson's mold precisely; as Earl Pomeroy observed, "during the great depression, the old idea that the West led the nation in opportunity and in democracy seemed out of date."[90]

William Rowley goes further, arguing not just that reform failed to jell in the 1930s but that much of the West actively resisted the New Deal,[91] though with one hand out for federal expenditures on public works.

The third dimension that requires a great deal more attention is the impact of World War II on both voting patterns and state policies.[92] For the eastern part of the nation, World War II seems not to have greatly changed previous political patterns; in the West, however, the war had a far greater impact both economically and socially—and, in all likelihood, politically.[93] The changes initiated by the war continued afterward, with rapid expansion of western metropolitan areas, especially the suburbs. By the Eisenhower elections (1952 and 1956), all the western states voted Republican for president.

The Republican West

After a brief resurgence by western Democrats from 1958 through the mid-1960s, voting in most of the West returned to patterns of Republican preponderance; since 1948, Democratic presidential candidates have found it virtually impossible to win more than a few western states. In 1960, John F. Kennedy carried only four of the nineteen (Hawaii, Nevada, New Mexico, and Texas). Johnson took all but Arizona in 1964. In the nationally close elections of 1968 and 1976, nearly all the West voted Republican: only three of the nineteen western states (Hawaii, Texas, and Washington) voted for Hubert Humphrey in 1978, and Jimmy Carter carried only one western state (Texas) in 1976. *None* of the western states voted Democratic in 1972, 1980, or 1984; and only Washington and Oregon voted Democratic in 1988. Clinton, however, carried eight of the nineteen western states in 1992.

During this period, the West has become a centrally important—even dominant—element in the national Republican party, producing fourteen of its past eighteen presidential candidates[94] and, since the 1960s, many of its most powerful Senate leaders, notably Robert Dole, Jake Garn, Barry Goldwater, Orrin Hatch, Mark Hatfield, Bob Packwood, and John Tower. Historians need to begin to address some of the questions their social science colleagues have been raising about this change and to place it into historical perspective.[95]

A number of political scientists have written recently on western political realignment, but they have agreed neither on the nature of the realignment nor even on its existence. Those who deny a major realignment readily acknowledge that parts of the mountain West have shifted significantly toward the Republicans. Ronald J. Hrebenar and Robert C. Benedict have concluded that Utah, Wyoming, Idaho, and Arizona are now the most Republican states in the West (their definition of the West did not the include the six states between North Dakota and Texas)—but seem to attribute this primarily to a distrust of government. Their analysis ignores ethnoreligious dimensions to voting behavior, even though these four states are among the five states with the largest proportions of Mormons.[96]

Most historians seem to have left the politics of the past thirty years to political scientists and sociologists, but it is time to begin the task of placing western political change into historical perspective. One clear pattern throughout the West—one that began in the West—is the separation of state and national voting. Thus, many western states that never deliver their presidential votes to Democrats nonetheless elect Democratic majorities to their state legislatures and regularly elect Democrats as governor or as United States senator.[97] This ticketsplitting is, in fact, one evidence of the disintegration of political parties, a process that western progressives carried further than in other parts of the nation; the West, as a consequence, presents a range of opportunities for the study of the transition from party politics to media politics.[98]

Studying Western Politics in the Twentieth Century

One way to think of research opportunities in twentieth-century western politics is to visualize a grid with issues and policies along one dimension, participants along a second, and political structures on a third. Each cell, then, has the potential for a study over time that includes an issue, one or more participants, and various structures and levels of decisionmaking. Some of the cells in such a grid already boast a rich and rewarding literature. Others clearly need more work. To visualize western politics in such a grid may suggest new questions: Where were women in the politics of resource development? How did various ethnic groups respond to the politics of water? What roles did African-American men and women play in the moral reforms of the early twentieth century?

Although such a grid may point to topics where little work has been undertaken, western political history should not be pushed into total fragmentation. Historians should continue to seek broader patterns as well as exploring case studies.[99]

One broad pattern that should occupy historians is the transition from Bryan to Reagan, from seeing government as Savior to seeing it as Satan. Clearly, that did not affect all westerners: not all embraced regulation or government ownership in the early twentieth century, and not all rejected them in the late twentieth century. Yet the change is important: in the early twentieth century, progressive wings of both parties mustered strong support in the West. Among major western political leaders of the early twentieth century, few made their mark as conservatives; late in the twentieth century, by contrast, American conservative leadership has largely passed from New England Republicans and Deep South Democrats to western Republicans.

What brought this transition? Part of the answer lies in a better understanding of westerners' attitudes toward private concentrations of economic power, attitudes that have moved from the Populists' demand for government ownership, to progressives' argument for regulation, to current conservatives' demand for a free market. Another part of the answer is to be found in the increasingly peripheral role of rural voters such as those who created Populism, the Nonpartisan League, and the Farmer-Labor movement, and whose votes swelled the totals of progressives in both parties during the first half of the century. Other parts of the answer may be found in the thinking of the western Democrats and Republican progressives who turned against Roosevelt and the New Deal by the late 1930s.[100] Other elements are likely to be found in the many strings that came attached to federal development dollars. Still another element may be the very success of federal development projects (including defense spending) in bringing prosperity to some who then came to resent federal taxes and regulations. Coupled to this transition is the emergence of the central paradox in western politics: condemnation of federal taxation and intervention and the simultaneous demand for federal expenditures on development projects.[101]

As noted earlier, Donald Worster and Norris Hundley present quite different conclusions regarding the nature of politics and, by implication, the state. Their disagreement reflects larger patterns of scholarly discourse on the nature and role of the state in American history. Over the past fifteen years or so, some scholars, especially political scientists, have turned to the study of political institutions. This "new institutionalism" has attracted the attention of some historians who have followed the lead of, especially, Theda Skocpol in studying the nature of the state and the process of statebuilding. Where most earlier analysts focused on the political behavior of individuals and groups and treated institutions as the arenas in which conflicting group demands were negotiated, the new institutionalists have focused on institutions and have presented them as relatively autonomous. This new institutionalism has been challenged as some scholars have asserted the explanatory virtues of the older, pluralist model. Case studies of western politics can provide useful insights into this discourse on the nature of the state.[102]

Finally, there is another and centrally important dimension to considerations of twentieth-century western politics: the concept of the West itself. What is it that makes the West a *political* arena in the twentieth century? Only a few historians have tried to explore twentieth-century western politics through a distinctly regional approach. In other cases, historians who have recently sought to revise interpretations of the West have said little explicitly regarding twentieth-century western politics.[103]

At some point, however, historians must ask if it is more rewarding to see the West as one region or as several. Only by case studies will the material appear for such a determination, but if historians continue to think of themselves as *western* historians, then surely they must turn their attention consciously to defining the political dimensions of the West for the twentieth century.

Notes

1. The ninety-eighth meridian is presented as the eastern boundary of the West by, for example, Walter Prescott Webb, "The American West, Perpetual Mirage," *Harper's Magazine* 214 (May 1957): 25–31; Gerald D. Nash, *The American West in the Twentieth Century: A Short History of an Urban Oasis* (Englewood Cliffs, N.J.: Prentice-Hall, 1973; repr., Albuquerque: University of New Mexico Press, 1977); Michael P. Malone, *Historians and the American West* (Lincoln: University of Nebraska Press, 1987); and Michael P. Malone and Richard W. Etulain, *The American West: A Twentieth-Century History* (Lincoln: University of Nebraska Press, 1989); but not all of these authors include Alaska and Hawaii.

2. Not all of the West includes all of these characteristics—the coastal Northwest does not lack for water; there are not high proportions of Mormons *everywhere* in the West, nor is this true of Asians, Latinos, and Native Americans; and some parts of the West have significant manufacturing economies. Some of these characteristics are to be found in the eastern part of the nation: a significant agricultural economy in much of the South and the Midwest; the presence of many Latinos in Florida, Latinos and Asians in New York City, and American Indians in upstate New York; and a significant tourist economy in Florida. It is the *combination* of these environmental, economic, and social factors with chronological and political factors that provides this definition of the West.

3. For an examination of urban rivalries, especially those involving military and naval spending, but also including transportation facilities, see Roger Lotchin, "The Darwinian City: The Politics of Urbanization in San Francisco Between the World Wars," *Pacific Historical Review* 48 (August 1979): 357–81, and Lotchin, *Fortress California, 1910–1961: From Warfare to Welfare* (New York: Oxford University Press, 1992). For westerners' changing attitudes toward railroads, see William F. Deverell, *Railroad Crossing: Californians and the Railroad, 1850–1910* (Berkeley and Los Angeles: University of California Press, 1994).

4. See, for example, Kendrick A. Clements, "Politics and the Park: San Francisco's Fight for Hetch Hetchy, 1908–1913," *Pacific Historical Review* 48 (May 1979): 183–215; Clements, "Engineers and Conservationists in the Progressive Era," *California History* 58 (Winter 1979–1980): 282–303.

5. U.S. Public Land Law Review Commission, *One Third of the Nation's Land* (Washington, D.C.: Government Printing Office, 1970), 327.

6. Samuel P. Hays, *Conservation and the Gospel of Efficiency: The Progressive Conservation Movement, 1890–1920* (Cambridge: Harvard University Press, 1959).

7. For examples, see Charles McKinley, *Uncle Sam in the Pacific Northwest* (Ber-

keley: University of California Press, 1952); or George Sundborg, *Hail Columbia: The Thirty Year Struggle for Grand Coulee Dam* (New York: Macmillan, 1954).

8. Norris Hundley, jr., *Water and the West: The Colorado River Compact and the Politics of Water in the American West* (Berkeley and Los Angeles: University of California Press, 1975), and *The Great Thirst: Californians and Water, 1770s–1990s* (Berkeley and Los Angeles: University of California Press, 1992); William L. Kahrl, *Water and Power: The Conflict over Los Angeles' Water Supply in the Owens Valley* (Berkeley and Los Angeles: University of California Press, 1982); Robert Kelley, *Battling the Inland Sea: American Political Culture, Public Policy, and the Sacramento Valley, 1850–1986* (Berkeley and Los Angeles: University of California Press, 1989); Donald J. Pisani, *From the Family Farm to Agribusiness: The Irrigation Crusade in California and the West, 1850–1931* (Berkeley and Los Angeles: University of California Press, 1984), and *To Reclaim a Divided West: Water, Law, and Public Policy, 1848–1902* (Albuquerque: University of New Mexico Press, 1992); Marc Reisner, *Cadillac Desert: The American West and Its Disappearing Water* (New York: Viking Penguin, 1986); Karen L. Smith, *The Magnificent Experiment: Building the Salt River Reclamation Project* (Tucson: University of Arizona Press, 1986); and Donald Worster, *Rivers of Empire: Water, Aridity, and Growth of the American West* (New York: Pantheon Books, 1985).

9. Worster, *Rivers of Empire*, 7.

10. Hundley, *The Great Thirst*, xvi.

11. I have capitalized *Populism* to refer to the Populist Party of the 1890s, and shall capitalize *Progressive* only to refer to the Progressive Party. With a lower-case initial letter, *progressivism* refers to the broad range of politics, policies, and politicians usually denoted that way. With regard to progressivism, this is the practice followed by, for example, Arthur S. Link and Richard L. McCormick in *Progressivism* (Arlington Heights, Ill.: Harlan Davidson, 1983).

12. The standard treatment is still Robert L. Morlan, *Political Prairie Fire: The Nonpartisan League, 1915–1922* (Minneapolis: University of Minnesota Press, 1955).

13. Paul Kleppner, "Politics without Parties: The Western States, 1900–1984," in *The Twentieth-Century West: Historical Interpretations*, ed. Gerald D. Nash and Richard W. Etulain (Albuquerque: University of New Mexico Press, 1989), 317–21.

14. Robert E. Firth, *Public Power in Nebraska: A Report on State Ownership* (Lincoln: University of Nebraska Press, 1962).

15. The West, especially the Pacific Northwest, is often seen as supportive of public power; see, for example, Nash, *American West in the Twentieth Century*, 111–12.

16. David Schap, *Municipal Ownership in the Electric Utility Industry* (New York: Praeger Publishers, 1986).

17. Kleppner, "Politics without Parties."

18. Lawrence Goodwyn, *Democratic Promise: The Populist Moment in America* (New York: Oxford University Press, 1976).

19. For a general survey of the development of cooperatives up to 1920, with little attention to politics, see Joseph G. Knapp, *The Rise of American Cooperative Enterprise: 1620–1920* (Danville, Ill.: Interstate Printers and Publishers, 1969). Of greater interest is Victoria Saker, "'Benevolent Monopoly': The Legal Transforma-

tion of Agricultural Cooperation, 1890–1943" (Ph.D. diss., University of California, Berkeley, 1990).

20. See George Mowry, *The California Progressives* (Berkeley: University of California Press, 1951), 149. Mansell Blackford's *The Politics of Business in California, 1890–1920* (Columbus: Ohio State University Press, 1977) deals in part with these issues; *California Progressivism Revisited*, ed. William Deverell and Tom Sitton (Berkeley and Los Angeles: University of California Press, 1994), does not. Jules Tygiel, *The Great Los Angeles Swindle: Oil, Stocks, and Scandal during the Roaring Twenties* (New York: Oxford University Press, 1994), includes some treatment of California's regulation of corporations.

21. From Table 14.6, in Kenneth K. Wong, "State and Local Government Institutions and Education Policy," in *Politics and Public Policy in the Contemporary American West*, ed. Clive S. Thomas (Albuquerque: University of New Mexico Press, 1991), 369.

22. From Table 8, in Jack S. Blocker, Jr., *Retreat from Reform: The Prohibition Movement in the United States, 1890–1913* (Westport, Conn.: Greenwood Press, 1976), 237–38.

23. For state studies, see Robert Smith Bader, *Prohibition in Kansas: A History* (Lawrence: University Press of Kansas, 1986); Norman Clark, *The Dry Years: Prohibition and Social Change in Washington* (Seattle: University of Washington Press, 1965); Jimmie Lewis Franklin, *Born Sober: Prohibition in Oklahoma, 1907–1959* (Norman: University of Oklahoma Press, 1971); Jeanne Bozzell McCarty, *The Struggle for Sobriety: Protestants and Prohibition in Texas, 1919–1935* (El Paso: Texas Western Press, University of Texas, 1980); and Gilman Ostrander, *The Prohibition Movement in California, 1848–1933* (Berkeley: University of California Press, 1957). For examples of the use of prohibition as an independent variable in political analysis of the time period, see Michael P. Rogin and John L. Shover, *Political Change in California: Critical Elections and Social Movements, 1890–1936* (Westport, Conn.: Greenwood Press, 1970); and Robert W. Cherny, *Populism, Progressivism, and the Transformation of Nebraska Politics, 1885–1915* (Lincoln: University of Nebraska Press, 1981).

24. Timberlake, *Prohibition and the Progressive Movement, 1900–1920* (Cambridge: Harvard University Press, 1963), esp. 166–67; Blocker, *Retreat from Reform*, esp. 236–40.

25. For just one example, see Klaus J. Hansen, *Mormonism and the American Experience* (Chicago: University of Chicago Press, 1981).

26. For example, Gordon Shepherd and Gary Shepherd, *A Kingdom Transformed: Themes in the Development of Mormonism* (Salt Lake City: University of Utah Press, 1984), include only five index citations to politics, two of them in notes, for a book of 286 pages. A few dissertations provide more attention, notably Q. Michael Croft, "Influence of the L.D.S. Church on Utah Politics, 1945–1985" (University of Utah, 1985); Donald Bruce Gilchrist, "An Examination of the Problems of the L.D.S. Church Influence in Utah Politics, 1890–1916" (University of Utah, 1967); and Jo Ann Barnett Shipps, "The Mormons in Politics: The First Hundred Years" (University of Colorado, 1965). See also Robert Gottlieb, *America's Saints: The Rise of Mormon Power* (New York: Putnam's, 1984).

27. I have generally used *Latino* throughout this essay, but I employ *Hispanic* when dealing with census data, because that has been the term employed by the Census Bureau.

28. U.S. Department of Commerce, Bureau of the Census, "Resident Population Distribution for the United States, Regions, and States, by Race and Hispanic Origin: 1990," Census Bureau Press Release CB91-100 (April 1991).

29. Among recent works on this subject are Frederick E. Hoxie, *A Final Promise: The Campaign to Assimilate the Indians, 1880–1920* (Lincoln: University of Nebraska Press, 1984); Lawrence C. Kelly, *The Assault on Assimilation: John Collier and the Origins of Indian Policy Reform* (Albuquerque: University of New Mexico Press, 1983); H. Craig Miner, *The Corporation and the Indian: Tribal Sovereignty and Industrial Civilization in Indian Territory, 1865–1907* (Columbia: University of Missouri Press, 1976); Kenneth R. Philp, *John Collier's Crusade for Indian Reform, 1920–1954* (Tucson: University of Arizona Press, 1977); Margaret Szasz, *Education and the American Indian: The Road to Self-Determination, 1928–1972* (Albuquerque: University of New Mexico Press, 1974); Graham D. Taylor, *The New Deal and American Indian Tribalism: The Administration of the Indian Reorganization Act, 1934–1945* (Lincoln: University of Nebraska Press, 1980); and Richard White, *The Roots of Dependency: Subsistence, Environment, and Social Change among the Choctaws, Pawnees, and Navajos* (Lincoln: University of Nebraska Press, 1983). More general works include Robert L. Bee, *The Politics of American Indian Policy* (Cambridge, Mass.: Schenkman Publishing Co., 1982); George Pierre Castile and Robert L. Bee, eds., *State and Reservation: New Perspectives on Federal Indian Policy* (Tucson: University of Arizona Press, 1992); James S. Olson and Raymond Wilson, *Native Americans in the Twentieth Century* (Provo: Brigham Young University Press, 1984); Donald Lee Parman, *Indians and the American West in the Twentieth Century* (Bloomington: Indiana University Press, 1994); and John H. Moore, ed., *The Political Economy of North American Indians* (Norman: University of Oklahoma Press, 1993).

30. For example, see, Marjane Ambler, *Breaking the Iron Bonds: Indian Control of Energy Development* (Lawrence: University Press of Kansas, 1989); Stephen Cornell, *The Return of the Native: American Indian Political Resurgence* (New York: Oxford University Press, 1988); Vine Deloria and Clifford M. Lytle, *The Nations Within: The Past and Future of American Indian Sovereignty* (New York: Pantheon Books, 1984); Augie Fleras and Jean Leonard Elliott, *The "Nations Within": Aboriginal-State Relations in Canada, the United States, and New Zealand* (Don Mills, Ont.: Oxford University Press, 1992); Loretta Fowler, *Arapahoe Politics, 1851–1978: Symbols in Crises of Authority* (Lincoln: University of Nebraska Press, 1982); Peter Iverson, *The Navajo Nation* (Westport, Conn.: Greenwood Press, 1981); James J. Lopach, Margery Hunter Brown, and Richmond L. Clow, *Tribal Government Today: Politics on Montana Indian Reservations* (Boulder: Westview Press, 1990); Howard L. Meredith, *Modern American Indian Tribal Government and Politics* (Tsaile, Ariz.: Navajo Community College Press, 1993); Sharon O'Brien, *American Indian Tribal Governments* (Norman: University of Oklahoma Press, 1989); Ernest L. Schusky, ed., *Political Organization of Native North Americans* (Washington: University Press of America, 1980); Theodore W. Taylor, *The Bureau of Indian Affairs* (Boulder: Westview Press, 1984); Robert H. White, *Tribal Assets: The Rebirth of Native America*

(New York: Henry Holt, 1990); and Peter M. Whiteley, *Deliberate Acts: Changing Hopi Culture through the Oraibi Split* (Tucson: University of Arizona Press, 1988). See also Tim J. Watts, *American Indian Tribal Autonomy and American Society in the 1980s: A Bibliography* (Monticello, Ill.: Vance Bibliographies, 1988).

31. See, for example, Mario Barrera, *Race and Class in the Southwest: A Theory of Racial Inequality* (Notre Dame, Ind.: University of Notre Dame Press, 1979); Douglas E. Foley, with Clarice Mota, Donald E. Post, and Ignacio Lozano, *From Peones to Politicos: Class and Ethnicity in a South Texas Town, 1900–1987* (Austin: University of Texas Press, 1988); Benjamin Marquez, *LULAC: The Evolution of a Mexican American Political Organization* (Austin: University of Texas Press, 1993), and *Power and Politics in a Chicano Barrio: A Study of Mobilization Efforts and Community Power in El Paso* (Lanham, Md.: University Press of America, 1985); and Maurilio Vigil, *Chicano Politics* (Washington: University Press of America, 1978). See also Mary Kaye Donahue, *Studies on the Mexican American Voter as a Political Force: A Bibliographic Essay* (Monticello, Ill.: Vance Bibliographies, 1984).

32. Mario T. García, *Mexican Americans: Leadership, Ideology, and Identity, 1930–1960* (New Haven: Yale University Press, 1989); Juan Gómez-Quiñones, *Chicano Politics: Reality and Promise, 1940–1990* (Albuquerque: University of New Mexico Press, 1990).

33. David Montejano, *Anglos and Mexicans in the Making of Texas, 1836–1986* (Austin: University of Texas Press, 1987).

34. For studies that include treatment of political patterns, see, for example, Rodolfo Acuña, *A Community under Siege: A Chronicle of Chicanos East of the Los Angeles River, 1945–1975* (Los Angeles: Chicano Studies Research Center Publications, University of California at Los Angeles, 1984); Ricardo Romo, *East Los Angeles: History of a Barrio* (Austin: University of Texas Press, 1983); Nancie L. González, *The Spanish-Americans of New Mexico: A Heritage of Pride* (Albuquerque: University of New Mexico Press, 1967); and Maurilio Vigil, *Los Patrones: Profiles of Hispanic Political Leaders in New Mexico History* (Washington: University Press of America, 1980).

35. Roger Daniels, *The Politics of Prejudice: The Anti-Japanese Movement in California and the Struggle for Japanese Exclusion* (Berkeley and Los Angeles: University of California Press, 1962), *Concentration Camps USA: Japanese Americans and World War II* (New York: Holt, Rinehart and Winston, 1971), and *The Decision to Relocate the Japanese Americans* (Philadelphia: J. B. Lippincott Company, 1975); Alexander Saxton, *The Indispensable Enemy: Labor and the Anti-Chinese Movement in California* (Berkeley and Los Angeles: University of California Press, 1971); Michael Kazin, *Barons of Labor: The San Francisco Building Trades and Union Power in the Progressive Era* (Urbana and Chicago: University of Illinois Press, 1987).

36. Sucheng Chan, *Asian Californians* (San Francisco: MTL/Boyd and Fraser, 1991); Chan, *Asian Americans: An Interpretive History* (Boston: Twayne Publishers, 1990); Ronald Takaki, *Strangers from a Different Shore* (Boston: Little, Brown and Company, 1989).

37. Yuji Ichioka, *The Issei: The World of the First Generation Japanese Immigrants, 1885–1924* (New York: Free Press, 1988), esp. 156–254. Other works that treat politics include Roger Daniels, *Asian America: Chinese and Japanese in the*

United States since 1850 (Seattle: University of Washington Press, 1988); Timothy P. Fong, *The First Suburban Chinatown: The Remaking of Monterey Park, California* (Philadelphia: Temple University Press, 1994); Bill Ong Hing, *Making and Remaking Asian America through Immigration Policy, 1850–1990* (Stanford, Calif.: Stanford University Press, 1993); Hyung-chan Kim, *A Legal History of Asian Americans, 1790–1990* (Westport, Conn.: Greenwood Press, 1994); Bill Hosokawa, *Nisei: The Quiet Americans* (New York: Morrow, 1969); Douglas Warren Lee, "Political Development in Chinese America, 1850–1911" (Ph.D. diss., University of California, Santa Barbara, 1979); Victor Low, *The Unimpressible Race: A Century of Educational Struggle* (San Francisco: East/West Publishing Co., 1982); and John Modell, *The Economics and Politics of Racial Accommodation: The Japanese of Los Angeles, 1900–1942* (Urbana: University of Illinois Press, 1977).

38. Very little has been done on Filipino immigrants, and only a bit more on south Asian immigrants; see Arthur Wesley Helweg and Usha M. Helweg, *An Immigrant Success Story: East Indians in America* (Philadelphia: University of Pennsylvania Press, 1990); and Joan M. Jensen, *Passage from India: Asian Indian Immigrants in North America* (New Haven: Yale University Press, 1988).

39. For example, Edward G. Carmines and James A. Stimson, *Issue Evolution: Race and the Transformation of American Politics* (Princeton, N.J.: Princeton University Press, 1989), do not treat region as a variable, and both California and Texas are missing from the index. For an award-winning study of black and Hispanic political participation in several California communities, see Rufus P. Browning, Dale Rogers Marshall, and David H. Tabb, *Protest Is Not Enough: The Struggle of Blacks and Hispanics for Equality in Urban Politics* (Berkeley and Los Angeles: University of California Press, 1984). A number of recent studies treat aspects of African-American politics in parts of the West: Albert S. Broussard, *Black San Francisco: The Struggle for Racial Equality in the West, 1900–1954* (Lawrence: University Press of Kansas, 1993); Rudolph M. Lapp, *Afro-Americans in California*, 2d ed. (San Francisco: Boyd and Fraser Publishing Co., 1987); Delores Nason McBroome, *Parallel Communities: African-Americans in California's East Bay, 1850–1963* (New York: Garland Publishing, 1993); Raphael Sonenshein, *Politics in Black and White: Race and Power in Los Angeles* (Princeton, N.J.: Princeton University Press, 1993); and Jim Schutze, *The Accommodation: The Politics of Race in an American City* [Dallas] (Secaucus, N.J.: Citadel Press, 1986).

40. This religious data and that reported earlier is for the mid-twentieth century and is taken from National Council of the Churches of Christ in the U.S.A., *Churches and Church Membership in the United States*, Series B, Nos. 5–8 (1956). For more recent data, see Martin B. Bradley et al., eds., *Churches and Church Membership in the United States, 1990* (Atlanta: Glenmary Research Center, 1992).

41. The major treatments of the suffrage campaigns in the western states are: Alan P. Grimes, *The Puritan Ethic and Woman Suffrage* (New York: Oxford University Press, 1967); Sandra L. Myres, "Suffering for Suffrage," chap. 8 of *Westering Women and the Frontier Experience, 1800–1915* (Albuquerque: University of New Mexico Press, 1982), 213–37; and Beverly Beeton, *Women Vote in the West: The Woman Suffrage Movement, 1869–1896* (New York: Garland Publishing, 1986). None

of the three offers any serious analysis of voting behavior, although Grimes presents an analysis of legislative roll-call voting.

42. Kleppner, "Politics without Parties"; Paula Baker, "The Domestication of Politics: Women and American Political Society, 1780–1920," *American Historical Review* 89 (June 1984): 620–47.

43. The two book-length studies of this sort are very old: Helen L. Sumner, *Equal Suffrage: The Results of an Investigation in Colorado* (New York: Harper and Brothers, 1909); and William Forest Sprague, *Women and the West: A Short Social History* (Boston: Christopher Publishing House, 1940). Sprague provides little more than an introductory survey of the subject of politics. The biographies of women political leaders are of interest: for example, Ruth Barnes Moynihan, *Rebel for Rights: Abigail Scott Duniway* (New Haven: Yale University Press, 1983); Anne Bail Howard, *The Long Campaign: A Biography of Anne Martin* (Reno: University of Nevada Press, 1985); Hannah Geffen Josephson, *Jeannette Rankin, First Lady in Congress: A Biography* (Indianapolis: Bobbs-Merrill, 1974); Kevin S. Giles, *Flight of the Dove: The Story of Jeannette Rankin* (n.p.: Touchstone Press, 1980). For a recent study by political scientists, see Paul Schumaker and Nancy Elizabeth Burns, "Gender Cleavages and the Resolution of Local Policy Issues," *American Journal of Political Science* 32 (1988): 1070–95, which deals with Lawrence, Kansas.

44. For example, see John D'Emilio, *Sexual Politics, Sexual Communities: The Making of a Homosexual Minority in the United States, 1940–1970* (Chicago: University of Chicago Press, 1983); and Barry D. Adam, *The Rise of a Gay and Lesbian Movement* (Boston: Twayne Publishers, 1987).

45. G. William Domhoff, *The Bohemian Grove and Other Retreats: A Study of Ruling-Class Cohesiveness* (New York: Harper and Row, 1974).

46. An essay as long as this one could be done on the historiography of Populism and the directions that it might take in the future, but most of Populism lies outside the chronological constraints of this essay. Two new surveys of Populism have appeared recently: Gene Clanton, *Populism: The Humane Preference in America, 1890–1900* (Boston: Twayne Publishers, 1991); and Robert C. McMath, Jr., *American Populism: A Social History, 1877–1898* (New York: Hill and Wang, 1993).

47. Kazin, *Barons of Labor.*

48. Susan Englander, *Class Coalition and Class Conflict in the California Woman Suffrage Movement, 1907–1912: The San Francisco Wage Earners' Suffrage League* (Lewiston, N.Y.: Mellen Research University Press, 1992).

49. See, for example, Daniel A. Cornford, *Workers and Dissent in the Redwood Empire* (Philadelphia: Temple University Press, 1987); Richard E. Lingenfelter, *The Hardrock Miners: A History of the Mining Labor Movement in the American West, 1863–1893* (Berkeley and Los Angeles: University of California Press, 1974); George G. Suggs, *Colorado's War on Militant Unionism: James H. Peabody and the Western Federation of Miners* (Detroit: Wayne State University Press, 1972); and Jules Tygiel, *Workingmen in San Francisco, 1880–1901* (New York: Garland, 1992). See also Garin Burbank, *When Farmers Voted Red: The Gospel of Socialism in the Oklahoma Countryside, 1910–1924* (Westport, Conn.: Greenwood Press, 1976).

50. Richard Boyden's forthcoming study, tentatively entitled *The San Fran-*

cisco Machinists from Depression to Cold War, 1930–1950 (Urbana: University of Illinois Press), is a welcome start on this task. Despite the sweep of Gerald D. Nash's *The American West Transformed: The Impact of the Second World War* (Lincoln: University of Nebraska Press, 1985), it contains very little on unions or politics.

51. We need a study of the post-1941 period to complement that of Cletus Daniels in *Bitter Harvest: A History of California Farmworkers, 1870–1941* (Ithaca, N.Y.: Cornell University Press, 1981). Two works cover parts of this topic: Ellen Casper, "A Social History of Farm Labor in California with Special Emphasis on the United Farm Workers Union and California Rural Legal Assistance" (Ph.D. diss., New School for Social Research, 1984), and J. Craig Jenkins, *The Politics of Insurgency: The Farm Worker Movement in the 1960s* (New York: Columbia University Press, 1985).

52. William Issel has found that the unions, especially CIO unions, played an important role in defining the postwar agenda of San Francisco politics regarding both race relations and housing policy; see Issel, "Liberalism and Urban Policy in San Francisco from the 1930s to the 1960s," *Western Historical Quarterly* 22 (November 1991): 431–50. For the enormous political impact of wartime unionization in Hawaii, see Sanford Zalburg, *A Spark Is Struck! Jack Hall and the ILWU in Hawaii* (Honolulu: University Press of Hawaii, 1979).

53. Arthur M. Schlesinger, Jr., *The Age of Roosevelt: The Politics of Upheaval* (Boston: Houghton Mifflin Company, 1960), chap. 2. The major treatments are Abraham Holtzman, *The Townsend Movement: A Political Study* (New York: Bookman Associates, 1963); and Jackson K. Putnam, *Old-Age Politics in California from Richardson to Reagan* (Stanford, Calif.: Stanford University Press, 1970).

54. Recent biographies include LeRoy Ashby and Rod Gramer, *Fighting the Odds: The Life of Senator Frank Church* (Pullman: Washington State University Press, 1994); Richard Coke Lower, *A Bloc of One: The Political Career of Hiram W. Johnson* (Stanford, Calif.: Stanford University Press, 1993); Richard Lowitt, *Bronson M. Cutting: Progressive Politician* (Albuquerque: University of New Mexico Press, 1992); Ross R. Rice, *Carl Hayden: Builder of the American West* (Lanham, Md.: University Press of America, 1994).

55. The list includes some figures who are still living, and for whom papers may not be fully available; for others, however, there are large manuscript collections, either open or soon to be opened. Any of the following should soon find a biographer: Carl Albert, Thomas Bradley, Edmund G. "Pat" Brown, Quentin Burdick, John Nance Garner, Barry Goldwater, Ernest Gruening, Henry Jackson, George McGovern, Warren Magnuson, Mike Mansfield, Wayne Morse, John Tower, and Burton K. Wheeler.

56. Populists established the initiative and referendum in South Dakota, the first state to adopt it, and former Populists played an important role in its adoption in Oregon. Elsewhere, it was progressives who led in promoting direct democracy.

57. Based on Table 3.1 in David B. Magleby, *Direct Legislation: Voting on Ballot Propositions in the United States* (Baltimore: Johns Hopkins University Press, 1984), 38–39.

58. Based on Table 4-4 in Austin Ranney, "The United States of America," in *Referendums: A Comparative Study of Practice and Theory*, ed. David Butler and Austin Ranney (Washington, D.C.: American Enterprise Institute for Public Policy Research, 1978).

59. R. McGreggor Cawley, *Federal Land, Western Anger: The Sagebrush Rebellion and Environmental Politics* (Lawrence: University Press of Kansas, 1993).

60. Thomas, *Politics and Public Policy in the Contemporary American West*, 15, 37–40, and throughout; see also Kleppner, "Politics without Parties," 330–31; and Malone and Etulain, *American West*, 276.

61. Lewis L. Gould, *Progressives and Prohibitionists: Texas Democrats in the Wilson Era* (Austin: University of Texas Press, 1973); Chandler Davidson, *Race and Class in Texas Politics* (Princeton, N.J.: Princeton University Press, 1990). Other interesting recent works include Evan Anders, *Boss Rule in South Texas: The Progressive Era* (Austin: University of Texas Press, 1982); Darlene Clark Hine, *Black Victory: The Rise and Fall of the White Primary in Texas* (Millwood, N.Y.: KTO Press, 1979); George Norris Green, *The Establishment in Texas Politics: The Primitive Years, 1938–1957* (Westport, Conn.: Greenwood Press, 1979).

62. Table E, U.S. Department of Commerce, Bureau of the Census, *State and Metropolitan Area Data Book 1991* (Washington: Government Printing Office, 1991), 204.

63. See, esp., Carl Abbott, *The Metropolitan Frontier: Cities in the Modern American West* (Tucson: University of Arizona Press, 1993), *The New Urban America: Growth and Politics in Sunbelt Cities* (Chapel Hill: University of North Carolina Press, 1981), and *Portland: Planning, Politics, and Growth in a Twentieth-Century City* (Lincoln: University of Nebraska Press, 1983). See also Richard M. Bernard and Bradley R. Rice, eds., *Sunbelt Cities: Politics and Growth since World War II* (Austin: University of Texas Press, 1983); Joe R. Feagin, *Free Enterprise City: Houston in Political-Economic Perspective* (New Brunswick, N.J.: Rutgers University Press, 1988); David R. Johnson et al., *The Politics of San Antonio* (Lincoln: University of Nebraska Press, 1983); Bradford Luckingham, *Phoenix: The History of a Southwestern Metropolis* (Tucson: University of Arizona Press, 1989); Orville D. Menard, *Political Bossism in Mid-America: Tom Dennison's Omaha, 1900–1933* (Lanham, Md.: University Press of America, 1989); Eugene P. Moehring, *Resort City in the Sunbelt: Las Vegas, 1930–1970* (Reno: University of Nevada Press, 1989); and Carol Estes Thometz, *The Decision-Makers: The Power Structure of Dallas* (Dallas: Southern Methodist University Press, 1963).

Studies of California cities include Richard Edward DeLeon, *Left Coast City: Progressive Politics in San Francisco, 1975–1991* (Lawrence: University Press of Kansas, 1992); Robert M. Fogelson, *The Fragmented Metropolis: Los Angeles, 1850–1930* (Cambridge: Harvard University Press, 1967); William Issel and Robert W. Cherny, *San Francisco, 1865–1932: Politics, Power, and Urban Development* (Berkeley and Los Angeles: University of California Press, 1986); Marilynn Johnson, *The Second Gold Rush: Oakland and the East Bay in World War II* (Berkeley and Los Angeles: University of California Press, 1993); Judd Kahn, *Imperial San Francisco: Politics and Planning in an American City, 1897–1906* (Lincoln: University of Nebraska Press, 1979); Norman M. Klein and Martin J. Schiesl, eds., *Twentieth Century Los Angeles: Power,*

Promotion, and Social Conflict (Claremont, Calif.: Regina Books, 1990); Rob Kling, Spencer Olin, and Mark Poster, eds., *Postsuburban California: The Transformation of Orange County since World War II* (Berkeley and Los Angeles: University of California Press, 1991); Terrence J. McDonald, *The Parameters of Urban Fiscal Policy: Socioeconomic Change and Political Culture in San Francisco, 1860–1906* (Berkeley and Los Angeles: University of California Press, 1986); and Frederick M. Wirt, *Power in the City: Decision Making in San Francisco* (Berkeley and Los Angeles: University of California Press, 1974).

64. Nash and Etulain, *Twentieth-Century West*, 293.

65. The most extensive summary of politics for the entire West is included in chaps. 2, 3, and 7 of Malone and Etulain, *American West*. Works that incorporate politics into larger studies of part or all of the West include Nash, *American West in the Twentieth Century*; Earl Pomeroy, *The Pacific Slope: A History of California, Oregon, Washington, Idaho, Utah, and Nevada* (New York: Alfred A. Knopf, 1965); and Carlos A. Schwantes, *The Pacific Northwest: An Interpretive History* (Lincoln: University of Nebraska Press, 1989).

The essays in Thomas, *Politics and Public Policy in the Contemporary American West*, focus almost entirely on current politics. Among work by historians, Kleppner's "Politics without Parties" is the most ambitious and interesting effort to analyze an aspect of western politics for the entire twentieth century. William D. Rowley, "The West as Laboratory and Mirror of Reform," in Nash and Etulain, *Twentieth-Century West*, 339–57, is another interesting effort to deal with western politics as something more than a collection of separate states' politics. F. Alan Coombs, "Twentieth-Century Politics," in Malone, *Historians and the American West* 300–322, surveys work up to the early 1980s and largely confirms the comments of Nash and Etulain.

66. The major statements are Walter Dean Burnham, *Critical Elections and the Mainsprings of American Politics* (New York: W. W. Norton and Company, 1970); and William Nisbet Chambers and Walter Dean Burnham, eds., *The American Party Systems: Stages of Political Development*, 2d ed. (New York: Oxford University Press, 1975). A recent adaptation of this paradigm at the national level is in Eldon J. Eisenach, "Reconstituting the Study of American Political Thought in a Regime-Change Perspective," *Studies in American Political Development* 4 (1990): 169–230. Malone and Etulain, in *American West*, use much the same periodization; so does Kleppner, in "Politics without Parties," but he collapses all the postwar period into one era.

67. The Border states, previously reliably Democratic, became more competitive.

68. For a somewhat different treatment of the degree of competitiveness, see Kleppner, "Politics without Parties."

69. I should stress that these are separate factors, and that I do not mean to suggest that Populism was limited to the silver issue.

70. The bibliographies in Clanton's *Populism* and McMath's *American Populism* include most state studies of Populism published before the mid-1980s; in addition, see Mary Ellen Glass, *Silver and Politics in Nevada: 1892–1902* (Reno: University of Nevada Press, 1969); William J. Gaboury, *Dissension in the Rockies: A*

History of Idaho Populism (New York: Garland Publishing, 1988); Jeffrey Ostler, *Prairie Populism: The Fate of Agrarian Radicalism in Kansas, Nebraska, and Iowa, 1880–1892* (Lawrence: University Press of Kansas, 1993).

71. Quoted in William E. Leuchtenburg, *Franklin D. Roosevelt and the New Deal: 1932–1940* (New York: Harper and Row, 1963), 82. See also John Brennan, *Silver and the First New Deal* (Reno: University of Nevada Press, 1969).

72. Rogin and Shover, *Political Change in California*; see also R. Hal Williams, *The Democratic Party and California Politics, 1880–1896* (Stanford, Calif.: Stanford University Press, 1973).

73. Cherny, *Populism, Progressivism, and the Transformation of Nebraska Politics*, esp. chaps. 7–9.

74. For examples, see Worth R. Miller, "Building a Progressive Coalition in Texas: The Populist-Reform Democrat Rapprochement, 1900–1907," *Journal of Southern History* 52 (May 1986): 163–82; and David R. Berman, *Reformers, Corporations, and the Electorate: An Analysis of Arizona's Age of Reform* (Niwot: University Press of Colorado, 1992). For state politics during the progressive era, see, for example, Anders, *Boss Rule in South Texas*; Cherny, *Populism, Progressivism, and the Transformation of Nebraska Politics*; Danney Goble, *Progressive Oklahoma: The Making of a New Kind of State* (Norman: University of Oklahoma Press, 1980); Colin B. Goodykoontz, *The Progressive Movement in Colorado, 1910–1912* (University of Colorado Studies in the Social Sciences, v.1, no.2, pt.2, 1941); Gould, *Progressives and Prohibitionists*; Mowry, *California Progressives*; Robert Sherman La Forte, *Leaders of Reform: Progressive Republicans in Kansas, 1900–1916* (Lawrence: University Press of Kansas, 1974); Spencer C. Olin, Jr., *California's Prodigal Sons: Hiram Johnson and the Progressives, 1911–1917* (Berkeley and Los Angeles: University of California Press, 1968), Carlos A. Schwantes, *Radical Heritage: Labor, Socialism, and Reform in Washington and British Columbia, 1885–1917* (Seattle: University of Washington Press, 1979).

75. Berman's study of Arizona, *Reformers, Corporations, and the Electorate*, is a good model for this sort of analysis. For overviews of the progressive era in the West or in parts of the West, see Malone and Etulain, *American West*, 54–66; Nash, *American West in the Twentieth Century*, 42–49; Pomeroy, *Pacific Slope*, chap. 8; Schwantes, *Pacific Northwest*, chap. 14. See also Rowley, "West as Laboratory and Mirror of Reform," esp. 341–47.

76. Kleppner, "Politics without Parties," 310.

77. Kleppner's analysis should be a starting point for further work; see ibid., 310–11.

78. Norman D. Brown, *Hood, Bonnet, and Little Brown Jug: Texas Politics, 1921–1928* (College Station: Texas A & M University Press, 1984); Arnon Gutfeld, *Montana's Agony: Years of War and Hysteria, 1917–1921* (Gainesville: University Presses of Florida, 1979); Frances W. Schruben, *Kansas in Turmoil, 1930–1936* (Columbia: University of Missouri Press, 1969); Robert E. Burke, *Olson's New Deal for California* (Berkeley: University of California Press, 1953); Michael P. Malone, *C. Ben Ross and the New Deal in Idaho* (Seattle: University of Washington Press, 1970).

79. Malone and Etulain, *American West*, 94–107, provide a good summary of key events, but they present only minimal analysis of changes. Much the same is

true of Nash, *American West in the Twentieth Century*, 105–16, and ch. 3; Pomeroy, *Pacific Slope*, chap. 9; and Schwantes, *Pacific Northwest*, chap. 15.

80. Malone and Etulain, *American West*, 106.

81. Richard Lowitt, *The New Deal and the West* (Bloomington: Indiana University Press, 1984).

82. Rogin and Shover, *Political Change in California*, chap. 5; James Gregory and Nancy Quam-Wickham are preparing detailed studies of California voting behavior during the 1930s that should provide a clearer picture of the nature and extent of that realignment. Kleppner has presented a starting point for a regional analysis in "Politics without Parties," 313–25.

83. From 1890 through 1938, Republicans won eleven gubernatorial victories, Democrats won eleven, and Populists with Democratic support won three.

84. See the treatment of this in Malone and Etulain, *American West*, 278–80.

85. Malone and Etulain, *American West*, 103–6; Nash, *American West in the Twentieth Century*, 170–75; Pomeroy, *Pacific Slope*, 242–52; Schwantes, *Pacific Northwest*, 304–11.

86. Burke, *Olson's New Deal*.

87. As quoted in G. Scott Thomas, *The Pursuit of the White House: A Handbook of Presidential Election Statistics and History* (Westport, Conn.: Greenwood Press, 1987), 415, with citation to John Gunther, *Inside the U.S.A.* (New York: Harper and Brothers, 1946), 87.

88. Kleppner provides a starting point; see "Politics without Parties," 317–24.

89. James T. Patterson, *The New Deal and the States: Federalism in Transition* (Princeton: Princeton University Press, 1969), 153–54.

90. Pomeroy, *Pacific Slope*, 251.

91. Rowley, "West as Laboratory and Mirror of Reform," 351.

92. For an overview, see Nash, *American West in the Twentieth Century*, 209–11.

93. The major treatment is Nash, *American West Transformed*, but he includes little consideration of the political impact of wartime changes. Malone and Etulain provide one paragraph in *American West*, 118–19; Rowley provides the beginning of an analysis in "West as Laboratory and Mirror of Reform," 353–54. Regarding Nash, see also Paul Rhode, "The Nash Thesis Revisited: An Economic Historian's View," *Pacific Historical Review* 63 (1994): 363–92; more generally, see that entire issue of *Pacific Historical Review*, a special issue entitled *Fortress California at War: San Francisco, Los Angeles, Oakland, and San Diego, 1941–1945*, ed. Roger W. Lotchin.

94. Republican presidential candidates from the West: Hoover twice, Landon, Eisenhower twice, Nixon three times, Goldwater, Reagan twice, Bush twice, and Dole. Republican candidates from the East: Willkie, Dewey twice, and Ford. The only western Democratic candidates since 1928: Johnson, Humphrey (born in South Dakota), and McGovern.

95. Nash, *American West in the Twentieth Century*, 242–50; Pomeroy, *Pacific Slope*, 315–31; Schwantes, *Pacific Northwest*, 357–67.

96. For opposing views regarding the nature of western realignment, see Peter F. Galderisi et al., eds., *The Politics of Realignment: Party Change in the Mountain West* (Boulder: Westview Press, 1987); and Ronald J. Hrebenar and Robert C. Benedict, "Political Parties, Elections and Campaigns, II: Evaluation and Trends,"

chap. 6 in Thomas, *Politics and Public Policy in the Contemporary American West*, esp. 140–55. Pomeroy, *Pacific Slope*, 234–35, 318–19, puts the influence of Mormonism into a larger context.

97. Hrebanar and Benedict identify two western states as one-party Republican (Wyoming, Utah) and three as two-party Republican dominant (Oregon, Arizona, Idaho). All others they classify as more competitive. Kansas might fit their one-party Republican dominant model, but probably not any of the other Plains states.

California provides an excellent example of ticket splitting. Hrebenar and Benedict call California a two-party state with Democrats dominant. Nonetheless, California has voted Republican for president nine times since 1952 and Democratic only twice. It has usually elected Democratic majorities to its legislature since 1958, but the governorship has been closely competitive, with four Democratic victories and six Republican wins. Democrats have usually held a majority of statewide offices other than governor, but the attorney general's office has usually gone to law-and-order Republicans. Republicans have usually held one U.S. Senate seat and Democrats the other.

Nebraska provides another example. It has voted Republican in every presidential election since 1940, save only 1964, and usually by enormous margins; nonetheless, Democrats have won nine of the twelve gubernatorial elections since 1958, and have won every U.S. Senatorial election since 1976.

98. As is true of many other topics, a detailed analysis should begin with the work of Kleppner in "Politics without Parties."

99. For one effort to define western political cultures, see Malone and Etulain, *American West*, 272–83.

100. For specific examples, see Burton Wheeler, *Yankee from Montana* (Garden City, N.Y.: Doubleday, 1962), and Arthur F. Mullen, *Western Democrat* (New York: Wilfred Funk, 1940); for more general treatments, see Ronald L. Feinman, *Twilight of Progressivism: The Western Republican Senators and the New Deal* (Baltimore: Johns Hopkins University Press, 1981); and Otis L. Graham, *An Encore for Reform: The Old Progressives and the New Deal* (New York: Oxford University Press, 1967).

101. Brief treatments of some of these themes may be found in Kleppner, "Politics without Parties"; Rowley, "West as a Laboratory and Mirror for Reform"; and Malone and Etulain, *American West*, 271–94.

102. For an overview of the "new institutionalism," see David Brian Robertson, "The Return to History and the New Institutionalism in American Political Science," *Social Science History* 17 (1993): 1–36. For leading examples, see Theda Skocpol, "Bringing the State Back In: Strategies of Analysis in Current Research," in *Bringing the State Back In*, ed. Peter B. Evans, Dietrich Rueschmeyer, and Theda Skocpol (New York: Cambridge University Press, 1985); Skocpol, "Political Response to Capitalist Crisis: Neo-Marxist Theories of the State and the New Deal," *Politics and Society* 10 (1980): 155–201; and Skocpol, *Protecting Soldiers and Mothers: The Politics of Social Provision in the United States* (New York: Cambridge University Press, 1992); and Stephen Skowronek, *Building a New American State: The Expansion of National Administrative Capacities, 1877–1920* (New York: Cambridge University Press, 1982). For an explicit challenge to this view of an autonomous state,

see Melvyn Dubofsky, *The State and Labor in Modern America* (Chapel Hill: University of North Carolina Press, 1994); Hundley's conclusions regarding the politics of water in California fit very well with Dubofsky's pluralist views on the nature of federal labor policy making.

103. For example, see Patricia Nelson Limerick, *The Legacy of Conquest: The Unbroken Past of the American West* (New York: W. W. Norton and Company, 1987), although, to be sure, much of her account carries clear implications for the study of twentieth-century western politics.

5

Twentieth-Century Western Women

Research Issues and Possibilities

Glenda Riley

Compared to the literature concerning women in the nineteenth-century West, scholarship on twentieth-century western women is slight.[1] One explanation is that until recently few western historians defined the twentieth-century American West as a separate research area. Scholars seemed to consider only the nineteenth-century West as truly "western" enough for study; typically, most dismissed the modern West as simply part of recent American history. During the past three decades, however, a growing number of fine studies have alerted scholars to the possibility that the twentieth-century West is a distinctive region demanding particular attention, research, and methodology.[2]

This revolution in thinking is especially fortunate for those interested in today's most pressing questions—race and ethnicity. Diversity has long constituted an important focus for historians of western women, especially those who concentrated on the nineteenth century.[3] Recently, proliferating research reminds us that the twentieth-century West is also a rich mixture of racial and ethnic groups, which offers exciting and virtually limitless potential for raising and answering significant questions.[4]

One group of western women who demand increased attention is Native American women. Despite researchers' countless attempts to eradicate stereotypes and move beyond the "pathology and problems" approach, unanswered questions concerning American Indian women are legion.[5] How have their family structures and roles adapted and changed in the face of twentieth-century realities? Do Native American women embrace feminism, lean toward Indian activism, or develop their own positions?[6] How active are they in tribal affairs compared to their participation in local, state, and national politics?[7]

Less obvious topics include comparative studies between varying types of Indian women, as well as inquiry into mixed-blood women, whether of cross-tribal or cross-racial heritage.[8] Also, Indian women's folklore, songs, and family histories offer much to be retrieved and analyzed.[9] Other questions include the significance of feminine identity, cross-gender practices, and lesbianism.[10] And how many cultural beliefs and practices—such as creating herbal medicines, speaking native languages, and engaging in traditional crafts—have Indian women conserved in the face of an overwhelming tide of Anglo-American settlement, prejudicial attitudes, and pressures to "Americanize"?[11]

Numerous Spanish-heritage women were also indigenous to areas that are now part of the United States. Moreover, as part of the fastest-growing ethnic group in the United States, such women both deserve and demand study. Historians Vicki Ruiz and Sarah Deutsch have supplied useful and provocative examples for additional research, which must be directed toward modifications in Latinas' lives and attitudes as the West changed, how their relationships with Latino men adapted, how their interactions with women and men of other groups altered, and the cost to them of Anglo-American expansion into formerly Mexican territories. Another focus must be the question of how, when, and why capitalists and industrialists exploited Latinas, and the nature and extent of this exploitation. Latinas' fortitude and determination—meaning how they responded to and coped with their changing environment, what options they created or chose, and which of their mores and traditions survive—are also significant issues.[12]

In addition to indigenous Spanish-background women, a sizeable number of Latinas immigrated to the United States, many within the past several decades. Thus, queries regarding immigrant women in general must be applied to Latinas in particular. How do women's roles in immigrant communities change after migration to the West? How does immigration affect household division of labor? Does immigration significantly alter roles and restraints within the family? How much and why do women's attitudes change after migration to the West? How much and why do their legal rights change? What about second-generation women; in particular, do they experience a radically different phenomenon than their mothers?[13] And, of utmost importance, do different types of Latinas—such as Puerto Ricans, Costa Ricans, and Hondurans—adapt to, and influence, the West in different or in basically similar ways?

In considering Latinas, scholars must, as historian Patricia Zavella warns, remember that Latin women differ by background, class, and ideology. In addition, Antonia Castañeda maintains that historians must reexamine their assumptions and their "racial, class and gender positions" for omissions and unconscious bias.[14] Such awareness is just in the process of emerging; even writers of the mid-1980s had barely begun to struggle with it. In the 1990s developing an understanding of the historical experiences of women of color is crucial to comprehension of twenti-eth-century western women, and will flourish best in an aura of empathy and cooperation.

In addition to Latinas, many African-American women were also im-migrants to the American West; others are native born. Research issues regarding African-American women include, for example, child-bearing rates and practices, political participation, economic endeavors, experi-ences with discriminatory treatment, contributions, and involvement in families and communities.[15] Historian Lawrence B. de Graaf's study in 1980 of black women in the Rocky Mountain and Pacific Coast states between 1850 and 1920 offers an admirable model for much-needed sta-tistical studies of the decades after 1920 as well as illuminating the great need for additional statistical studies based on census data. De Graaf dis-covered that black women in these western areas between 1850 and 1920 bore fewer children, and were slightly older on the average than black southern women. They lived in urban rather than in rural areas and en-dured widespread segregation policies, lack of civil rights, and frequent harassment. They also worked at low-paid and exhausting domestic and agricultural tasks. De Graaf's conclusion that "black women would long remain an invisible segment of western society whose lives and accom-plishments would remain known only within the confines of their race" is still too true.[16]

Obviously, more research must be done and more thought given to framing analytical issues regarding twentieth-century black women in the American West. Historian Anne M. Butler has demonstrated how much waits to be discovered. In a creative study of African-American women in western prisons, Butler has shown that useful data exists in places other than libraries and archives. More recently, Paul R. Spickard's study of south-ern California black women's work during World War II indicates research possibilities in an area bedeviled by lack of traditional documentary re-sources.[17]

Another topic that needs exploration is African-American women's involvement in public movements ranging from club work to contempo-rary feminism. Sudie Rhone, an African-American woman commenting on women's service clubs in Cheyenne, Wyoming, remarked that women's groups were racially segregated during the early years of the twentieth century. According to her, the Searchlight Club, founded in 1904, was the only service group in Cheyenne for black women. Rhone explained that although black women could have joined white women's clubs, they vir-tually never did. She believed that prejudice and discriminatory practices kept black and white women effectively segregated.[18]

As Rhone's comments suggest, groups of women in the twentieth-century West were often discrete entities with their own values, attitudes, cultures, and activities. Thus, we must ask such questions as: Did black women target the same problems as white women or attack race-related problems instead? Did they ever join with white women or, as Sudie Rhone maintained, typically limit themselves to working only with other African-American women? An especially important issue is raised by this last problem, for if African-American women were largely segregated, how much of their segregation derived from prejudice on the part of white, western clubwomen. Scholars have shown that the National Association of Colored Women, organized in 1896, claimed fifty thousand members by 1915. These black clubwomen were affiliated with twenty-eight state federations and over one thousand individual clubs. One such group was the Montana Federation of Negro Women's Clubs in Butte; another existed in Kansas.[19] Were there others in the West? And did those in such densely populated West Coast cities as Los Angeles and Oakland experience the same patterns as those on the Plains?

Asian women, many of whom were relatively recent arrivals in the American West, also deserve extensive research.[20] We need to know far more about their work, marriages and families, education, and religious beliefs. For instance, have they maintained their own traditional religious beliefs or tended to adopt mainstream American ones? And to what extent have they blended their religious and other values with others?

Also, what can scholars learn from Asian-American women's writings? Historian Valerie Matsumoto has demonstrated the richness of literary works of 1930s Nisei women writers. Matsumoto revealed that literature offers insight into "critical questions regarding relations among racial ethnic groups, the impact of regional influences on ethnic culture, and the challenges faced by women seeking their niche in both mainstream U.S. society and the ethnic community."[21] This insight suggests a plethora of similar studies, ranging from the writing of such authors as Maxine Hong Kingston to Kitty Tsui's autobiographical revelation of lesbianism, to the memories of women who lived in such World War II internment camps as California's Tule Lake and Wyoming's Heart Mountain.[22]

Of course, Asian-American women are diverse in themselves, for they include Chinese, Japanese, Korean, Filipino, Vietnamese, and Hmong women. They also settled in vastly different western states, including Hawaii, California, Oregon, and Washington.[23] As a result of Asian-American women's heterogeneity, scholars must shun the common trap of colonizing Asian-American women, as well as other groups of women of color, as consistent, definable entities. Information about Chinese women cannot be generalized to Vietnamese, nor that about Japanese to Filipino. Rather, each group must be studied in its own right.

Another danger in researching racial and ethnic groups of women is the tendency to test their experiences against existing models of Anglo-American, white, middle-class women's history. For instance, the cult of domesticity is a white, middle-class construct that has limited applicability to Native American, Spanish-heritage, African-American, and Asian-American women.[24] Often, its usage is also ineffective and insulting, for it ignores and denies the validity of such women's cultural values and beliefs. A similar problem occurs when researchers attempt to judge other groups of women against white, middle-class feminist models.[25] Feminist goals and expectations had far different meanings for white women than for women of color; suffrage was important to some groups of women while the prevention of economic exploitation, rape, and frequent childbirth were far more meaningful to others.

Clearly, scholars must develop new frameworks and approaches to fit the cultures and values of women other than those of Anglo Americans. It also would be useful to master women's native languages and to study their literature if they are not already part of a scholar's cultural heritage. Studying an anthology such as *This Bridge Called My Back* is sure to convey to a would-be researcher the sense of disillusionment, powerlessness, and rage that many non-Anglo women have felt through the years.[26] Native language sources would similarly reveal the joys, laughter, and celebrations of specific groups of women.

Yet another strategy is a comparative examination of the effect of various races and ethnicities of women on each other and on the larger American culture. It can be theorized, for example, that women are more receptive than men to adopting portions of other women's ways; that a Chicana employer will often readily accept her Indian-woman cook's methods and cuisine. It would also be revealing to know more about regional and state variations among Latinas and African-American, Asian-American, and Native American women—specifically whether region has more or less influence on women's lives than did their own ethnic or racial backgrounds.

Race and ethnicity are clearly significant, but other characteristics also create differences among western women. Such elements as age, religion, education, marital status, and sexual preference can prove crucial, for, depending upon the combination of variables, each woman sees and experiences the West in a slightly different way.[27]

Another very different aspect of western women's diversity derives from the specific era under consideration. The phrase "twentieth-century West" is so concise and appealing that it is easy to forget that it delineates a one-hundred-year period; one hundred years marked by more changes than any preceding century in world history. The American West of the early twentieth century differs vastly from that of midcentury and more widely still from that of the late twentieth century.

Moreover, the term *twentieth century* is more convenient for historians writing about the era than it was for the women living it. Women did not necessarily change their ways or ideas in 1900. Consequently, a historian of the twentieth century has to reach backward into the nineteenth century to understand more recent trends, and often has to compare patterns in the two centuries to understand twentieth-century developments.

Yet another type of diversity stems from the geographic region being studied. Because the twentieth-century West constitutes nearly two-thirds of the nation's land area, numerous variations are present. Historians Joan Jensen and Dorothy Schwieder repeatedly note that experiences of western rural women contrast, often sharply, with those of western urban women.[28] Yet we still lack, among other things, a definitive study of women homesteaders on the Great Plains during the early twentieth century.[29] By the beginning of World War I, homesteading on the Great Plains was popular among large numbers of women. One body of evidence regarding "girl homesteaders," as they were often called, is found in farm and other journals that regularly carried articles discussing and debating women homesteaders. Favorite topics were the feasibility and "social righteousness" of women farming on their own. Although some popular writers demurred, at least one concluded that homesteading provided the "perfect occupation for women who have a taste for country life."[30]

Urban women in the twentieth-century West also experienced particular problems and phenomena. Historian Karen Anderson argues that "women have acted in various ways to claim the city as a place of empowerment for themselves," yet have received little historical attention. From the work of Carl Abbott to that of Gerald Nash, Anderson states, urban women's lives and activities have gone largely unnoted and unexplored.[31]

State boundaries provide another organizing principle for studies of western women. In Oklahoma, for example, how many women, especially single, divorced, and widowed women, were Sooners and Boomers? Did Native American women in Oklahoma generally receive the allotments due them? And how many of these women received proposals of marriage because they were about to get allotments or already owned land? The contributions of Oklahoma's African-American women in raising families, founding black towns, working the land, and in paid employment also beg for investigation.[32]

Another possibility for state studies involves the varying types of legislation that affect women. For instance, more nurse practitioners live and work in western states with hospitable legislation than in those with hostile laws. This situation suggests at least one hypothesis that needs investigation: professional women are grouped in, and attracted to, certain western areas more as a result of favorable laws than other factors.

Given all the diversities among twentieth-century western women, the ultimate question becomes what *is* a western woman? Is she someone who is born in the region, has chosen to live there, or lives there as a result of someone else's decision? How long does she have to live in the West before she is a western woman? Or is her "westernness" more a matter of adopting a special set of "western" attitudes?

A second cause for the relative neglect of twentieth-century western women's history is that women's historians have tended to focus first upon topics of northeastern and national importance and have only gradually branched out to other regions of the country. The "New England bias" of early women's historians is now a widely recognized phenomenon. Still, many studies that claim to include all American women continue to give short shrift to western women.[33]

This situation demands that historians of twentieth-century western women give the issue of what can be termed essentialism—that is, whether western women are essentially the same as, or different from, American women in other regions—high priority on their research agendas. More specifically, we must explore whether twentieth-century western women are significantly different from those in the Northeast, South, and Midwest. We must also ask whether gender issues and configurations are dissimilar, or perhaps even unique, in the West. We must establish whether modern western women constitute a particular type of female deserving of study in her own right. And we must determine whether studies focusing upon twentieth-century western women will illuminate and expand knowledge of women and the West in a useful manner.

The few historians who have approached the question of essentialism have offered various conclusions regarding the nature of twentieth-century western women. As a case in point, in 1978 historian D'Ann Campbell found that the values of the young western women she sampled contrasted noticeably with those of northeastern and southern women. According to poll data from 1943, women in the Pacific Coast states appeared more secular and less interested in the issue of women's morality than other American women.[34]

More recently, however, historian Karen Anderson speculated that western women are much like those in other parts of the country. "The historical work done so far," she wrote in 1989, "indicates that western women have not differed substantially from women elsewhere in the nation in their labor force status, political rights and roles, or family roles and status. . . . Given these preliminary conclusions, it seems likely that western history will be changed more by the inclusion of gender than women's history will be altered by a new additional regional perspective, but each will profit by a more inclusive approach to its subject matter."[35]

It is critical to test such assumptions before concocting sweeping hypotheses and conclusions about twentieth-century western women—for what if, after all, we are simply studying women's history rather than *western* women's history? If western women are the same as other American women, we can relax and feel comfortable with nationally focused studies of women and gender. But if western women are, as I suspect, indeed different, a whole plethora of regional studies are necessary.

Scholars can attack the essentialist-versus-nonessentialist issue by conducting additional detailed studies of women and gender within the West itself. Only after they have established the details and experiences of western women's lives can they compare western women to other groups such as American women in general, or to northeastern, southern, and midwestern women in particular.[36]

One specific example of a research question is the way(s) western women conceive of, and utilize, their environment. We know, for example, that many women supported the activities of John Muir, joined Muir's expeditions, encouraged the development of a national-park concept, and formed naturalists' clubs, but we know little about their role in the Sierra Club, in Greenpeace, and other environmental-reform movements. Do western women lean toward the conservationist side, hoarding and preserving natural resources, or do they tend to consume, creating mounds of trash as they go? Perhaps recent arrivals react differently to the western environment than native-born women, or there may be in operation an outdoor aesthetic of sorts that shapes the way western women in general view environment-related issues. Or we might discover a wide variety of approaches among various races, ethnicity, ages, and educational levels of western women—a variety that would belie the concept of a unified western women's view of the environment.[37]

Another important research question that addresses essentialism concerns western women's roles in producing and supporting culture. Do modern western women read a particular type of literature? Do they write a particular type of literature? prefer certain films? produce distinctive scripts and poems? produce characteristic drawings, prints, and paintings? report news through their own slant? write their special brand of history? In other words, is their work influenced by region? If so, how so and how much?[38] Western women's support of the arts and cultural organizations is also unclear. We simply do not have enough information on western women's attitudes and participation in cultural activities to draw any conclusions.[39]

At the same time that researchers gather detailed information on modern western women, the process of conducting comparative studies must accelerate. Although the next logical step in resolving the issue of western women's distinctiveness is contrasting western women with their counterparts in other regions, such studies are scant in number. We do know, of course, that western women obtained the right to vote before those in other regions, but the reason for this achievement remains clouded. The attainment of suffrage could mean that western women were more determined to vote than women in the Northeast, South, and Midwest; that they were organized more effectively; that they were more suffrage-minded; or that they had greater opportunity to gain access to political participation in areas of the nation where the public sphere was relatively undeveloped. The attainment of women's suffrage in the West could simply reflect suffragists' political organization, or lack thereof, in many western states.[40] Or it could indicate that western men—who were, after all, the voters and legislators who made the suffrage decision—were for a variety of reasons more amenable to the idea of women voting than were men in other regions of the country.

We also know that more western women obtained, and continue to obtain, divorces than women elsewhere in the nation. Even discounting the number of migratory divorces secured by citizens of other states, the rate of divorce among western women is noticeably higher than among northeastern, southern, and midwestern women. Again, the meaning of this phenomenon is unclear. Does it indicate that western women are more contentious and aggressive or less submissive and accepting than women in other regions of the country? Perhaps western cultural attitudes underwrite the high divorce rate; widespread economic opportunities for women make it possible for them to divorce in large numbers; western states' permissive legislation and western judges' liberal attitudes encourage women to solve their marital difficulties by way of the divorce court; or women themselves have a greater role in shaping legal provisions and practices in the West.

Clearly, we have to ask and answer many questions before we understand how western, northeastern, southern, and midwestern women *compare*. Some of the most important questions relate to women's work: Do western women workers tend to earn more or less than women in other regions? Do they have more or less awareness of themselves as wage earners? Are they more or less active in labor organizations?[41] Is the link between work and domestic roles different or similar?[42] What is the role of technology in western women's work?[43] Do western women establish their own businesses more or less frequently? And does the West offer women more or fewer economic opportunities than the East?[44]

Other comparative topics are almost infinite in number. They include: How do western women's periodicals and magazines compare with those in other regions? Do western women adopt notably different fashions than women in other regions? Are greater numbers of them lesbian in orientation? Are western women more politically involved? Do they push to join such traditionally male associations as Rotary, Lions, and Kiwanis? Are they more active in women's groups and social-service organizations? Do they commit more crimes? Do more of them engage in prostitution? Do they join orders of women religious or become ministers more often? And, if so, are western religious orders and churches more open and liberating for women?[45]

Yet another focus for comparative studies is the effect of national events and trends upon women in the various regions of the country. How did the depression beginning in 1929, World War I and World War II, the women's New Deal, urbanization, industrialization, the Vietnam era, the civil rights movement, and contemporary pacifism and feminism disrupt and shape the lives of western women in contrast to those of other American women? And did such movements as pacifism and feminism have more impact in the reputedly egalitarian West?[46]

Another slightly different aspect of comparative studies concerns differences not between western women and those in other regions, but between western women and men. How can scholars study such crucial subjects as home, family, wage work, politics, and sexual orientation without considering men? We also need to know if western women essentially differ from their male counterparts. And in what ways are western women similar to western men? Optimally, historians of western men will provide research and analysis, but as yet men's-studies bibliographies reveal little study of western men.[47]

Granted, the intersection of region and gender is difficult to study because it often confounds precise dissection. It is a fairly straightforward matter to identify differences between women and men, but it is far more difficult to document the nature of such differences, why they occur, and what kinds of behavior, attitudes, and policies they reflect or cause.

One specific and long-standing debate concerning women and men is linked to their varied motives for relocating in the West. Historians have failed to agree on an answer for nineteenth-century western settlers and generally have failed to inquire into the motives of twentieth-century western migrants. Scholars can only make educated guesses whether women and men both choose the West because of job opportunities, improved climate, spousal pressures, children's needs and desires, and economic opportunities, or whether they have a contrasting set of motivations. It would be especially helpful to know how many and what type of women believed that westward migration was a liberating experience.

Of course, such comparative investigations carry dangers. It is especially easy to get immersed in discovering differences and forget to ask *why* they exist. In addition, it is frequently simpler to discover dissimilarities, which are often more readily apparent, than to identify underlying similarities. Among others, political scientist Virginia Sapiro warns against the urge to overestimate differences between groups of women: "Although employment rates of women in the United States are among the highest in the industrialized non-Communist world, the degree of occupational segregation is similar, and in some countries—France and Germany, for example—the earning gap between women and men is smaller than in the United States."[48] Emphasizing differences between western women and men, while ignoring their similarities, can be similarly inaccurate and misleading.

A third reason some scholars may have avoided researching twentieth-century western women is that the topic demands an analysis of continuity and change. At present, historians of women have no generally accepted definition of these concepts. Neither term is defined, for example, in handbooks or dictionaries of feminist theory.[49] As a result, historians seldom agree on whether certain events or occurrences in women's lives constitute continuity or change. For instance, if women wageworkers still think of themselves as wives and mothers first and as only temporary, supplemental breadwinners rather than wage earners in their own right, has their status and awareness changed significantly? Or have these women's attitudes and roles remained much the same as when they worked within the home?

Myriad topics speak to the issue of continuity and change. Western women's altering roles in such professions as teaching, nursing, law, photography, and the military beg for analysis.[50] In addition, women's participation in farm organizations can provide insight into continuity and change. Tracing women's roles, participation, and power through the Granger movement, Farmers' Alliance, and Populist Party could very well reveal an increase in the number of women's planks, a clear growth of women's influence, and a corresponding decline of women's auxiliary groups.[51] And comparing the views of such women activists as Annie LaPorte Diggs with such male writers as Sockless Jerry Simpson could help explain why women's contributions either increased, or failed to do so.

Another similar issue that begs for attention is women's roles in the Wobblies. Were women simply supportive of men's activities or did they have their own agenda? Did any women oppose strikes and if so, why? Did first-generation women differ notably from their daughters and granddaughters in their views and participation? And how were western-women Wobblies similar to, or different from, their eastern counterparts?

The results of women's reform activities over time also remain clouded. One key question is whether women's clubs and reform activities reinforced traditional gender segregation or whether they broke down old stereotypes and offered new opportunities to women. For instance, rural canning projects in North Dakota were an example both of modernization and domestication. On the one hand, such projects taught women new techniques of preserving food, yet, on the other, they encouraged women to continue preserving foodstuffs in their homes in true cottage-industry style. Another related question is whether women reformers achieved an upward trajectory in their efforts, or operated in a series of peaks and valleys. One way to attack this issue would be a study of Mormon women leaders beginning during the 1880s and 1890s, when their participation was high, and continuing through the early twentieth century, when Mormon women's influence and activities seemed to succumb to new limitations. Another would be an examination of progressive-era women from the 1890s through the New Deal years.

Yet another puzzling instance of continuity versus change is apparent in relationships between western women and men. At first glance, many observers would maintain that western women's roles and status clearly improved over the course of the twentieth century. Yet when such factors as increasing female poverty, crime against women, wife abuse, and backlash against feminism and affirmative-action programs are taken into account, one must wonder how far women have progressed.

A fourth cause underlying the relative neglect of twentieth-century western women has been the sluggish growth of western family history. In a 1991 plea for increased attention to western families, Virginia Scharff poignantly asked, "is anybody home on the range?" Yet, in reality, western families provide the milieu in which daily lives and gradual changes are played out. Scharff has even argued that "we might describe the history of the trans-Mississippi West as a continuing struggle among individuals and groups to define, establish, or defend, or avoid, escape, or reconstitute their homes and families as they saw fit."[52]

Certainly, within western families the number of relationships and interactions are almost legion. Historian John Mack Faragher has stressed, for example, the study of "relations of reproduction and work within the family, the structures of domestic authority, and the relationship of both sexes to the public world."[53] In addition, studying family dynamics can also reveal alterations in domestic work roles, expectations of wives and husbands, childbearing and child-raising patterns, conflicts between women and men, and thousands of other aspects of human interrelationships.[54]

Intermarriage in the twentieth-century West is another subject generally neglected by historians. Yet intermarriage abounded in the West from the beginning of Anglo exploration and settlement to the present. In addition to disparate westerners who marry each other, another critical-research area concerns westerners who marry abroad and return with their spouses to the West. For example, numerous U.S. servicemen married Japanese women during World War II and brought their wives back to the United States after the war.[55]

Of course, families also include children. Certainly, in this arena critical topics include birth control, fertility, prenatal care, childbirth, and child rearing.[56] In the latter realm, Mormon parents and their children differ markedly from Hispanic families, just as Asian families differ from Anglos. What parents teach children, how they discipline them, whether they educate them, and whether they hire them out as wageworkers demonstrates a good deal about family structures, but also helps explain long-term patterns of behavior by girls and boys who one day become parents with their own marriages to manage and their own children to train.[57]

Another consideration is the treatment of children, including those of color, in such public institutions as schools and hospitals.[58] And despite recent scholarly interest in western children, we still know little about children's play at home and in public.[59]

In addition, family life and sexuality had an underside. Yet topics ranging from rape and spousal abuse in the West have received minimal attention.[60] Moreover, families shift and change, often through separation, desertion, divorce, or death.[61] For example, millions of western women move from the status of wife to widow each year, widows who are dependent upon pensions, life insurance, charity, or their own earning abilities. But what is the *experience* of widowhood, then, in the twentieth-century West? Does society shunt these women aside so that they lead largely invisible lives, or are they generally active and involved? Do they join forces with single and divorced women to improve the position of all unmarried women, or do they accept their situation with equanimity?[62] And what of women in Sunbelt retirement communities? How many women live on their own and how do their lives compare to other types of western women?

Other traumatic family situations need scholarly work, notably those whose suffering came from outside. In Asian split families, for example, wives and children lived in their homelands, while husbands lived in the United States because U.S. immigration exclusion policies prohibited entry of wives and children.[63]

A fifth factor underwriting some researchers' hesitancy to delve into the twentieth-century West stems from an attack on biography by scholars who believe it is more significant to study movements and trends in history rather than the individuals caught up in them. As a result, biography is currently unfashionable in certain circles, yet to other scholars the life stories of famous and not-so-famous people punctuate modern western history. To these researchers, individuals shaped movements and trends, provided leadership, exercised individual will, and left their marks on the American West. In the case of western women, women's biographies help explain the complexities of the lives of differing racial, ethnic, and other groups of women. Women's biographies also allow study of how women contributed to, or were affected by, prevailing western myths.[64] Moreover, biographical studies reveal individual motivations, the deeper meanings of a woman's life, and how a particular woman exerted her will and influence despite a political and economic system that often proved restrictive.[65]

The issue of women's agency is especially gaining importance for biographers. Rather than simply discussing victimization, exploitation, and cultural dissolution, historians of western women now analyze their subjects' will, force, or power. In other words, historians are pursuing understanding of the ways in which women who were categorized, stereotyped, or typecast resisted "oppression," responded, spoke out, influenced policy, and utilized education to implement change.[66] The question of agency is particularly important for western women of color, who have long been regarded as little more than victims, but are now viewed as people fully capable of action.[67] Numerous Latinas, for example, influenced, shaped, and implemented labor policies, even becoming what one scholar termed "unlikely strikers."[68]

In other ways as well, women's biography is rapidly becoming more revealing than ever before. In *Writing a Woman's Life*, feminist author Carolyn Heilbrun pointed to the year 1973 as a turning point for the writing of women's biography. Earlier prohibitions against writing about women's anger, their desire for power and control, personal fantasies, relations with and love for women, and the reality of their marriages began to lessen at about that time. In other words, some women's biographies began to be more revealing and frank.[69]

Many possible subjects for honest and agency-oriented biographies of twentieth-century western women spring to mind. Among them are author Mary Austin (especially an analysis of her feminist thought); Charlotta Spears Bass of Los Angeles, who became editor in 1912 of the *California Eagle*, the oldest black newspaper on the West Coast, and in 1952 was the first black woman to run for the vice presidency of the United States; intellectual and writer Ina Coolbrith; Annie La Porte Diggs of Kansas, a Farmers' Alliance activist and a magnetic speaker known for her religious liberalism and populist ideas; Dr. Ruth Flowers, who achieved in 1924 the distinction of being the first black woman to graduate from the University of Colorado; Grace Raymond Hebard of Wyoming, important early twentieth-century historian, suffragist, and writer; Susan LaFlesche, Native American physician and reformer in Nebraska; Louise Pound, a professor and well-known athlete at the University of Nebraska; Berkeley Ph.D. Millicent Shinn who, as assistant editor of the *Overland Monthly* and a writer, delved into contemporary issues; Sarah Breedlove Walker, known as Madam Walker, who developed "The Walker Method" of styling African-American women's hair in 1905; Alma White, founder of the Pillar of Fire Church in Denver in 1901; and Aldina de Azavala, Texas author whose stories preserve Hispanic legends and culture.[70] Even well-known western women such as Elaine Goodale Eastman, Sister Aimee McPherson, Georgia O'Keeffe, and Jeanette Rankin, all of whom have been the focus of several previous biographies, would benefit from scrutiny as western women and from an assessment of region on their ideas and work.[71]

In a similar vein, women's autobiographies, both personal and published, must be interpreted and analyzed in the context of growing knowledge and theory about both women and the modern West. Such analysis can demonstrate how western women establish meanings and values that make sense of their lives and their world; it would also help pinpoint the effect of region on western women's thinking and actions. Because an autobiography—especially of a woman of color—is one place where a woman often admits more fully than her mother and grandmother her inner feelings about her lack of, and desire for more, autonomy; her personal thoughts about men and gender relationships; and her particular experiences of the family, workplace, and public networks, it has the potential to answer some of the questions tugging at the minds of historians of western women.[72] As historian Judy Lensink argues, women's other private writings and oral-history interviews also provide valuable texts. Literary criticism and cultural studies can help us move women from the periphery to the center of our research and writing.[73]

In pursuing both biography and autobiography, scholars must especially delve into the inner lives of more women of color. Such Native American women as Maria Martinez and Gertrude Bonnin cry out for interpretive works. Although some argue that necessary sources are nonexistent, others fairly point out that such women as Martinez can be studied in terms of her pots, her place in women's history, her impact on the Pueblo economy, and her role as cultural broker.[74] Other examples that offer plentiful resources are Latina labor organizers Emma Tenayuca, Dolores Huerta, Jesse López de la Cruz, and Raquel Rivera Hernández.[75]

A final deterrent to historians who wish to delve into the rich and exciting research possibilities offered by twentieth-century western women is current scholarly politics and polemics, notably political correctness, deconstructionism, feminist activism, and the debate concerning women's studies versus gender studies. Taking one side or the other in these controversies can affect the slant of research questions, shape the design of studies, influence the choice of methodologies, and help determine the dissemination and thrust of findings.[76]

For instance, historians must ask themselves if they wish to research and write "objective" studies of twentieth-century western women, or intend to mold their work to assist the goals of contemporary feminism? At the present time, historians are divided on this question. Some scholars argue for the acceptance of women's words and experiences as accurate representations of their lives, as well as for a rigorous use of sources, including artifacts and historic sites. Although most historians would support the importance of the feminist movement and a feminist perspective in historical research, they might object to letting their research serve feminism rather than the cause of knowledge. One difficulty with this approach is that by hewing so closely to sources, historians sometimes overlook a crucial point or critical insight that could result from a more liberal application of feminist theory.

On the other side of the debate are historians who argue that because we cannot possibly ascertain the literal truth about the past, we can, or perhaps should, interpret the past in light of contemporary issues. In their view, western women's history *should* serve feminism. One danger in this approach is the possibility of devaluing women's domestic labor by judging it against men's work as the normative standard. Another is the tendency to take women's words and actions out of their historical context.

Given this controversy, historians of twentieth-century western women must decide whether their work will serve a relatively abstract scholarship, assist current causes, or combine the best of these approaches by incorporating both philosophies in a reasonable and rational manner.

As historians confront such dilemmas for themselves, scholarship will perhaps move to another—and welcome—stage. In the United States, scholars and laypeople have thus far experienced three stages in the evolution of their attitudes toward specific groups of people. During the first, one group of people often demeaned and looked down on others. Race, ethnicity, gender, religion, age, and a host of other characteristics provided ample reasons to dislike others, criticize them, and treat them in a discriminatory manner.

During the second phase, people "discovered" the fascinating history, culture, and contributions of formerly disparaged groups. People actively sought out diversity, discovered and explored differences among peoples, valued such divergences, and sought to improve intergroup relationships.

Today, in a third stage, we are struggling with—or against—the concerns raised during stage two: how diversity and fairness can be incorporated into American life. In a future fourth stage, we may search instead for similarities among groups and identify the qualities that unify whites and blacks, men and women, English and Spanish speakers, and other categories of people as human beings, as Americans, and as westerners. Although researching topics relating to twentieth-century western women is important and worthwhile, using such topics to pioneer this fourth stage may prove ultimately more important to historians and lay Americans alike.

Notes

The author would like to thank Susan H. Armitage, Anne M. Butler, Elizabeth Jameson, Joan M. Jensen, Howard R. Lamar, and Virginia Scharff for reading the manuscript and offering provocative comments and helpful suggestions.

1. That scholarship on twentieth-century western women is gradually catching up with work on nineteenth-century women is indicated in Pat Devejian and Jacqueline J. Etulain, comps., *Women and Family in the Twentieth-Century American West: A Bibliography* (Albuquerque: Center for the American West, University of New Mexico, 1990).

2. Notably, see Earl Pomeroy, *The Pacific Slope* (New York: Alfred Knopf, 1965); Gerald D. Nash, *The American West in the Twentieth Century: A History of an Urban Oasis* (Englewood Cliffs, N.J.: Prentice-Hall, 1973), Gene Gressley, *The Twentieth-*

Century West: A Potpourri (Columbia: University of Missouri Press, 1977); Richard Lowitt, *The New Deal and the West* (Bloomington: Indiana University Press, 1984); Gerald D. Nash, *The American West Transformed: The Impact of the Second World War* (Bloomington: Indiana University Press, 1985); and Gerald D. Nash and Richard W. Etulain, eds., *The Twentieth-Century West: Historical Interpretations* (Albuquerque: University of New Mexico Press, 1989).

3. See Joan M. Jensen and Darlis A. Miller, "The Gentle Tamers Revisited: New Approaches to the History of Women in the American West," *Pacific Historical Review* 49 (May 1980): 173–214; Elizabeth Jameson, "Toward a Multicultural History of Women in the Western United States," *Signs* 13 (Summer 1988): 761–91; and Glenda Riley, *A Place to Grow: Women in the American West* (Arlington Heights, Ill.: Harlan Davidson, 1992).

4. See, for example, Carol K. Coburn, "Ethnicity, Religion, and Gender: The Women of Block, Kansas, 1868–1940," *Great Plains Quarterly* 8 (Fall 1988): 222–32; Joan M. Jensen, "Crossing Ethnic Barriers in the Southwest: Women's Agricultural Extension Education, 1914–1940," *Agricultural History* 60 (Spring 1986): 169–81; Rosalinda Méndez González, "Distinctions in Western Women's Experience: Ethnicity, Class, and Social Change," in *The Women's West*, ed. Susan Armitage and Elizabeth Jameson (Norman: University of Oklahoma Press, 1987), 237–51; Antonia I. Castañeda, "Gender, Race, and Culture: Spanish-Mexican Women in the Historiography of Frontier California," *Frontiers* 11 (Winter 1990): 8–20; and Karen Anderson, "Work, Gender, and Power in the American West," *Pacific Historical Review* 62 (November 1992): 481–99.

5. For insightful early studies of Native American women, see Rayna Green, "The Pocahontas Perplex: The Image of Indian Women in American Culture," *Massachusetts Review* 16 (Autumn 1975); and Green, "Native American Women," *Signs* 6 (Winter 1980): 248–67.

6. For ideas, see Rebecca Tsosie, "Changing Women: The Cross-Currents of American Indian Feminine Identity," *American Indian Culture and Research Journal* 12 (1988): 1–37; and Gail H. Landsman, "The 'Other' as Political Symbol: Images of Indians in the Woman Suffrage Movement," *Ethnohistory* 39 (Summer 1991): 247–84. See also Nancy Shoemaker, "The Rise or Fall of Iroquois Women," *Journal of Women's History* 2 (Winter 1991): 39–57; and Beatrice Medicine, "North American Indigenous Women and Cultural Domination," *American Indian Culture and Research Journal* 17 (1993): 121–30.

7. For a nineteenth-century example, see Ted C. Hinkley, "Glimpses of Societal Change among Nineteenth-Century Tlingit Women," *Journal of the West* 32 (July 1993): 12–24. See also Terry P. Wilson, "Osage Women, 1870–1980," in Sucheng Chan, *Peoples of Color in the American West*, ed. Sucheng Chan, Douglas Henry Daniels, Mario T. García. and Terry P. Wilson (Lexington, Mass.: D. C. Heath, 1994), 182–97.

8. For comparative studies, see Betty J. Harris, "Ethnicity and Gender in the Global Periphery: A Comparison of Basotho and Navajo Women," *American Indian Culture and Research Journal* 14 (1990): 15–38; and Martha Harroun Foster, "Of Baggage and Bondage: Gender and Status among Hadatsa and Crow Women," *American Indian Culture and Research Journal* 17 (1993): 121–53. For mixed-blood

women, see Jacqueline Peterson and Jennifer S. H. Brown, eds., *The New Peoples: Being and Becoming Métis in North America* (Lincoln: University of Nebraska Press, 1985).

9. Studies that provide models in recapturing such lore are Rayna Green, *That's What She Said: Contemporary Poetry and Fiction by Native American Women* (Bloomington: Indiana University Press, 1984); H. Henrietta Stockel, *Women of the Apache Nation: Voices of Truth* (Reno: University of Nevada Press, 1991); Ruth McDonald Boyer and Narcissus Duffy Gayton, *Apache Mothers and Daughters: Four Generations of a Family* (Norman: University of Oklahoma Press, 1992); and Virginia Giglio, *Southern Cheyenne Women's Songs* (Norman: University of Oklahoma Press, 1994).

10. See, for example, Evelyn Blackwood, "Sexuality and Gender in Certain Native American Tribes: The Case of Cross-Gender Females," *Signs* 10 (Autumn 1984): 27–42; and Rebecca Tsosie, "Changing Women: The Cross-Currents of American Indian Feminine Identity," *American Indian Culture and Research Journal* 12 (1988): 1–37.

11. See Beatrice Medicine, "American Indian Family: Cultural Change and Adaptive Strategies," *Journal of Ethnic Studies* 8 (Winter 1981): 13–23; Robert A. Trennert, "Educating Indian Girls at Non-reservation Boarding Schools, 1878–1920," *Western Historical Quarterly* 13 (July 1982): 271–90, and "Victorian Morality and the Supervision of Indian Women Working in Phoenix, 1906–1930," *Journal of Social History* 22 (Fall 1988): 113–28; Terry P. Wilson, "Osage Indian Women during a Century of Change, 1870–1890," *Prologue* 14 (Winter 1982):185–201; Ann Metcalf, "Navajo Women in the City: Lessons from a Quarter-Century of Relocation," *American Indian Quarterly* 6 (Spring/Summer 1982): 71–89; Alison Bernstein, "A Mixed Record: The Political Enfranchisement of American Indian Women during the Indian New Deal," *Journal of the West* 23 (July 1984): 13–20; and Sandra K. Schackel, "'The Tales Those Nurses Told!': Public Health Nurses among the Pueblo and Navajo Indians," *New Mexico Historical Review* 65 (April 1990): 225–49.

12. Vicki Ruiz, *Cannery Women, Cannery Lives: Mexican Women, Unionization, and the California Food Processing Industry, 1930–1950* (Albuquerque: University of New Mexico Press, 1987); Sarah Deutsch, *No Separate Refuge: Culture, Class, and Gender on an Anglo-Hispanic Frontier in the American Southwest, 1880–1940* (New York: Oxford University Press, 1987). See also Tatcho Mindiola, "The Cost of Being a Mexican Female Worker in the 1970 Houston Labor Market," *Aztlan* 11 (Fall 1980): 231–47; Paul S. Taylor, "Mexican Women in Los Angeles Industry in 1928," *Aztlan* 11 (Spring 1980): 99–131; Patricia Zavella, "'Abnormal Intimacy': The Varying Networks of Chicana Cannery Workers," *Feminist Studies* 11 (Fall 1985): 541–57; Marianne L. Stoller, "The Hispanic Women Artists of New Mexico: Present and Past," *El Palacio* 92 (Summer/Fall 1986): 21–25; Elizabeth Martinez and Ed McCaughan, "Chicanas and Mexicanas within a Transnational Working Class," in *Between Borders: Essays on Mexicana/Chicana History*, ed. Adelaida R. del Castillo (Encino, Calif.: Floricanto Press, 1990), 31–60; and Maria Herrera-Sobek, *The Mexican Corrido: A Feminist Analysis* (Bloomington: Indiana University Press, 1990).

13. For immigration issues, see Robert R. Alvarez, Jr., *Familia: Migration and*

Adaptation in Baja and Alta California, 1800–1975 (Berkeley: University of California Press, 1987); Rosalinda M. González, "Chicanas and Mexican Immigrant Families, 1920–1940: Women's Subordination and Family Exploitation," in *Decades of Discontent: The Women's Movement, 1920–1940* (Westport, Conn.: Greenwood Press, 1983), 59–84; Suzanne O'Dea Schenken, "The Immigrants' Advocate: Mary Treglia and the Sioux City Community House, 1921–1959," *Annals of Iowa* 50 (Fall 1989/Winter 1990): 181–213; and George F. Sánchez, "'Go after the Women': Americanization and the Mexican Immigrant Woman, 1915–1929," in *Unequal Sisters: A Multicultural Reader in U.S. Women's History*, ed. Ellen Carol DuBois and Vicki L. Ruiz (New York: Routledge, 1990), 250–63. Examples of studies that explored early Chicanas changing legal rights are Rosalind Z. Rock, "'Pido y Suplico': Women and the Law in Spanish New Mexico," *New Mexico Historical Review* 65 (April 1990): 145–59; and Gloria Ricci Lothrop, "Rancheras and the Land: Women and Property Rights in Hispanic California," *Southern California Quarterly* 76 (Spring 1994): 59–84.

14. Patricia Zavella, "Reflections on Diversity among Chicanas," *Frontiers* 12 (Spring 1991): 75; and Antonia I. Castañeda, "Women of Color and the Rewriting of Western History: The Discourse, Politics, and Decolonization of History," *Pacific Historical Review* 61 (November 1992): 501–33.

15. For the importance of black communities, see Nupur Chaudhuri, "'We All Seem Like Brothers and Sisters': The African-American Community in Manhattan, Kansas, 1865–1940," *Kansas History* 14 (Winter 1991–92): 270–88.

16. Lawrence B. de Graaf, "Race, Sex, and Region: Black Women in the American West, 1850–1920," *Pacific Historical Review* 49 (May 1980): 285–314.

17. Anne M. Butler, "Still in Chains: Black Women in Western Prisons, 1865–1910," *Western Historical Quarterly* 20 (February 1989): 19–35; Paul R. Spickard, "Work and Hope: African American Women in Southern California during World War II," *Journal of the West* 33 (July 1993): 70–79.

18. Sudie Rhone, Interview, November 8, 1979, University of Wyoming, American Heritage Center, Laramie.

19. Marilyn Dell Brady, "Kansas Federation of Colored Women's Clubs, 1900–1930," *Kansas History* 9 (Spring 1986): 19–30; Brady, "Organizing Afro-American Girls' Clubs in Kansas in the 1920s," *Frontiers* 9 (1987): 69–73.

20. This argument is eloquently made in Gail M. Nomura, "Significant Lives: Asian and Asian Americans in the History of the U.S. West," *Western Historical Quarterly* 25 (Spring 1994): 69–88.

21. Valerie Matsumoto, "Desperately Seeking 'Deirdre': Gender Roles, Multicultural Relations, and Nisei Women Writers of the 1930s," *Frontiers* 12 (1991): 31.

22. That the necessary source materials are available is demonstrated by Arthur A. Hansen, *Japanese American World War II Evacuation Oral History Project, Part I: Internees* (Westport, Conn.: Meckler Publishing, 1991). See also Sandra C. Taylor, "Leaving the Concentration Camps: Japanese Americans and Resettlement in the Intermountain West," *Pacific Historical Review* 60 (May 1991): 169–94.

23. For studies that concentrate on specific groups, see Yuji Ichioka, "*Amerika Ndeshiko*: Japanese Immigrant Women in the United States, 1900–1924," *Pacific*

Historical Review 49 (May 1980): 339–57; Annie Soo, "The Life, Influence, and Role of Chinese Women in the U.S., Specifically the West, 1906–1966," in *The Life, Influence, and Role of the Chinese in the U.S., 1776–1960* (n.p.: Conference Proceedings of the Second National Conference on Chinese American Studies, 1981); Evelyn Nakano Glenn, *Issei, Nisei, War Brides: Three Generations of Japanese American Women in Domestic Service* (Philadelphia: Temple University Press, 1986); and Benson Tong, *Unsubmissive Women: Chinese Prostitutes in Nineteenth-Century San Francisco* (Norman: University of Oklahoma Press, 1994).

24. See González, "Chicanas and Mexican Immigrant Families," 59–84; and Robert L. Griswold, "Anglo Women and Domestic Ideology in the American West in the Nineteenth and Early Twentieth Centuries," in *Western Women: Their Land, Their Lives*, ed. Lillian Schlissel, Vicki L. Ruiz, and Janice Monk (Albuquerque: University of New Mexico Press, 1988), 15–33. For further discussion of differentiations, see Cynthia Fuchs Epstein, *Deceptive Distinctions: Sex, Gender, and the Social Order* (New Haven: Yale University Press, 1988); and Sandra Lipsitz Bem, *The Lenses of Gender: Transforming the Debate on Sexual Inequality* (New Haven: Yale University Press, 1993).

25. See Sylvia Gonzales, "The White Feminist Movement: The Chicana Perspective," *Social Science Journal* 14 (April 1977): 67–76; Martha Cotera, "Feminism: The Chicana and Anglo Versions, A Historical Analysis," in *Twice a Minority, Mexican American Women*, ed. Margarita B. Melville (St. Louis, Mo.: C. V. Mosby Company, 1980), 217–34; Ruth Ann Alexander, "Elaine Goodale Eastman and the Failure of the Feminist Protestant Ethic," *Great Plains Quarterly* 8 (Spring 1988): 89–101; Alma Garcia, "The Development of Chicana Feminist Discourse, 1970–1980," in DuBois and Ruiz, *Unequal Sisters*, 418–31; and Antonia I. Castañeda, "The Political Economy of Nineteenth Century Stereotypes of Californianas," in del Castillo, *Between Borders*, 213–36.

26. Cherrie Moraga and Gloria Anzaldua, eds., *This Bridge Called My Back: Writings by Radical Women of Color* (Latham, N.Y.: Women of Color Press, 1984). See also Vicki L. Ruiz, "Texture, Text and Context: New Approaches in Chicano Historiography," *Mexican Studies / Estudios Mexicanos* 2 (Winter 1986): 145–52, and "'And Miles to go . . . ': Mexican Women and Work, 1930–1985," in Schlissel, Ruiz, and Monk, *Western Women*, 117–36; and Rosaura Sánchez, "The History of Chicanas: A Proposal for a Materialist Perspective," 1–29, J. Jorge Klor de Alva, "Chicana History and Historical Significance: Some Theoretical Considerations," 61–86, and Juan Gómez-Quiñones, "Questions within Women's Historiography," 87–97, all in del Castillo, *Between Borders*.

27. For example, see Laurie K. Mercier, "We Are Women Irish: Gender, Class, Religious, and Ethnic Identity in Anaconda, Montana," *Montana: The Magazine of Western History* 44 (Winter 1994): 28–41.

28. Dorothy Schwieder, "Education and Change in the Lives of Iowa Farm Women, 1900–1940," *Agricultural History* 60 (Spring 1986): 200–215; Schwieder and Deborah Fink, "Plains Women: Rural Life in the 1930s," *Great Plains Quarterly* 8 (Spring 1988): 79–88; Joan M. Jensen, "Canning Comes to New Mexico: Women and the Agricultural Extension Service, 1914–1919," *New Mexico Historical Review* 57 (October 1982): 361–86, "'I've Worked, I'm Not Afraid of Work': Farm Women

in New Mexico, 1920–1940," *New Mexico Historical Review* 61 (January 1986): 27–52, "New Mexico Farm Women, 1900–1940," in *Labor in New Mexico: Unions, Strikes, and Social History since 1881*, ed. Robert Kern (Albuquerque: University of New Mexico Press, 1983), 61–81; Jensen, *Promise to the Land: Essays on Rural Women* (Albuquerque: University of New Mexico Press, 1991); Deborah Fink, *Agrarian Women: Wives and Mothers in Rural Nebraska, 1880–1940* (Chapel Hill: University of North Carolina Press, 1992).

29. Colorado women homesteaders have received the most attention. See Julie Jones-Eddy, *Homesteading Women: An Oral History of Colorado, 1890–1950* (New York: Twayne, 1992); and Katharine Harris, *Long Vistas: Women and Families on Colorado Homesteads* (Niwot: University Press of Colorado, 1993). For other areas of the West, see Janet E. Schulte, "Proving Up and Moving Up: Jewish Homesteading Activity in North Dakota, 1900–1920," *Great Plains Quarterly* 10 (Fall 1990): 228–44; Sherry L. Smith, "Single Women Homesteaders: The Perplexing Case of Elinore Pruitt Stewart," *Western Historical Quarterly* 22 (May 1991): 163–83; H. Elaine Lindgren, *Land in Her Own Name: Women as Homesteaders in North Dakota* (Fargo: North Dakota Institute for Regional Studies, North Dakota State University, 1991); Erling N. Sannes, "'Free Land for All': A Young Norwegian Woman Homesteads in North Dakota," *North Dakota History* 60 (Spring 1993): 24–28; and Sherry L. Smith, "A Woman's Life in the Teton Country: Homesteader with an Unconventional View," *Montana: The Magazine of Western History* 44 (Summer 1994): 18–33.

30. H. W. Doyle, "She Farms Alone," *Country Gentleman* 83 (August 10, 1918): 36–37; A. May Holoday, "The Lure of the West for Women," *Sunset* 38 (March 1917): 61. See also Paula M. Bauman, "Single Women Homesteaders in Wyoming, 1880–1930," *Annals of Wyoming* 58 (Spring 1986): 39–53; Glenda Riley, "Introduction," in Edith Eudora Kohl, *Land of the Burnt Thigh* (St. Paul: Minnesota Historical Society Press, 1986), ix–xxxii; and Sherry L. Smith, "Single Women Homesteaders: The Perplexing Case of Elinore Pruitt Stewart," *Western Historical Quarterly* 22 (May 1991): 163–83.

31. Karen Anderson, "Western Women: The Twentieth-Century Experience," in Nash and Etulain, *Twentieth-Century West*, 100–101.

32. See Malvena Thurman, ed., *Women in Oklahoma: Century of Change* (Oklahoma City: Oklahoma Historical Society, n.d.), which includes Cherokee women, Osage women, women's suffrage, and black women in elected office. For another example of a state study, see Joan M. Jensen and Gloria R. Lothrop, *California Women* (San Francisco: Boyd and Fraser, 1987).

33. For examples of publications that include western women, see the *Journal of Women's History*; Kathryn Kish Sklar and Thomas Dublin, eds., *Women and Power in American History: A Reader* (Englewood Cliffs, N.J.: Prentice-Hall, 1990); and Nancy Cott, ed., *History of Women in America* (Westport, Conn.: Meckler Corp., forthcoming). Among those that overlook western women are Sara M. Evans, *Born for Liberty: A History of Women in America* (New York: Free Press, 1989); and Mary Beth Norton, ed., *Major Problems in Women's History* (Lexington, Mass.: D. C. Heath, 1989).

34. D'Ann Campbell, "Was the West Different? Values and Attitudes of Young

Women in 1943," *Pacific Historical Review* 47 (August 1978): 453–63.

35. Anderson, "Western Women," in Nash and Etulain, *Twentieth-Century West*, 114. See also Anderson, "Work, Gender, and Power in the American West."

36. Excellent examples of regional or subregional studies include Mary Melcher, "Women's Matters: Birth Control, Prenatal Care, and Childbirth in Rural Montana, 1910–1940," *Montana: The Magazine of Western History* 41 (Spring 1991): 47–56; and George M. Blackburn and Sherman L. Richards, "Unequal Opportunity on a Mining Frontier: The Role of Gender, Race, and Birthplace," *Pacific Historical Review* 62 (February 1993): 19–38. See also Maureen Ursenbach Beecher and Kathryn L. MacKay, "Women in Twentieth-century Utah," in *Utah's History*, ed. Richard D. Poll (Provo, Utah: Brigham Young University Press, 1978), 563–86; John R. Sillito, "Women and the Socialist Party in Utah, 1900–1920," *Utah Historical Quarterly* 49 (Summer 1981): 220–38; Joan M. Jensen, "'Disfranchisement Is a Disgrace'": Women and Politics in New Mexico, 1900–1940," *New Mexico Historical Review* 56 (January 1981): 5–35; and Jensen, "The Campaign for Women's Community Property Rights in New Mexico, 1940–1960," in *New Mexico Women: Intercultural Perspectives*, ed. Joan Jensen and Darlis A. Miller (Albuquerque: University of New Mexico Press, 1986), 333–55.

37. See Vera Norwood, "The Photographer and the Naturalist: Laura Gilpin and Mary Austin in the Southwest," *Journal of American Culture* 5 (Summer 1982): 1–28; Norwood and Janice Monk, eds., *The Desert Is No Lady: Southwestern Landscapes in Women's Writing and Art* (New Haven, Conn.: Yale University Press, 1987); Lewis L. Gould, *Lady Bird Johnson and the Environment* (Lawrence: University Press of Kansas, 1988); and Carol Greentree, "Harriett Barnhart Wimmer: A Pioneer San Diego Woman Landscape Architect," *Journal of San Diego History* 34 (Summer 1988): 223–39.

38. See Barbara Meldrum, "Images of Women in Western American Literature," *Midwest Quarterly* 17 (Spring 1976): 252–67; Kathleen Fraser, "On Being a West Coast Woman Poet," *Women's Studies* 5 (1977): 153–60; Madelon E. Heatherington, "Romance without Women: The Sterile Fiction of the American West," *Georgia Review* 33 (Fall 1979): 643–56; Lawrence L. Lee and Merrill J. Lewis, eds., *Women, Women Writers, and the West* (Troy, N.Y.: Whitston, 1979); Helen Winter Stauffer and Susan J. Rosowski, eds., *Women and Western American Literature* (Troy, N.Y.: Whitston, 1982); Melody Graulich, "Violence against Women in Literature of the Western Family," *Frontiers* 7 (1984): 14–20; Ruth Ann Alexander, "South Dakota Women Writers and the Blooming of the Pioneer Heroine, 1922–1939," *South Dakota History* 14 (Winter 1985): 281–307; June O. Underwood, "Western Women and True Womanhood: Culture and Symbol in History and Literature," *Great Plains Quarterly* 5 (Spring 1985): 93–106; Levi Peterson, *Juanita Brooks: Mormon Woman Historian* (Salt Lake City: University of Utah Press, 1988); Tey Diana Rebolledo, Erlinda Gonzales-Berry, and Teresa Márquez, eds., *Las Mujeres Hablan: An Anthology of Nuevo Mexicana Writers* (Albuquerque: Academia/El Norte Publications, 1988); Barbara A. Babcock and Nancy J. Parezo, *Daughters of the Desert: Women Anthropologists and the Native American Southwest, 1880–1980* (Albuquerque: University of New Mexico Press, 1988); and Gladys Talcott Rife, "Personal

Perspectives in the 1950s: Iowa's Rural Women Newspaper Columnists," *Annals of Iowa* 49 (Spring 1989): 661–82.

39. See Raye Price, "Utah's Leading Ladies of the Arts," *Utah Historical Quarterly* 38 (Winter 1970): 65–85.

40. For antisuffrage, see Billie Barnes Jensen, "'In the Weird and Wooly West': Anti-Suffrage Women, Gender Issues, and Woman Suffrage in the West," *Journal of the West* 32 (July 1993): 41–51.

41. See, for example, Dennis A. Deslippe, "'We Had an Awful Time with Our Women': Iowa's United Packinghouse Workers of America, 1945–75," *Journal of Women's History* 5 (Spring 1993): 10–32; and Michael J. Lewandowski, "Democracy in the Workplace: Working Women in Midwestern Unions, 1943–1945," *Prologue* 25 (Summer 1993): 157–69.

42. Louise Lamphere, Patricia Zavella, and Felipe Gonzales, with Peter B. Evans, *Sunbelt Working Mothers: Reconciling Family and Factory* (Ithaca: Cornell University Press, 1993).

43. See, for example Katherine Jellison, "Women and Technology on the Great Plains, 1910–40," *Great Plains Quarterly* 8 (Summer 1988): 145–57, and Jellison, *Entitled to Power: Farm Women and Technology, 1913–1963* (Chapel Hill: University of North Carolina Press, 1993); Jane Adams, "Resistance to 'Modernity': Southern Illinois Farm Women and the Cult of Domesticity," *American Ethnologist* 20 (February 1993): 89–113; and Angela E. Davis, "'Valiant Servants': Women and Technology on the Canadian Prairies, 1910–1940," *Manitoba History* 25 (Spring 1993): 33–42.

44. See Melissa Hield, "'Union-Minded': Women in the Texas ILGWU, 1933–1950," *Frontiers* 4 (Summer 1979): 59–70; Miriam B. Murphy, "Women in the Utah Work Force from Statehood to World War II," *Utah Historical Quarterly* 50 (Spring 1982): 139–59; Clementina Durán, "Mexican Women and Labor Conflict in Los Angeles: The ILGWU Dressmakers' Strike of 1933," *Aztlán* 15 (Spring 1984): 145–61; Glenna Matthews, "The Fruit Workers of the Santa Clara Valley: Alternative Paths to Union Organization during the 1930s," *Pacific Historical Review* 54 (February 1985): 51–70; Ruiz, *Cannery Women, Cannery Lives*; Patricia Zavella, "The Impact of 'Sun Belt Industrialization' on Chicanas," in Armitage and Jameson, *Women's West*, 291–304; Barbara Kingsolver, *Holding the Line: Women in the Great Arizona Mine Strike of 1983* (Ithaca, N.Y.: ILR Press, 1989); Micaela di Leonardo, "The Myth of the Urban Village: Women, Work, and Family among Italian-Americans in Twentieth-Century California," in Armitage and Jameson, *Women's West*, 277–89; Lucy Eldersveld Murphy, "Business Ladies: Midwestern Women and Enterprise, 1850–1880," *Journal of Women's History* 3 (Spring 1991): 65–89; Anderson, "Work, Gender, and Power in the American West"; William Strobridge, "A Turn-of-the-Century Sister's Act: Mariposa's Wells Fargo Ladies," *The Californians* 11 (November/December 1993): 6–15; Elizabeth Maret, *Women of the Range: Women's Role in the Texas Beef Cattle Industry* (College Station: Texas A & M University Press, 1993); and Michael Bargo, "Women's Occupations in 1870," *Journal of the West* 32 (January 1993): 30–45.

45. For women's literature, see the suggestive study by Sherilyn Cox Bennion,

Equal to the Occasion: Women Editors of the Nineteenth-Century West (Reno: University of Nevada Press, 1990). For prostitution, see John S. McCormick, "Red Lights in Zion: Salt Lake City's Stockade, 1908–11," *Utah Historical Quarterly* 50 (Spring 1982): 168–81; Anne P. Diffendal, "Prostitution in Grand Island, Nebraska, 1870–1913," *Heritage of the Great Plains* 16 (Summer 1983): 1–5; Mary Murphy, "The Private Lives of Public Women: Prostitution in Butte, Montana, 1878–1917," *Frontiers* 7 (1984): 30–35; Priscilla Wegars, "'Inmates of Body Houses': Prostitution in Moscow, Idaho, 1885–1910," *Idaho Yesterdays* 33 (Spring 1989): 25–37. For involvement in public service, see Peggy Pascoe, *Relations of Rescue: The Search for Female Moral Authority in the American West, 1874–1939* (New York: Oxford University Press, 1990); and Susan C. Peterson and Beverly Jensen, "The Red Cross Call to Serve: The Western Response from North Dakota Nurses," *Western Historical Quarterly* 21 (August 1990): 321–40. For women religious and women religious leaders, see Sister M. Evangeline Thomas, "The Role of Women Religious in Kansas History, 1841–1981," *Kansas History* 4 (Spring 1981): 53–63; Susan C. Peterson, "Adapting to Fill a Need: The Presentation Sisters and Health Care, 1901–1961," *South Dakota History* 17 (Spring 1987): 1–22; Peterson and Courtney Ann Vaughn-Roberson, *Women with Vision: The Presentation Sisters of South Dakota, 1880–1985* (Urbana: University of Illinois Press, 1988); Cynthia Tucker Grant, *Prophetic Sisterhood: Liberal Women Ministers of the Frontier, 1880–1930* (Boston: Beacon Press, 1990); Thomas W. Spalding, "Frontier Catholicism," *Catholic Historical Review* 77 (July 1991): 470–84; and Michael E. Engh, "Mary Julia Workman, The Catholic Conscience of Los Angeles," *California History* 72 (Spring 1993): 2–19.

46. Richard Lowitt, in *New Deal and the West*, has demonstrated that women were active in program administration at the state level. Many more questions remain to be asked of the New Deal and the other events mentioned. Examples of such studies include JoAnn Ruckman, "'Knit, Knit, and then Knit': The Women of Pocatello and the War Effort of 1917–1918," *Idaho Yesterdays* 26 (Spring 1982): 26–36; Dorothy Schwieder, "South Dakota Farm Women and the Great Depression," *Journal of the West* 24 (October 1985): 6–18; Clarice F. Pollard, "WAACs in Texas during the Second World War," *Southwestern Historical Quarterly* 93 (July 1989): 61–74; Kathleen E. B. Manley, "Women of Los Alamos during World War II: Some of Their Views," *New Mexico Historical Review* 65 (April 1990): 251–66; Joan M. Jensen, "When Women Worked: Helen Marston and the California Peace Movement, 1915–1945," *California History* 67 (June 1988): 118–31, 147–48; Karen Ward, "From Executive to Feminist: The Business Women's Legislative Council of Los Angeles, 1927–1932," *Essays in Economic and Business History* 7 (1989): 60–75; and Karen J. Blair, "The Limits of Sisterhood: The Woman's Building in Seattle, 1908–1921," *Frontiers* 8 (Spring 1984): 45–52.

47. See, for example, Rupert Wilkinson, *American Tough: The Tough-Guy Tradition and American Character* (Westport, Conn.: Greenwood Press, 1984); and David Savran, *Communists, Cowboys, and Queers: The Politics of Masculinity in the Work of Arthur Miller and Tennessee Williams* (Minneapolis: University of Minnesota Press, 1992).

48. Virginia Sapiro, *Women in American Society* (Palo Alto, Calif.: Mayfield Publishing Company, 1986), 434.

49. See, for example Maggie Humm, *Dictionary of Feminist Theory* (Columbus: Ohio State University Press, 1990).

50. Solid studies of professional groups exist, but not overviews. See Kathleen Underwood, "Schoolmarms on the Upper Missouri," *Great Plains Quarterly* 11 (Fall 1991): 225–33; Carol Cornwall Madsen, "Sisters at the Bar: Utah Women in Law," *Utah Historical Quarterly* 61 (Summer 1993): 208–32; Donna M. Lucey, "Evelyn Cameron: Pioneer Photographer and Diarist," *Montana: The Magazine of Western History* 41 (Summer 1991): 42–55; and Susan C. Peterson and Amy K. Rieger, "'They Needed Nurses at Home': The Cadet Nurse Corps in South Dakota and North Dakota," *South Dakota History* 23 (Summer 1993): 122–32.

51. See, for example, Donald B. Marti, *Women of the Grange: Mutuality and Sisterhood in Rural America, 1866–1920* (Westport, Conn.: Greenwood Press, 1991).

52. Virginia Scharff, "Gender and Western History: Is Anybody Home on the Range?" *Montana: The Magazine of Western History* 41 (Spring 1991): 64. See also Susan Armitage, "Women and Men in Western History: A Stereoptical Vision," *Western Historical Quarterly* 16 (October 1985): 384–87.

53. John Mack Faragher, "Twenty Years of Western Women's History," *Montana: The Magazine of Western History* 41 (Spring 1991): 73.

54. See Betty García-Bahne, "La Chicana and the Chicano Family," in *Essays on la Mujer*, ed. Rosaura Sánchez and Rosa Martinez Cruz (Los Angeles: Chicano Studies Center, 1977), 30–47; Ann Schofield, "The Women's March: Miners, Family, and Community in Pittsburg, Kansas, 1921–1922," *Kansas History* 7 (Summer 1984): 159–68; Katherine Harris, "Sex Roles and Work Patterns among Homesteading Families in Northeastern Colorado, 1873–1920," *Frontiers* 7 (1984): 43–49; Peggy Pascoe, "Gender Systems in Conflict: The Marriages of Mission-Educated Chinese American Women, 1874–1939," *Journal of Social History* 22 (Summer 1989): 631–52; and Sally M. Miller, "California Immigrants: Case Studies in Continuity and Change in Societal and Familial Roles," *Journal of the West* 33 (July 1993): 25–34.

55. Teresa K. Williams, "Marriage between Japanese Women and U.S. Servicemen since World War II," *Amerasia Journal* 17 (1991): 135–54; and Beth Bailey and David Farber, *The First Strange Place: The Alchemy of Race and Sex in World War II Hawaii* (New York: Free Press, 1993). See also Peggy Pascoe, "Race, Gender, and Intercultural Relations: The Case of Interracial Marriage," *Frontiers* (Winter 1991): 5–18; and Staff of the Asian American Studies Center, University of California, Los Angeles, "Antimiscegenation Laws and the Filipino, 1920s–1960s," in Chan, Daniels, García, and Wilson, eds., *Peoples of Color in the American West*, 288–99.

56. See, for example, Charles R. King, "The Woman's Experience of Childbirth on the Western Frontier," *Journal of the West* 29 (January 1990): 76–84; Mary Melcher, "Women's Matters: Birth Control, Prenatal Care, and Childbirth in Rural Montana, 1910–1940," *Montana: The Magazine of Western History* 41 (Spring 1991): 47–56; Deborah Fink and Alicia Carriquiry, "Having Babies or Not: Household Composition and Fertility in Rural Iowa and Nebraska, 1900–1910," *Great Plains Quarterly* (Summer 1992): 157–68; and Lee L. Bean, Geraldine P. Mineau, and Douglas L. Anderton, "High-Risk Childbearing: Fertility and Infant Mortality on the American Frontier," *Social Science History* 16 (Fall 1992): 337–63.

57. See George N. Otey, "New Deal for Oklahoma's Children: Federal Day Care Centers, 1933–1946," *Chronicles of Oklahoma* 62 (Fall 1984): 296–311; Gilbert G. Gonzalez, "Segregation of Mexican Children in a Southern California City: The Legacy of Expansionism and the American Southwest," *Western Historical Quarterly* 16 (January 1985): 55–76; Sara A. Brown and Robie O. Sargent, "Children in the Sugar Beet Fields of the North Platte Valley of Nebraska, 1923," *Nebraska History* 67 (Fall 1986): 256–303; James H. Conrad, "Aid to Families with Dependent Children in Texas, 1941–1981," in *For the General Welfare: Essays in Honor of Robert H. Bremner,* ed. Frank Annunziata et al. (New York: Peter Lang, 1989), 337–60; Elliott West, *Growing Up With the Country: Childhood on the Far Western Frontier* (Albuquerque: University of New Mexico Press, 1989); Elizabeth Hampsten, *Settlers' Children: Growing Up on the Great Plains* (Norman: University of Oklahoma Press, 1991); Ken Driggs, "Who Shall Raise the Children? Vera Black and the Rights of Polygamous Utah Parents," *Utah Historical Quarterly* 60 (Winter 1992): 27–46; and Julie Hemming Savage, "Hannah Grover Hegsted and Post-Manifesto Plural Marriage," *Dialogue: A Journal of Mormon Thought* 26 (Fall 1993): 101–17.

58. Devon A. Mihesuah, "Too Dark to be Angels: The Class System among the Cherokees at the Female Seminary," *American Indian Culture and Research Journal* 15 (1991): 29–52, and Mihesuah, *Cultivating the Rosebuds: The Education of Women at the Cherokee Female Seminary, 1851–1909* (Champaign: University of Illinois Press, 1993); K. Tsianina Lomawaima, "Domesticity in the Federal Indian Schools: The Power of Authority over Mind and Body," *American Ethnologist* 20 (May 1993): 227–40; Rickey Hendricks, "Feminism and Maternalism in Early Hospitals for Children: San Francisco and Denver, 1875–1915," *Journal of the West* 32 (July 1993): 61–69; and Rickey L Hendricks and Mark S. Foster, *For a Child's Sake: History of the Children's Hospital, Denver, Colorado, 1910–1990* (Niwot: University Press of Colorado, 1994).

59. See, for example Jean Cochrane, "Children of the Farm: Work and Play on the Frontier," *Beaver* 72 (August/September 1992): 12–18.

60. See, for example, Betsy Downey, "Battered Pioneers: Jules Sandoz and the Physical Abuse of Wives on the American Frontier," *Great Plains Quarterly* 12 (Winter 1992): 31–49; and Joan M. Jensen, "The Death of Rosa: Sexuality in Rural America," *Agricultural History* 67 (Fall 1993): 1–12.

61. See Paula Petrik, "If She Be Content: The Development of Montana Divorce Law, 1865–1907," *Western Historical Quarterly* 18 (July 1987): 261–91; and Glenda Riley, *Divorce: An American Tradition* (New York: Oxford University Press, 1991), 85–107.

62. See Arlene Scadron, ed., *On Their Own: Widows and Widowhood in the American Southwest, 1848–1939* (Urbana: University of Illinois Press, 1988).

63. A case study is found in Haiming Liu, "The Trans-Pacific Family: A Case Study of Sam Chang's Family History," *Amerasia Journal* 18 (1992): 1–34.

64. Examples of image makers are found in Michael Allen, "The Rise and Decline of the Early Rodeo Cowgirl: The Career of Mabel Strickland, 1916–1941," *Pacific Northwest Quarterly* 83 (October 1992): 122–27; Kathryn Derry, "Corsets and Broncs: The Wild West Show Cowgirl, 1890–1920," *Colorado Heritage* (Sum-

mer 1992): 2–16; Richard A. Lutman, "A Woman to Live in Your Heart Forever: The Women of Zane Grey's West," *Journal of the West* 32 (January 1993): 62–68; Mary Lou LeCompte, *Cowgirls of the Rodeo: Pioneer Professional Athletes* (Champaign: University of Illinois Press, 1993); and Glenda Riley, *The Life and Legacy of Annie Oakley* (Norman: University of Oklahoma Press, 1994).

65. See, for example Valerie Sherer Mathes, *Helen Hunt Jackson and Her Indian Reform Legacy* (Austin: University of Texas Press, 1990); Julie Roy Jeffrey, *Narcissa Whitman* (Norman: University of Oklahoma Press, 1991); Debbie Mauldin Cottreel, *Pioneer Woman Educator: The Progressive Spirit of Annie Webb Blanton* (College Station: Texas A & M University Press, 1993); Sally M. Miller, *From Prairie to Prison: The Life of Social Activist Kate Richards O'Hare* (Columbia: University of Missouri Press, 1993); Emily Wortis Leider, *California's Daughter: Gertrude Atherton and Her Times* (Stanford, Calif.: Stanford University Press, 1993); and Shirley A. Leckie, *Elizabeth Bacon Custer and the Making of a Myth* (Norman: University of Oklahoma Press, 1993).

66. Studies of women who were stereotyped are found in Harold E. Hinds and Charles Tatum, "Images of Women in Mexican Comic Books," *Journal of Popular Culture* 18 (Summer 1984): 146–62; Sarah Carter, "Categories and Terrains of Exclusion: Constructing the 'Indian Woman' in the Early Settlement Era in Western Canada," *Great Plains Quarterly* 13 (Summer 1993): 147–61; and Linda Borish, "Was Woman's Constitution Less Robust?: Farm Women and Physical Health in the Agricultural Press, 1820–1870," *Canadian Journal of History and Sport* 25 (May 1994): 1–18. For examples of women who fought back, see Barbara J. Burt-Way, "Gender and Sustaining Political Ambition: A Study of Arizona Elected Officials," *Western Political Quarterly* 45 (March 1992): 11–25; and Sandra Schackel, *Social Housekeepers: Women Shaping Public Policy in New Mexico, 1920–1940* (Albuquerque: University of New Mexico Press, 1992).

67. See, for example Pascoe, *Relations of Rescue.*

68. Patricia Zavella, "The Impact of 'Sun-Belt' Industrialization on Chicanas," Working Paper Series No. 7, Stanford University Center for Chicano Research, September 1984, 1–25; and Irene Ledesma, "Unlikely Strikers: Mexican-American Women in Strike Activity in Texas, 1919–1974" (Ph.D. diss., Ohio State University, 1992). For similar studies of nineteenth-century western women, see Vicki Ruiz, "Dead Ends or Gold Mines? Using Missionary Records in Mexican-American Women's History," *Frontiers* 12 (1991): 33–56; and Carol Devens, *Countering Colonization: Native American Women and Great Lakes Missions, 1630–1900* (Berkeley: University of California Press, 1992).

69. Carolyn G. Heilbrun, *Writing a Woman's Life* (New York: W. W. Norton and Co., 1988), 11–19. For discussions of women's biography, see Jean Baker, "Writing Female Lives: The Case of Mary Todd Lincoln," *The Psychohistory Review* 17 (Fall 1988) 34–48; Personal Narratives Group, ed., *Interpreting Women's Lives: Feminist Theory and Personal Narratives* (Bloomington: Indiana University Press, 1989); Louise A. Tilly, "Gender, Women's History, and Social History," *Social Science History* 13 (Winter 1989): 439–80; Peter Stansky, "The Crumbling Frontier of History and Biography: Some Personal Remarks," *Pacific Historical Review* 61 (February 1990): 1–14; Kathleen Barry, "The New Historical Syntheses: Women's Biog-

raphy," *Journal of Women's History* 1 (Winter 1990): 77–105; Liz Stanley, "Moments of Writing: Is There a Feminist Auto/biography?" *Gender and History* 2 (Spring 1990): 58–67; Sara Alpern, Joyce Antler, Elisabeth Israels Perry, and Ingrid Winther Scobie, eds., *The Challenge of Feminist Biography: Writing the Lives of Modern American Women* (Urbana: University of Illinois Press, 1992); and Carolyn G. Heilbrun, "Is Biography Fiction?" *Soundings* 76 (Summer/Fall 1993): 293–304.

70. See, for example Janice B. MacKinnon and Stephen R. MacKinnon, *Agnes Smedley: The Life and Times of an American Radical* (Berkeley: University of California Press, 1988); Virginia Scharff, "The Independent and Feminine Life" (regarding Grace Raymond Hebard), in *Lone Voyagers*, ed. Geraldine Clifford (New York: Feminist Press, 1989); Valerie Sherer Mathes, "Susan LaFlesche Picotte, M.D.: Nineteenth-Century Physician and Reformer," *Great Plains Quarterly* 13 (Summer 1992): 172–86; and regarding another member of the LaFlesche clan: Lisa Emmerich, "Marguerite LaFlesche Diddock: Office of Indian Affairs Field Matron," *Great Plains Quarterly* 13 (Summer 1993): 162–71.

71. For ideas about Eastman, for example, see Ruth Ann Alexander, "Finding Oneself through a Cause: Elaine Goodale Eastman and Indian Reform in the 1880s," *South Dakota History* 22 (Spring 1992): 1–37.

72. For further discussion of the value of women's autobiography, see Personal Narratives Group, *Interpreting Women's Lives*.

73. Judy Nolte Lensink, "Beyond the Intellectual Meridian: Transdisciplinary Studies of Women," *Pacific Historical Review* 61 (November 1992): 463–65.

74. For ideas concerning cultural brokers, see Margaret Connell Szasz, ed., *Between Indian and White Worlds: The Cultural Broker* (Norman: University of Oklahoma Press, 1994).

75. See, for example Richard A. Garcia, "Dolores Huerta: Woman, Organizer, Symbol," *California History* 72 (Spring 1993): 56–71.

76. For a fuller discussion of the politics of writing women's history, see Virginia Scharff, "Else Surely We Shall All Hang Separately: The Politics of Western Women's History," *Pacific Historical Review* 61 (November 1992): 535–55.

6

Research Opportunities in Twentieth-Century Western Cultural History

Richard W. Etulain

Imagine a traveler entering the United States along the West Coast, zig-zagging north and south as he moves east, and emerging from the American West at the Mississippi River. When he returns home, his friends ask him to describe and evaluate what he has seen and experienced. For the careful observer wishing to provide more than superficial personal impressions, the request is neither an easy nor quickly completed task. He has traversed some of the country's most humid and arid regions, he has encountered substantial numbers of Indian, Hispanic, and Asian peoples, and he has likely passed through sprawling urban concentrations as well as immense open spaces. And if he were to make the same trip a decade later, notable changes will have marked much of the West. How can he give any sense of this huge region and its diverse, swiftly changing lifestyles?

Similar challenges face students and scholars endeavoring to define and describe the numerous cultures and cultural developments of the twentieth-century American West.[1] Diversities and changes so complicate and transform the scene that hesitant and overly cautious students are dissuaded from embarking on the daunting venture. Still, a few recent and illuminating conceptual paths and a handful or two of interpretive way stations encourage intrepid pioneers to set forth, to mark out larger and more exact trails through the region. Along the way, they are likely to realize that erecting new periodic, comparative, and contrasting sign-posts will not only guide their own pioneering journeys but also blaze trails for those who follow.

In the past, historians paid scant attention to cultural developments in the modern American West. Although Vernon Louis Parrington's monumental *Main Currents in American Thought* (1927, 1930) stimulated dozens of other scholars to consider major trends in American cultural history, the popularity of that work and the writings of other cultural historians dramatically declined after the 1950s. The field of cultural-intellectual historiography has not revived since that time, despite the increased interest in American "culture" during the last two decades. Moreover, specialists in the frontier and West have retarded the study of cultural history in two other ways. Typically, from Frederick Jackson Turner forward they have overlooked most cultural activities and, secondly, only since the 1960s have they emphasized the twentieth-century West. Together, these trends have been large barriers to the study of cultural developments in the post-1900 West.[2]

This essay, attempting to surmount these earlier barriers and to build on the few scattered interpretations available on western American culture, is divided into two major parts. The first section briefly structures western cultural history into frontier, regional, and postregional periods, thereby suggesting one mental map for scholars studying the modern West. Also noted are specific subtopics that merit special attention. Part two focuses on western subregionalism and comparative regions. Here, attention is called to three other ways of studying western cultural history, including mention of numerous projects needing further study. If heeded, these research agendas on western subregionalism, comparisons among western, southern American, and Canadian cultures, and linkages between western and national American cultural trends will greatly enrich understanding of western American cultures. Along the way, in the text and the footnotes, other research opportunities within this large subject are briefly noted.

Early in the twentieth century—indeed well into the 1920s—frontier themes and images dominated western American culture and powered major trends in historiography, literature, art, and popular culture.[3] Echoing emphases of the nineteenth century, the historical writings of Frederick Jackson Turner and Frederic Logan Paxson, and the fiction of Owen Wister, Zane Grey, Hamlin Garland, and Jack London, for example, dramatized initial contacts and conflicts with new lands and peoples. In their essays and books, Turner and Paxson depicted pioneers battling Indians and unsettled wilderness in order to conquer new frontiers. They were not inclined to depict newcomers living in established communities in the trans-Mississippi West. Concurrently, novels like Wister's *The Virginian* (1902) and Grey's *Riders of the Purple Sage* (1912) introduced and solidified the ingredients of the popular Western, in which valiant cowboys or gunmen outdueled black-hatted opponents against wilderness backdrops serving as notable characters in the novels' plots.[4]

Artists Frederic Remington and Charles Russell were intrigued with similar themes in paintings they completed between the 1880s and 1920s.

If Remington's depictions of Indians, cowboys, and soldiers nearly always focused on action and adventure scenes isolated from frontier farms or towns, Russell also treated cowboys in frenetic scenes in such well-known paintings as *A Bronc to Breakfast* (1908) and *In Without Knocking* (1909). These emphases were also familiar images in Hollywood Westerns from *The Great Train Robbery* (1903) through the 1920s. Sagebrush heroes like Broncho Billy Anderson, William S. Hart, and Tom Mix rode hard and fought valiantly against cowardly villains bent on disrupting nascent settlements. And particularly in Hart films like *Hell's Hinges* (1916), *The Toll Gate* (1920), and *Tumbleweeds* (1925), wilderness settings and lawless social conditions challenge heroic protagonists.[5] Indeed, in most of these historiographical, fictional, artistic, and cinematic cultural documents, an existing or closing frontier occupies the central narrative focus.

Even before the end of the 1920s, another cultural protagonist appeared on stage. Although regionalists did not drive earlier frontier emphases from the cultural scene, the West as region emerged as an alternative way of looking at western culture, a perspective that gained increasing popularity during the 1920s and 1930s.[6]

Prefigured by the notable historical and literary works of Josiah Royce, Mary Austin, and Willa Cather before 1920, regionalism surged on the scene soon after World War I. Above all, regionalists strove to show how postfrontier western settings and experiences shaped the histories and lives of westerners. Regionalists were convinced that their domain was no longer a Wild West of wilderness and Indian conflicts, but one in which the shaping power of varied physical terrains and racial/ethnic experiences were producing a new regional culture recognizably different from those in other sections of the United States. In *O Pioneers!* (1912), for instance, Willa Cather dramatically depicts the courage and stamina of Alexandra Bergson driving her to conquer the Nebraska Divide, helping to transform it from a frontier dominating immigrants into a rich agricultural setting dotted with fruitful farms and thriving communities hosting schools and churches. Cather's first major novel is a pioneering portrait of western culture maturing from frontier to region.[7]

During the interwar years, other historians, novelists, and artists furnished revealing treatments of a regional West. Frederick Jackson Turner's sectional (regional) thesis in 1925, Walter Prescott Webb's *The Great Plains* (1931), and the grassland histories of Kansan James Malin are premier illustrations of this new regionalism. At the same time, novelists like Vardis Fisher, H. L. Davis, Harvey Fergusson, and John Steinbeck used Pacific Northwest, Southwest, and California settings to produce memorable fictions about those western subregions. Among these novels, Steinbeck's *Grapes of Wrath* (1939), while a first-rank work of social criticism, is also an unforgettable regional novel, illustrating important western sociocultural experiences across the depression Southwest.

During the 1920s and 1930s, artists like Thomas Hart Benton, Grant Wood, and John Steuart Curry turned to regional settings and experiences for their artwork. Dubbed American Scene painters, this midwestern triumvirate and other like-minded artists such as Alexandre Hogue and Peter Hurd capitalized on small-town, farm and ranching, and other rural scenes to illuminate a Midwest and Southwest in transition from open, unsettled frontiers to regions spawning new cultural voices and identities.[8]

Moreover, several small magazines across the West, serving both as indexes of and outlets for this new regional outpouring, sprang up during the 1920s and 1930s. Part and parcel of a surging regionalism that flooded across the American South and West, the Canadian West, and even sections of Europe, these regional magazines encouraged historians, novelists, and painters to abandon earlier stereotypical emphases on a pioneer West of "uncivilized" Indians and courageous pioneers and to turn instead to a later West developing its own regional identity. Energetic editors such as B. A. Botkin (*Folk-Say*), John T. Frederick (*Midland*), and H. G. Merriam (*Frontier*), as well as other journals such as *Southwest Review, Prairie Schooner*, and *New Mexico Quarterly*, drew on as well as encouraged this surge of regionalism that deluged the West.[9] If earlier emphases on the West as frontier remained alive in the 1920s and 1930s, they now had to vie with competing visions of the West as developing region.

Then World War II stormed across the West, like a flash flood, redirecting previous frontier and regional themes and preparing the way for a new era of postregionalism. A generation later, in the 1960s and 1970s, emotional reactions to an unpopular war, political corruption, and rising expectations of ethnic groups and women sent another tidal wave through western American culture. If the Second World War brought millions of newcomers to the West to redefine the region through their varied backgrounds, as historians Earl Pomeroy and Gerald Nash have clearly shown,[10] the activism of the 1960s and 1970s enriched the regional cultural cauldron with still other spicy ingredients. Together, the war and "the 1960s" helped to revolutionize the cultural identity of the modern American West.[11] Recent historians, novelists, artists, and other purveyors of western culture are revealing reflectors of this new postregionalism.

For example, American Studies scholar Henry Nash Smith and historian Earl Pomeroy presented novel historiographical interpretations in the 1950s. Building a provocative case for closer scrutiny of myths and symbols that nineteenth-century Americans projected onto the American West, Smith, through wide-ranging, interdisciplinary research in his provocative volume *Virgin Land*, revolutionized scholars' understanding of the roles that ideas and ideology played in shaping western culture. Meanwhile, Pomeroy urged scholars to reexamine persisting eastern influences on the American West. He asserted, in his pathbreaking essay "Toward a Reorientation of Western History: Continuity and Environment," that these incoming cultural currents "bulked at least as large" as new frontier influences in shaping western culture. In staking this novel claim, Pomeroy encouraged students to be less caught up in viewing the West as a radical, innovating frontier that reshaped every incoming influence.[12]

Other nonwesterners and westerners were simultaneously depicting the West as neither frontier nor region in their fiction. One group of novelists, including newcomers Nathanael West, Aldous Huxley, and James M. Cain in the 1930s, and the Beat writers Jack Kerouac and Allen Ginsberg after the war, were convinced that the West, especially California, was no longer the Eden, the El Dorado, and the Big Rock Candy Mountain that earlier frontier and regional writers claimed. Even Steinbeck's *Grapes of Wrath* implied that California as a land of milk and honey was a cruel hoax.

Artist Georgia O'Keeffe and architect Frank Lloyd Wright were other outsiders who imported earlier training and experiences to the West, fell in love with western settings, and invigorated western culture by utilizing modernistic and minimalistic techniques to deal with western scenes and places. O'Keeffe, influenced by her art-school training and the dominance of Alfred Stieglitz, drew on her abundant skills with bright colors, sharp lines, and eye-catching forms to give new significance to New Mexico churches, crosses, and desert bones. Similarly, Wright, equally independent and individualistic, displayed his innovative and iconoclastic temperament in such western structures as Taliesin West near Phoenix, the Marin County Civic Center in California, and the Price Tower in Bartlesville, Oklahoma. Together, O'Keeffe and Wright represent a strain of western postregionalism less reflective of place than of nonwestern experiences adapted to western scenes.[13]

Other happenings in the postwar generation illustrated the West shrugging off its colonialism even while it pioneered new cultural trends. Abstract expressionist painters, increased evidences of evangelical religious groups (for example, the launching of Oral Roberts's career and the founding of Fuller Seminary), and the establishing of California's Master Plan of higher education epitomized pacesetting cultural trends between World War II and the earlier 1960s.

Then new transforming sociocultural trends disrupted the West in the later 1960s and early 1970s, as they did other regions of the country. These upheavals may not have been as upsetting as those during and immediately following World War II, but they nonetheless injected additional change and diversity into the western cultural bloodstream. Mounting discontent with an unpopular war and what seemed to be unresponsive federal, state, and local governments in dealing with urban, racial-ethnic, and family and poverty issues reoriented earlier sociocultural trends even while they ushered in new ones.

For the first time, a chorus of ethnic literary voices were heard throughout the region. Native American novelists N. Scott Momaday, Leslie Silko, and James Welch dramatized controversies over reservations, white urban life, and the history and culture of the Indian past, even while Rudolfo Anaya, Tomás Rivera, and Denise Chávez reminded readers of the notable divergent experiences of Hispanics in the region. Indeed, these authors and their novels were startling reminders that the West of Indians and Hispanics differed markedly from the culture that many European Americans considered typical of the region.[14]

No less noteworthy were the enlarged contributions of women to western literature. Even though Mary Austin, Willa Cather, and Mari Sandoz published notable essays, nonfiction, and novels before the 1960s, Tillie Olsen, Joan Didion, Native Americans Leslie Silko and Louise Erdrich, and Asians Maxine Hong Kingston and Amy Tan, as well as more recent authors Marilynne Robinson and Barbara Kingsolver, represent the mounting importance of women's voices, diversifying and enriching the canon of western writing. Erdrich's four novels depicting Indian and small-town experiences in the northern Plains, for instance, are revealing portraits of women's attitudes toward family, culture, and the environment that too often were missing from most earlier western fiction.[15]

Similar strains of change and diversity mark recent trends in western historiography. Beginning in the 1970s, many historians, but particularly those of minority backgrounds, produced an avalanche of new books about diverging racial/ethnic experiences in the West. For example, Albert Camarillo, Mario García, Vicki Ruiz, and Ramón Gutiérrez authored several volumes, often innovative in approach and organization, examining Spanish-speaking peoples across the Southwest from the sixteenth into the twentieth centuries. Although Native American historians have been less active in writing monographs or syntheses of their western experiences, non-Indians Francis Paul Prucha, Richard White, Robert Utley, and Brian W. Dippie, among many others, have written superb studies of Indian policy, Indian cultures, and white–Indian conflicts. At the same time, the books and essays of Frederick C. Luebke, David Emmons, and William A. Douglass supply much-needed analytical studies of European immigrant groups.[16]

In several other areas, historians reveal how much our views of the West as frontier or as emerging region have changed in the last generation. Following national—in fact international—trends, western specialists have launched a blizzard of articles and books on women and families, urban and community experiences, and environmental topics. Taken together, these numerous studies create a more complex western past.

This tentative periodization of western American culture suggests an agenda for a multitude of new studies. Although Franklin Walker, Kevin Starr, and several members of the Western Literature Association have produced pathbreaking studies, western historians generally have paid scant attention to western literature, and most western literary studies beg for sound, extensive historical underpinnings.[17] If we lack a well-integrated literary history of the West, one demonstrating how historical and cultural changes have shaped frontier, regional, and postregional trends in western writing, we also need wide-reaching studies treating the varied roles of ethnic groups, women and families, environmental themes, and popular figures such as the cowboy and outlaw in western prose and poetry.[18]

In the field of western historiography the lacunae are equally numerous. Despite all the significant studies of Frederick Jackson Turner, we still need a book-length analytical study of his frontier and regional ideas. Similarly, the existing studies of Walter Prescott Webb and Herbert Eugene Bolton, although satisfactory biographies, are not probing interpretations of their regional themes nor comparative evaluations of their places in American or western historiography. The same may be said for the works and concerns of Frederic Logan Paxson, James Malin, and Ray Billington. Moreover, although a few scattered essays treat the significance of Henry Nash Smith and Earl Pomeroy and trends in western historiography since World War II, no one has yet produced a major work on this half-century of historical writing.[19]

Unfortunately, even fewer studies focus on western art, religion, education, and popular culture. Artists like Remington, Russell, Benton, Wood, and O'Keeffe have received merited book-length attention, but only Patricia Janis Broder attempts a full overview of twentieth-century western art, and it fails to link artistic trends to historical developments in the post-1900 West.[20] A new generation of western scholars ought to study these frontier-regional-postregional transformations in western art as well as supply more comprehensive studies of how western artists illustrate or break from national and global artistic trends. Studies of western religion and education are even less numerous. A few denominations and notorious ministers have received article-length attention, but the regional or postregional dimensions of these topics have yet to be studied. Similarly, scholars have examined individual colleges and universities, a handful of leading educators, and a few other topics concerning schools and schooling in the modern West, but for the most part the field of western educational history is virtually uncultivated.[21] Finally, we lack, and very much need, a study like Smith's *Virgin Land* of the twentieth-century West. Scattered monographs treat popular cultural topics like rodeos, dude ranches, and gambling and resort meccas, but no one has yet essayed a synthetic study of these diverse topics. Meanwhile, on Hollywood we have three or four overviews, hundreds of books on individual stars, movies, and companies, but nearly all fail to treat the so-called dream factory as one reflection of regional and postregional trends.[22]

   This division of western American culture into frontier, regional, and postregional periods is but one way to conceptualize the region's culture. Equally promising is to view the West as a series of subregions in which cultural currents owe as much or more to developments within these sub-Wests as they do to larger regional, national, or worldwide trends. One need mention only a handful or two of these subregional topics that merit initial or additional consideration.

   Actually, historians have been more aware of the signal importance of western subregionalism than most accounts suggest. Early on, Turner, Webb, and Malin, for example, pinpointed dynamic differences among sections or regions, and more recent studies by journalists, anthropologists, and geographers reiterate the significance of sub-Wests in the post–World War II era. Pathbreaking studies of the Great Plains or the Kansas grasslands are now joined by books on the Power Shift, the Westward Tilt, the Sunbelt, and the Nine Nations of North America, all of which counter the tendency of other scholars to homogenize the West into one sprawling region.[23] As William G. Robbins notes in a recent provocative essay, shifting economic forces have so transformed the modern West that earlier patterns of colonialism, cores and peripheries, and regional rivalries no longer hold; new subregional competitions have replaced the previous interregional showdowns.[24]

   In the last decade or two, historians exhibit larger understandings of these subregional differences in the West. For instance, Frederick Luebke, Sarah Deutsch, David Emmons, and David Montejano, in several notable books and essays, examine the ways in which ethnic diversity, cohesion, and assimilation are, in part, products of subregional differences.[25] Similarly, Donald Worster and Richard White demonstrate the central importance of subregionalism to an understanding of the environmental history of the West. Equally illuminating are new studies of subregional influences on women and families throughout the West.[26]

   Literary scholars are likewise commenting on the significance of western subregionalism. Even though the Bay Area continues to enjoy its reputation as a notable western literary community, Los Angeles, northern New Mexico, and parts of Texas and Montana clamor for well-deserved attention as significant literary colonies. On the other hand, why is it, Wallace Stegner asks, that other sections of the West lack prominent literary traditions.[27] In answer, no one well acquainted with the cultural contours of the modern West will claim a uniform literary output, in quantity or quality, throughout the region. Even though urban areas and several university campuses have played host to important literary activity, unusual locations such as Taos, New Mexico, Missoula, Montana, and Denton, Texas, are buzzing with literary activity.

Subregional patterns also help to define and explain some religious currents in the modern West. If Mormon worldviews dramatically influence culture in the central West, increasing numbers of Southern Baptists, Pentecostals, and other fundamentalists/evangelicals are stalking the Southwest, from Texas to California. If Roman Catholics remain strong in the northern West from the Dakotas through Montana, especially in older mining and European immigrant areas, they are also expanding in the Southwest, where mushrooming Mexican populations swell Catholic church numbers. Meanwhile, the Pacific Northwest, along with Nevada and Alaska, contains the lowest percentage of church-affiliated people of any area in the entire nation.[28]

For scholars attracted to these subregional themes, numerous projects await them. Historians and literary critics are just beginning to demonstrate, for example, how ethnicity, gender, and environmental diversity have flavored the historiography and fiction of the Great Plains, the Southwest, the Great Basin, and the Pacific Northwest. Nor should ambitious students of western subregional cultures overlook the varying artistic contributions apparent in the Midwest, Pacific Northwest, and Southwest. Here, too, ethnic identity has played an increasing role in modifying and enriching western culture. In this regard, future studies of Indian painting and other arts should avoid homogenizing the work of Plains, southwestern, and northern Rockies tribes under one rubric of "Native American art."

Consider, too, the fruitful possibilities for studies of religious experiences and organizations and schools and schooling throughout the West. But one must reiterate that close examinations of Catholic experiences in the upper Plains, the Rocky Mountains, and along the southwestern border, of conservative Lutherans in the Midwest, fundamentalists in Texas, and a wide assortment of evangelical groups in California are likely to be as revealing for subregional differences as for denominational unities.[29] And California higher education, Mormon seminaries in the Great Basin area, and bilingual efforts across the Southwest are other examples of western subregionalism beckoning researchers.

Among the several studies of western subregions, two are especially provocative models for subsequent research. Beginning as early as the 1950s, but especially in the 1960s and 1970s, geographer D. W. Meinig published a series of essays and books on the Columbia Plain, Texas, the Southwest, and Mormon cultural cores.[30] Like so many cultural/historical geographers, Meinig particularly illuminates how shifting cultural landscapes, mobile populations, ethnic diversities, and sprawling transportation grids encourage endless cultural changes in western subregions.

Another stimulating paradigm for the study of western subregionalism is James Gregory's immensely useful study of Okie culture in California, *American Exodus*.[31] Moving far beyond John Steinbeck's and Carey McWilliams's first portraits of the migrants, Gregory examines the religious, musical, and political legacies as well as the "plain-folk American" values of the Okies and traces the shaping power of these subcultural themes on sections of California. Utilizing a rich variety of sources, including literary and folkloric materials, census records, field notes and songs, Gregory fashions a pathbreaking study of subregional popular culture.

With Meinig and Gregory as their guides, those intrigued with western subregional cultures are faced with numberless research opportunities. A dozen or so examples should suffice. The Basques of Boise, scattered rural Mormon communities throughout the intermountain West, dozens of European ethnic settlements dotting the Plains, newly arrived survivalist and Aryan Nation groups in the Pacific Northwest, struggling agricultural and ranching enclaves in the northern West, the snowbird and retiree groups of the Southwest—all are worthy topics for subregional studies. And, if one wishes, the cultural distinctiveness of most western states remains to be chronicled. Consider the unique recent happenings in Oregon, which one journalist aptly describes as "Regionalism, tending toward Sectionalism,"[32] or the long-standing cultural complexities of New Mexico, including its century-and-a-half simmering stews of Indians, Hispanics, and Anglos, now spiced with new sociocultural ingredients of thousands of newcomers in the past two generations. One might also center on Arizona and Idaho, cultures perched on international boundaries, surrounded by states so unlike them culturally, and continually competing with cultural hegemonies to their west.[33] Finally, other scholars should undertake cultural histories of the West's two behemoths, Texas and California. No one has yet tackled the demanding task of trying to understand Texas, but Kevin Starr is well into chronicling California cultures throughout the twentieth century in his sprightly written, multivolume series.[34]

Clearly, then, scholars interested in the twentieth-century West will find dozens of projects awaiting them if they attempt to study the region's cultural history through its frontier, regional, or postregional stages and if they wish to examine the cultural contours of its many subregions. Interregional comparisons offer still other research opportunities. No scholar, for example, has thoroughly compared the modern American West and South or the American and Canadian Wests. Comparative frontiers we have, but not comparisons of postfrontier or regional cultures.[35] A limited number of samples comparing the West and South or the Wests of the United States and Canada indicates how abundant are the possibilities for comparative cultural studies.

Witness the differing conclusions, for example, historians and regional writers arrive at in attempting to define the South and the West. When a clear line of southern historians and journalists from U. B. Phillips through Wilbur J. Cash and C. Vann Woodward point to race as the central theme of southern history, they break camp from western historians who usually stress Frederick Jackson Turner, the frontier, or western exceptionalism. Obviously, both historiographical traditions, under pronounced revisionist pressures during the last decade or so, are diverging from these earlier emphases, but students of the South and West have yet to discover how much comparative historiographical studies can tell us about the cultures of the two regions.

Nor have scholars set about to compare the literary traditions of the West and South. At first glance, premier western novelists like Willa Cather, John Steinbeck, and Wallace Stegner seem far removed from the thematic emphases, the stylistic mannerisms, and the predominant tones and moods of southerners such as William Faulkner, Robert Penn Warren, and Flannery O'Connor. Yet all these authors have produced redolent regional fiction. Consider, too, the central importance of the southern literary manifesto, *I'll Take My Stand* (1930), whose Agrarian creators attacked mounting industrial, scientific, and rationalistic emphases in the South.[36] The West produced no such risk-taking literary tract, although historians Walter Prescott Webb and Bernard DeVoto also lashed out at alien cultural influences invading the West in the 1930s.[37] Equally provocative are the dissimilar myths of the two regions. If Margaret Mitchell's novel *Gone with the Wind* (and its cinematic twin), Erskine Caldwell's racy rural realism, and the historical romances of black author Frank Yerby reflect deep-seated, strongly held mythic notions among southerners, the fictional Westerns of Zane Grey and Louis L'Amour and the Hollywood Horse Operas starring John Wayne and Clint Eastwood are equally revealing mythic documents about the West. No one, in essay or book form, has provided much-needed comparative studies of these regionalistic literary and popular cultural trends.[38]

Parallel gaps exist in scholarly examinations of religion and education in the South and West. American historians invariably emphasize the Protestant leanings of southerners, and their bent toward fundamentalism and other Bible Belt persuasions. Meanwhile, westerners are depicted as more diversely religious: Catholic along the Mexican and Canadian borders and in European immigrant areas, Mormon in the central core, and increasingly evangelical, especially Southern Baptist and Pentecostal, from Arkansas and Texas to California. And the Golden State is nearly always singled out as the most yeasty religious region in the country, alive with cults, cranks, and Christians of all sorts. In the area of education, students of both regions increasingly study cultural conflicts leading to controversies over integration/segregation, public vs. private schools, and bilingualism and English Only in their colleges and schools. But, again, few of these studies are comparative. Even examinations of a Sunbelt stretching from Florida to California have yet to supply extensive comparisons and contrasts of southern and western churches and schools.

Other important topics may be less comparable. Southerners seem less concerned, for example, about water and irrigation problems, subjects likely to start a historiographical civil war among any group of westerners. Moreover, although southerners, like westerners, are experiencing increasing urbanization throughout their region, the South remains the most rural area of the country while the West beyond the one hundredth meridian is the nation's most urban section.[39] Westerners also seem more caught up in environmental questions and arguments over who controls the land than do their southern brethren, perhaps because the federal government owns so much of the West and so many Americans hold on to the West as the last ecological frontier. These topics and others dealing with gender and family relations, ethnic patterns, and violence and other social problems may be more comparable than we think, but until more comparative studies are undertaken, these questions remain unanswerable at this point.

Those interested in comparing cultures of the twentieth-century Wests of the United States and Canada face a different set of problems. Although numerous scholars have prepared comparisons of the frontier periods of the two Wests, little is yet available on the twentieth century.[40] Clearly, Canadian historians are a step or two ahead of Americanists in applying Turnerian themes to history north of the 49°, but neither group of historians has done much with post-1900 cultural borders. Similarly, literary scholars in Canada know much more about modern American western literature; only a handful of U.S. literary scholars exhibit much knowledge of Canadian western literature in the twentieth century. In addition to these needed comparative studies of western Canadian and American historiographical and literary developments, comparativists could tell us a good deal about the two Wests through focused studies of novelists like Willa Cather, Wallace Stegner, Robert Kroetsch, and critic Dick Harrison, whose writings often straddle and illuminate both sides of the literary border.[41]

What is true for the possibilities in comparing the Canadian and American Wests is largely true for comparisons with other world areas. A few scholars have essayed comparisons of western cultures with cultural trends in Mexico, Australia, New Zealand, Latin America, and South Africa; but none of these studies is extensive, thorough, or based on multi-archival research.[42] As a result, scholars entering these uncharted waters will experience the bittersweet joys of specialists pioneering new areas without having much information near at hand. Still, one must not underestimate how much such comparative studies will add to a larger understanding of culture in the modern American West.

In addition to these much-needed comparisons of western, southern, and Canadian western cultures, scholars should also examine western perceptions of the West, national conceptions of the West, and western cultural influences on the nation. Although these immense topics include dozens of research opportunities, only a few salient ones can be mentioned here.

For much of the period from 1900 to World War II, the West, as well as the nation, viewed the region primarily as a new frontier or cultural colony of the East. Ambitious students and scholars need to trace these general trends of opinion and to plot out how those views have changed markedly in the last half-century, as the most populous and powerful western subregions have been transformed and declared their cultural independence. Although historians Earl Pomeroy, Gerald D. Nash, and Gene Gressley deal with shifting economic linkages between the West and the nation in the twentieth century, cultural historians have yet to explore how these regional/national perceptions have shaped western cultural history.

Equally fruitful for future research is the topic of western cultural influences on the United States. Literary historians ought to focus on the impacts of western realists, regionalists, and ethnic writers on national literary trends, whereas historians could study the influences of such scholars as Herbert Eugene Bolton, James Malin, Henry Nash Smith, and the New Western historians, for example, on the country's larger historiographical trends. At the same time, students of art, religious, and educational history will discover numerous projects awaiting them in scrutinizing the impact of western regional and experimental art, denominational belief and growth patterns, and educational plans and policies especially on post–World War II America. Nor should one overlook the abundant research possibilities awaiting those studying the large influences of Beat, Hippie, and other popular groups on national cultural movements.

In studying these regional-national perceptions and regional cultural influences, students must reexamine earlier happenings as well as recent trends in western sociocultural life. For example, have other Americans continued to view the West as the "last best hope" to save American traditions, as did Theodore Roosevelt, Owen Wister, and Frederic Remington at the end of the nineteenth century? Do nonwesterners still see the West as a physical or psychological safety valve like many earlier generations? And are ambivalent, bittersweet eastern attitudes toward the West, so clear in the writings of Washington Irving, James Fenimore Cooper, Daniel

Webster, and Francis Parkman, still evident in eastern writings about the West in the twentieth century?

Answers to these questions and to the many others focusing on contemporary western cultures must not overlook the signal importance of the region's burgeoning ethnic populations. Scholars must see that most of the country's well-known Native American, Hispanic, and Asian novelists live or were reared in the West, which is also true of nearly all notable Indian and Chicano historians and painters. Few students of western and American cultures have evaluated the growing impact of these writers and artists on national cultural trends. When they begin to do so, these studies will greatly augment our understanding of multicultural contributions to regional and national cultural experiences.

Close students of historiographical trends in the United States understand that one generation's emphases are often the impetus for the next generation's revisionism. Such is the case with recent interpretations of the American West. If many historians from World War II to the mid-1960s turned out narrative histories of the frontier West, the next generation has challenged the periodizations, content, approaches, and points of view of the earlier historians.[43] Unfortunately, cultural history has not fared well in either period. This persisting oversight means that no subfield in modern western history is more replete with rich research opportunities. One hopes that ambitious scholars entering the field will find the frontier-regional-postregional periodizations, these suggested subregional topics, and the outlined comparative studies to be useful beginning points in a research area where so much remains to be done.[44]

Notes

1. I use "culture" in a more restrictive sense than do anthropologists, historians, and other scholars who employ the now-popular word to mean a society's total system of values and behavior. Instead, I focus on selected cultural topics such as historiography, fiction, painting, religion, education, and popular culture. I hope, however, by referring to such nonelite works as Zane Grey's and Louis L'Amour's Westerns, Charlie Russell's paintings, and ethnic cultural documents to avoid the excessive selectivity of too many earlier cultural historians. The concepts of "frontier," "region," and "postregion," as employed in this essay, receive extended treatment in Richard W. Etulain, *Re-imagining the Modern American West: A Century of Fiction, History, and Art* (Tucson: University of Arizona Press, 1996).

2. Brief overviews of western cultural activities are contained in Gerald D. Nash, *The American West in the Twentieth Century: A Short History of an Urban Oasis* (Englewood Cliffs, N.J.: Prentice-Hall, 1973); and Michael P. Malone and Richard W. Etulain, *The American West: A Twentieth-Century History* (Lincoln: University of Nebraska Press, 1989). The classic study of ideas and cultural predispositions that

shaped images of the nineteenth-century West is Henry Nash Smith, *Virgin Land: The American West as Symbol and Myth* (Cambridge, Mass.: Harvard University Press, 1950). The most recent discussions of western cultural history are those by Ferenc M. Szasz and Margaret Connell Szasz (religion), Brian Dippie (art), Thomas J. Lyon (literature), Charles S. Peterson (historiography), and Anne M. Butler (popular culture), in *The Oxford History of the American West*, ed. Clyde A. Milner II, Carol A. O'Connor, and Martha A. Sandweiss (New York: Oxford University Press, 1994). For a thorough listing of essays and books on western cultural and intellectual topics, see Richard W. Etulain et al., eds., *The American West in the Twentieth Century: A Bibliography* (Norman: University of Oklahoma Press, 1994).

3. Several components of frontier culture are treated in J. Golden Taylor and Thomas J. Lyon et al., eds., *A Literary History of the American West* (Fort Worth: Texas Christian University Press, 1987); William H. Goetzmann and William N. Goetzmann, *The West of the Imagination* (New York: W. W. Norton, 1986); and Lee Clark Mitchell, *Witnesses to a Vanishing America: The Nineteenth-Century Response* (Princeton, N.J.: Princeton University Press, 1981).

4. Christine Bold, *Selling the Wild West: Popular Western Fiction, 1860–1960* (Bloomington: Indiana University Press, 1987), is the most complete study, but consult the listings on the Western and on leading writers of Westerns in Richard W. Etulain and N. Jill Howard, eds., *A Bibliographical Guide to the Study of Western American Literature*, 2d ed. (Albuquerque: University of New Mexico Press, 1995). Jane Tompkins furnishes feminist perspectives on fictional and cinematic Westerns in her *West of Everything: The Inner Life of Westerns* (New York: Oxford University Press, 1992).

5. Among the many studies of Remington, consult Peggy and Harold Samuels, *Frederic Remington: A Biography* (New York: Doubleday, 1982), for an exceedingly thorough life-story. On Russell, see Frederic C. Renner, *Charles M. Russell* (Austin: University of Texas Press, 1966); and the many essays and edited books by Brian Dippie. The two most useful studies of the Hollywood Western are George N. Fenin and William K. Everson, *The Western: From Silents to the Seventies* (New York: Grossman, 1973); and Jon Tuska, *The Filming of the West* (Garden City, N.Y.: Doubleday, 1976). For sections on popular Western novels and films, consult John G. Cawelti, *Adventure, Mystery, and Romance: Formula Stories as Art and Popular Culture* (Chicago: University of Chicago Press, 1976).

6. Richard Maxwell Brown, "The New Regionalism in America, 1970–1981," in *Regionalism and the Pacific Northwest*, ed. William G. Robbins et al. (Corvallis: Oregon State University Press, 1983), 37–96; Merrill Jensen, ed., *Regionalism in America* (Madison: University of Wisconsin Press, 1951, 1965). The most recent study of American regionalism, which focuses more on the South than the West, is Robert L. Dorman, *Revolt of the Provinces: The Regionalist Movement in America, 1920–1945* (Chapel Hill: University of North Carolina Press, 1993).

7. Western literary regionalism is treated in Carey McWilliams, *The New Regionalism in American Literature* (Seattle: University of Washington Book Store, 1930); Fred Erisman, "Western Regional Writers and the Uses of Place," *Journal of the West* 19 (January 1980): 36–44, and Erisman, "The Changing Face of Western Literary Regionalism," in *The Twentieth-Century West: Historical Interpretations*, ed.

Gerald D. Nash and Richard W. Etulain (Albuquerque: University of New Mexico Press, 1989), 361–81.

8. Nancy Heller and Julia Williams, *The Regionalists* (New York: Watson-Guptill, 1976); Lea Rosson DeLong, *Nature's Forms/Nature's Forces: The Art of Alexandre Hogue* (Norman: University of Oklahoma Press, 1984); and Rick Stewart, *Lone Star Regionalism: The Dallas Nine and Their Circle, 1928–1945* (Austin: Texas Monthly Press, 1985).

9. No one has undertaken a much-needed study of western regional magazines. Until then, the story can be pieced together from Mary M. Tuppet, "A History of the *Southwest Review*: Toward an Understanding of Regionalism" (Ph.D. diss., University of Illinois, 1966); Paul Robert Stewart, "*The Prairie Schooner*: A Little Magazine's First Twenty-Five Years" (Ph.D. diss., University of Illinois, 1954); Milton M. Reigelman, *The Midland: A Venture in Literary Regionalism* (Iowa City: University of Iowa Press, 1975); and David William Pugh, "A Study in Literary, Social, and University History: The Life and Often Hard Times of the *New Mexico Quarterly*, 1931–1969" (Ph.D. diss., University of New Mexico, 1975).

10. Earl Pomeroy, *The Pacific Slope: A History of California, Oregon, Washington, Idaho, Utah, and Nevada* (New York: Alfred A. Knopf, 1965, 1991); Gerald D. Nash, *The American West Transformed: The Impact of the Second World War* (Bloomington: Indiana University Press, 1985).

11. Malone and Etulain, *American West*, 107–19, 170–218.

12. See the essays by Lee Clark Mitchell and Michael P. Malone on Henry Nash Smith and Earl Pomeroy in *Writing Western History: Essays on Major Western Historians*, ed. Richard W. Etulain (Albuquerque: University of New Mexico Press, 1991); Pomeroy, "Toward a Reorientation of Western History: Continuity and Environment," *Mississippi Valley Historical Review* 41 (March 1955): 579–600.

13. We still lack studies emphasizing the western influences on such cultural giants as O'Keeffe and Wright. Nearly all accounts of O'Keeffe play down her western years.

14. The best brief discussions of recent western ethnic writers are contained in Taylor and Lyon et al., *Literary History*.

15. Lawrence L. Lee and Merrill E. Lewis, eds., *Women, Women Writers, and the West* (Troy, N.Y.: Whiston, 1979); Helen Winter Stauffer and Susan J. Rosowski, eds., *Women and Western American Literature* (Troy, N.Y.: Whiston, 1982).

16. The most thorough account of these major trends in western historiography is Gerald D. Nash, *Creating the West* (Albuquerque: University of New Mexico Press, 1991). Also consult, Etulain, *Writing Western History*.

17. Some of these ideas and those in succeeding paragraphs draw on Richard W. Etulain, "The American Literary West and Its Interpreters: The Rise of a New Historiography," *Pacific Historical Review* 45 (April 1976): 311–48; and Etulain, "Shifting Interpretations of Western American Cultural History," in *Historians and the American West*, ed. Michael P. Malone (Lincoln: University of Nebraska Press, 1983), 414–32.

18. Several of these topics receive chapter-length treatment in Taylor and Lyon et al., *Literary History*. See also William W. Savage, Jr., *The Cowboy Hero: His Image in American History and Culture* (Norman: University of Oklahoma Press, 1979).

19. Ray A. Billington's brilliant biography, *Frederick Jackson Turner: Historian, Scholar, Teacher* (New York: Oxford University Press, 1973), emphasizes extrinsic details. The best recent analytical studies are William Cronon, "Revisiting the Vanishing Frontier: The Legacy of Frederick Jackson Turner," *Western Historical Quarterly* 18 (April 1987): 157–76; and the essays by Cronon and Michael Steiner in Etulain, *Writing Western History*. Also, see Nash, *Creating the West*; Martin Ridge, "The Life of an Idea: The Significance of Frederick Jackson Turner's Frontier Thesis," *Montana: The Magazine of Western History* 41 (Winter 1991): 2–13; and Wilbur R. Jacobs, *On Turner's Trail: One Hundred Years of Writing Western History* (Lawrence: University Press of Kansas, 1994).

20. Patricia Janis Broder, *The American West: The Modern Vision* (New York: Little, Brown and Company, 1984). For a capsule summary of recent western artistic trends, consult H. Wayne Morgan, "Main Currents in Twentieth-Century Western Art," in Nash and Etulain, *Twentieth-Century West*, 383–406.

21. The most illuminating study of western ministers is Ferenc M. Szasz, *The Protestant Clergy in the Great Plains and Mountain West, 1865–1915* (Albuquerque: University of New Mexico Press, 1988). Szasz is currently at work on a full-scale examination of religion in the modern West. Meanwhile, the most extensive listing is Richard W. Etulain, comp., *Religion in the Twentieth-Century American West: A Bibliography* (Albuquerque: Center for the American West, University of New Mexico, 1991). Also, see Ronald E. Butchart, "Education and Culture in the Trans-Mississippi West: An Interpretation," *Journal of American Culture* 3 (Summer 1980): 351–73.

22. The best overviews of Hollywood are Robert Sklar, *Movie-Made America: A Cultural History of American Movies* (New York: Random House, 1975, 1994); and Charles Higham, *The Art of the American Film* (Garden City, N.Y.: Anchor Press/Doubleday, 1973). Lary May supplies a model cultural analysis in his *Screening Out the Past: The Birth of Mass Culture and the Motion Picture Industry* (New York: Oxford University Press, 1980).

23. Kirkpatrick Sale, *Power Shift: The Rise of the Southern Rim and Its Challenge to the Eastern Establishment* (New York: Random House, 1975); Neil Morgan, *Westward Tilt: The American West Today* (New York: Random House, 1961, 1963); Joel Garreau, *The Nine Nations of North America* (Boston: Houghton Mifflin Company, 1981).

24. William G. Robbins, "The 'Plundered Province' Thesis and Recent Historiography of the American West," *Pacific Historical Review* 55 (November 1986): 577–97; Robbins expands on some of these ideas in his *Colony and Empire: The Capitalist Transformation of the American West* (Lawrence: University Press of Kansas, 1994). Also useful for studying western subregionalism is Raymond D. Gastil, *Cultural Regions of the United States* (Seattle: University of Washington Press, 1975).

25. Frederick C. Luebke, "Ethnic Group Settlement on the Great Plains," *Western Historical Quarterly* 8 (October 1977): 405–30, and Luebke, "Ethnic Minority Groups in the American West," in Malone, *Historians and the American West*, 387–413; Sarah Deutsch, *No Separate Refuge: Culture, Class, and Gender on an Anglo-Hispanic Frontier in the American Southwest, 1880–1940* (New York: Oxford University Press, 1987); David M. Emmons, *The Butte Irish: Class and Ethnicity in an American*

Mining Town, 1873–1925 (Urbana: University of Illinois Press, 1989); David Montejano, *Anglos and Mexicans in the Making of Texas, 1836–1986* (Austin: University of Texas Press, 1987).

26. Donald Worster, *Dust Bowl: The Southern Plains in the 1930s* (New York: Oxford University Press, 1979); Richard White, *Land Use, Environment, and Social Change: The Shaping of Island County* (Seattle: University of Washington Press, 1980), and White, *"It's Your Misfortune and None of My Own": A New History of the American West* (Norman: University of Oklahoma Press, 1991). The most important writing on women and family in the modern West is listed in Pat Devejian and Jacqueline J. Etulain, comps., *Women and Family in the Twentieth-Century American West: A Bibliography* (Albuquerque: Center for the American West, University of New Mexico, 1990).

27. Wallace Stegner and Richard W. Etulain, *Conversations with Wallace Stegner on Western History and Literature*, rev ed. (Salt Lake City: University of Utah Press, 1990), xvii–xx.

28. Douglas W. Johnson et al., *Churches and Church Membership in the United States, 1971: An Enumeration by Region, State and County* (Washington, D.C.: Glenmary Research Center, 1974); Bernard Quinn et al., *Churches and Church Membership in the United States, 1980* (Atlanta: Glenmary Research Center, 1982); Edwin Scott Gaustad, *Historical Atlas of Religion in America*, rev ed. (New York: Harper and Row, 1976).

29. For a very useful survey of western ethnic patterns, see Richard White, "Race Relations in the American West," *American Quarterly* 38, no. 3 (1986): 396–416, and White, *"It's Your Misfortune"*; Patricia Nelson Limerick, *Legacy of Conquest: The Unbroken Past of the American West* (New York: W. W. Norton, 1987). Also consult, Richard W. Etulain, "Regionalizing Religion: Evangelicals in the American West, 1940–1990," in *Religion and Culture: Historical Essays*, ed. Raymond M. Cooke and Richard W. Etulain (Albuquerque: Far West Books, 1991), 79–103.

30. D. W. Meinig, *The Great Columbia Plain: A Historical Geography, 1805–1910* (Seattle: University of Washington Press, 1968); Meinig, *Imperial Texas: An Interpretive Essay in Cultural Geography* (Austin: University of Texas Press, 1969); Meinig, *Southwest: Three Peoples in Geographical Change, 1600–1970* (New York: Oxford University Press, 1971); Meinig, "American Wests: Preface to a Geographical Interpretation," *Annals of the Association of American Geographers* 62 (June 1972): 159–84.

31. James N. Gregory, *American Exodus: The Dust Bowl Migration and Okie Culture in California* (New York: Oxford University Press, 1989).

32. David Sarasohn, "Regionalism, Tending toward Sectionalism," in Robbins et al., *Regionalism and the Pacific Northwest*, 223–36. See also Howard F. Stein and Robert F. Hill, eds., *The Culture of Oklahoma* (Norman: University of Oklahoma Press, 1993.

33. Carlos Schwantes, *In Mountain Shadows: A History of Idaho* (Lincoln: University of Nebraska Press, 1991); Richard W. Etulain, "Contours of Culture in Arizona and the Modern West," in *Arizona at Seventy-five: The Next Twenty-five Years* (Tucson: Arizona Historical Society, 1987), 11–53.

34. Kevin Starr, *Americans and the California Dream, 1850–1915* (New York:

Oxford University Press, 1973); Starr, *Inventing the Dream: California through the Progressive Era* (New York: Oxford University Press, 1985); Starr, *Material Dreams: California through the 1920s* (New York: Oxford University Press, 1990).

35. W. Turrentine Jackson, "A Brief Message for the Young and/or Ambitious: Comparative Frontiers as a Field for Investigation," *Western Historical Quarterly* 9 (January 1978): 5–18; Jerome O. Steffen, *Comparative Frontiers: A Proposal for Studying the American West* (Norman: University of Oklahoma Press, 1980). Walter Nugent furnishes a brief but very useful comparative overview in his "Comparing Wests and Frontiers," in Milner, O'Connor, and Sandweiss, *Oxford History of the American West*, 802–33.

36. Twelve Southerners, *I'll Take My Stand: The South and the Agrarian Tradition* (New York: Harper and Brothers, 1930); Richard H. King, *The Southern Renaissance: The Cultural Awakening of the American South, 1930–1955* (New York: Oxford University Press, 1980); Michael O'Brien, *The Idea of the American South, 1920–1941* (Baltimore: Johns Hopkins University Press, 1979).

37. Walter Prescott Webb, *Divided We Stand: The Crisis of a Frontierless Democracy* (New York: Farrar and Rinehart, 1937); Bernard DeVoto, "The West: A Plundered Province," *Harper's* 159 (August 1934): 355–64.

38. For an indispensable guide to books and essays on American regionalism, see Michael Steiner and Clarence Mondale, *Region and Regionalism in the United States: A Source Book for the Humanities and Social Sciences* (New York: Garland Publishing, 1988).

39. On recent southern culture, consult the collected essays in Joe P. Dunn and Howard L. Preston, eds., *The Future South: A Historical Perspective for the Twenty-first Century* (Urbana: University of Illinois Press, 1991); and the many pertinent entries in the superb reference volume edited by Charles Reagan Wilson and William Ferris, *Encyclopedia of Southern Culture* (Chapel Hill: University of North Carolina Press, 1989).

40. For a brief beginning piece on comparative regionalism, see Robin W. Winks, "Regionalism in Comparative Perspective," in Robbins et al., *Regionalism and the Pacific Northwest*, 13–36; also, consult Dick Harrison, *Crossing Frontiers: Papers in American and Canadian Western Literature* (Edmonton: University of Alberta Press, 1979).

41. Dick Harrison, *Unnamed Country: The Struggle for a Canadian Prairie Fiction* (Edmonton: University of Alberta Press, 1977); Howard Lamar, "Comparing Depressions: The Great Plains and Canadian Prairie Experiences, 1929–1941," in Nash and Etulain, *Twentieth-Century West*, 175–206.

42. For a very useful listing of comparative studies, see George Miles, "A Comparative Frontiers Bibliography," 317–33, and the other essays in *The Frontier in History: North America and Southern Africa Compared*, ed. Howard R. Lamar and Leonard Thompson (New Haven, Conn.: Yale University Press, 1981).

43. Nash, *Creating the West*; Etulain, *Writing Western History*, 335–58; Gene M. Gressley, "Whither Western History? Speculations on a Direction," *Pacific Historical Review* 53 (November 1984): 493–501, and Gressley, "The West: Past, Present, and Future," *Western Historical Quarterly* 17 (January 1986): 5–23; Michael P. Malone, "Beyond the Last Frontier: Toward a New Approach to Western American

History," *Western Historical Quarterly* 20 (November 1989): 409–27; William G. Robbins, "Western History: A Dialectic on the Modern Condition," *Western Historical Quarterly* 20 (November 1989): 429–49.

44. Howard Lamar's essay, "Much to Celebrate: The Western History Association's Twenty-Fifth Birthday," *Western Historical Quarterly* 17 (October 1986): 397–416, remains the most provocative call for research on western cultural topics. The two most recent overviews of western historiography are Brian W. Dippie, "The Winning of the West Reconsidered," *Wilson Quarterly* (Summer 1990): 70–85; and William G. Robbins, "Laying Siege to Western History: The Emergence of New Paradigms," *Reviews in American History* 19 (September 1991): 313–31. Several of these essays are reprinted in Patricia Nelson Limerick, Clyde A. Milner, II, and Charles E. Rankin, eds., *Trails: Toward a New Western History* (Lawrence: University Press of Kansas, 1991).

7

The Enduring Myth and the Modern West

Fred Erisman

One of the most compelling moments in the entire John Ford canon, if not in all Western films, occurs in *My Darling Clementine* (1946).[1] Midway through the film, Clementine Carter (Cathy Downs) cajoles Wyatt Earp (Henry Fonda), marshal of Tombstone, into walking her to church. The two stroll down the dusty main street to the strains of "Shall We Gather at the River," and the town's church, still under construction, looms larger and larger on the screen. At the church, Earp and Clementine find a celebration: the church floor is complete, the town is on its way to respectability, and the citizens are marking the occasion with a dance. As the impromptu party gets under way, Earp watches benevolently from the sidelines. Clementine, however, caught up in the music and gaiety, at last prevails on him to dance with her, and the two make an exuberant circuit of the dance floor, the whole joyous episode centered in the frame and punctuated with a solitary saguaro cactus silhouetted against the distant skyline.[2]

It is a remarkable sequence, rich in mythic icons and resonances, as Ford intended it to be. The church building, emblematic of community virtue, is a skeletal structure striving upward, its thrust topped by a prominent cross, the traditional emblem of Christianity. Dominating the foreground are two enormous American flags, linking the power of the State with that of the Church to establish a unifying force in a fragmented time. The background is dotted with saguaro cacti, invoking the regional landscape, its wildness, and its natural innocence. The townspeople are banded together in a ritualistic celebration of civic unity. Marshal Earp (the Law) embraces Clementine Carter (a nurse [Compassion] and, later, the schoolmarm, or Education), and their lurching dance accentuates the community's tentative progress toward a progressive society. All of the elements are fused into an organic whole by the auditory icon of "Shall We Gather at the River," an archetypically fundamental statement of Protestant faith in progress under the guidance of a benevolent God. It is, then, no wonder that, as Carl Bredahl observes, the scene is a central statement of the principal mythological elements of the American West.[3]

Myths, whatever their origin, are necessarily integral to the originating society. That they *reflect* pervasive social themes is clear, but (what is more important) equally clear is that they also *influence* the attitudes and operations of the society. As Richard Slotkin points out, these "stories, drawn from history . . . , have acquired through usage over many generations a symbolizing function that is central to the cultural functioning of the society that produces them." They go on, moreover, to become a "deeply encoded set of metaphors that may contain all of the 'lessons' we have learned from our history, and all of the essential elements of our world view." In those lessons and in those elements, in short, resides the "glue" that holds the society together, for it gives the society a frame of reference within which to judge itself and a vocabulary with which to make that judgment, providing in the process a concise, accessible statement of "the rules of the game" by which the society sees itself operating.[4]

Few myths in American life are so enduring, so influential, and so fruitful of research potential as that of the West. Growing out of the process of westward expansion and disseminated by the nation's popular culture from the earliest years of the nineteenth century, it has become for many Americans *the* means of explaining the "rules" of the national "game." Its expressions are many and varied, but three generalized components stand out as central. These are: the embodiment of a national hero, a belief in the diverse richness of the natural environment of the West, and a sense that the West as region functions in a special way in the vision of the national generally.[5] From these elements evolve the more particular manifestations that have shaped Americans' vision of the West— the ideal of the individualistic, self-determining westerner and the belief that the pristine western landscape offers unique opportunities for personal freedom and societal improvement. John Ford and his viewers responded to these mythic elements throughout much of the twentieth century, and the images still stir responses in the last years of the century. But they have not remained static, and in the manner in which they have adjusted to the "rules of the game" of an evolving society is a capsule history of the changing American scene, offering a challenging range of opportunities for further research into the workings of the western myth in contemporary society.

The "rules of the game" in American life explicitly define the traditional western hero. He is a white male no older than his mid-thirties. He normally lacks extensive formal education, but he possesses a wealth of

empirical knowledge and an intuitively profound sense of propriety, social values, and natural order. He is physically strong but soft-spoken;
modest about his abilities, he is, when motivated by principle or threat-
ened by enemies, capable of almost irresistible violence, assisted by the
firearms (rifle or pistol) that he wields with disciplined precision. Unmarried and unfettered by family or occupational ties, he is free to come and
go as he pleases, moving in and out of society with careless ease, his lack
of deep-seated social obligations accentuating the individualism that controls his every act.

Originating in James Fenimore Cooper's Natty Bumppo, or
Leatherstocking (introduced in *The Pioneers* [1825]), the hero undergoes a
steady metamorphosis as American society moves westward. From hunter
to trapper, from trapper to scout, from scout to pioneer, and from pioneer
to cowboy, he parallels the evolving pattern of settlement, an individualistic emblem for a social movement. His traits, developed and popularized in the dime novels of the mid-nineteenth century, gain tangible
expression in the Wild West shows of William F. Cody, and are crystal-
lized for all time by Owen Wister's *The Virginian* (1902). The later Western
film serves only to expand and reinforce the nature of this hero, with the
films of John Ford (and, secondarily, Howard Hawks and Sam Peckinpah)
providing the defining incarnation of the type.[6]

As the hero evolved, each succeeding generation found in his per-
sonification qualities to which it could respond. As Richard Slotkin observes, "Tom Sawyer got his sense of the game from Fenimore Cooper;
Horatio Alger's heroes got theirs from Ned Buntline; President Eisenhower
got his from pulp Westerns and Owen Wister; the generation following
got theirs from John Wayne."[7] And yet, ironically, as the western hero
became ever more inseparably a part of American society, his defining
traits grew increasingly at odds with the world of reality, with common
sense requiring that the image acknowledge the imperatives of technology, the society, and the changing world. "By the 1920s the coexistence
of modern twentieth-century and traditional nineteenth-century incli-
nations became noticeably strained," John Lenihan points out, and the
era undertook "to redefine values and goals that would accommodate
traditional and modern sensibilities."[8] Contradictory though the enterprise seemed, it contributed to the evolution and the durability of the
western hero.

One stimulus to the evolution was Charles A. Lindbergh's trans-At-
lantic flight of May 1927, which was on the surface a flawless extension
of the western ideal. The flight was achieved by a westerner. It was carried
out alone. It succeeded when more complex and more sophisticated efforts failed. It marked an American conquest of a new frontier, and it was
described almost immediately in the language of the western movement;
thus, one contemporary source announced, "Charles Lindbergh . . . is of

the stuff out of which have been made the pioneers that opened up the wilderness, first on the Atlantic coast, and then in our great West. His are the qualities which we, as a people, must nourish."[9] The myth in its original form lent itself readily to Lindbergh's achievement.

Yet underlying the reality of Lindbergh's flight were extraordinary facts that the myth took in its stride. Whatever the magnitude of Lindbergh's personal accomplishments, the flight was a triumph of far more than individualism. Technology played an essential role: without the machine (in itself, as a product of Ryan Airlines of San Diego, a western accomplishment) to carry out the feat, the flight would have been impossible. So, too, did cooperation and collaboration; without the concerted efforts of his backers, Lindbergh himself could not have acquired the machine and carried out his flight. And so, too, did the news media; without a global network of communication, print and radio, the news of Lindbergh's accomplishment could not have been disseminated to a receptive world.

The outcome, then, was a new version of the American myth that tacitly reconciled western individualism with sophisticated industrial technology and the elements of an interdependent society:

> Lindbergh, the self-reliant American individual, pioneered, but only in a complex machine produced by the engineering and mechanical skills of a team of hard-working experts funded by "progressive" businessmen. Man and machine and industrial organization were one. They were complementary, in perfect balance. None could survive, function, or achieve without the others. The Lindbergh myth triumphantly celebrated the inseparability of the individual and industrial society. The acceptance of Lindbergh as a national hero indicated that there are roles available for Americans—the spiritual if not physical descendants of the frontiersmen, the pioneers, and the cowboys—in the modern world of airplanes, automobiles, vast industries, and sprawling cities.

In Lindbergh and in the flyers, real and fictional, who followed him, the western hero took to the skies, still passionately individualistic yet taking in stride the requirements of a techno-industrial time.[10]

A second modification of the myth of the hero occurred as Americans strove to make their peace with the city. For all its appeal as the last stronghold of virgin land, the West quickly developed as an urban society, and the facts of city life became as imperatively real as they ever were on the East Coast.[11] Once more, however, the myth proved its adaptability, contributing essential elements to the figure of the private detective. In works like Dashiell Hammett's *The Maltese Falcon* (1930), set in San Francisco, or Raymond Chandler's *The Big Sleep* (1939), in Los Angeles, the private eye quietly emerged as an updating of the mythic western hero. Like the traditional western hero, the detective acted alone; he spoke for no organized agency of the larger society, and he had no compelling responsibilities to that society. But the private eye, like the Lindbergh figure, readily assimilated new circumstances. Rather than acting as the free-standing western hero of the myth, he acts openly and overtly as the agent of a private citizen. His allegiance is to his client, and while he is only one step removed from the "hired gun" of pulp Western fame, that step makes an enormous difference.[12]

For all his acceptance of the ugly realities of the city and its peoples, the private eye, like the western hero before him, works first and foremost from principle. Unlike the mythic hero, though, he has personal flaws, often serious ones, indicative of or created by the circumstances of urban life. These flaws are compensated for, nevertheless, by the essential integrity of his character. Thus, he is, as Raymond Chandler remarks,

> a man of honor, by instinct, by inevitability, without thought
> of it and certainly without saying it. He must be the best man
> in his world and a good enough man for any world. . . . The
> story is his adventure in search of a hidden truth, and it would
> be no adventure if it did not happen to a man fit for adventure.
> If there were enough like him . . . the world would be a very
> safe place to live in, and yet not too dull to be worth living in.[13]

In the manner in which he balances principle and expediency, idealism and practicality, the community and the individual, the private eye becomes a worthy descendent of the western hero of the past, enabling the myth to survive into the contradictory, complex, and dispiriting world of the present.

It is clear, then, that the evolving nature of the western hero calls for further research. That research, moreover, must address several issues. There is, first, the whole compelling issue of individualism. *Must* the western hero be an individualist? Or are other traits more pertinent to the demands of life now and in the future? We need to inquire. Next, given the increasingly interrelated nature of American society, *can*—and *should*—the hero *remain* an individualist? Can a fully socialized and acculturated person carry on the heroic myth? And if he or she can, what are the larger implications of the circumstance in defining "the rules of the game?"

Finally, what modifications have occurred (or *should* occur) in general American attitudes toward individualism and the hero? What new "heroic" traits might society of the next century require of its persons, and is there any evidence of the emergence of these traits? In a provocative study of Americans' informal social institutions, Ray Oldenburg notes that "incessant and excessive promotion of the individual and the idea that the good life is an individual accomplishment discourages collective effort, discounts collective effort, and obscures the fact that many good and necessary things can only result from collective effort."[14] His emphasis upon collective effort is one fraught with significance, for the whole issue of individual action vs. collective action in the West cries out for careful, extended examination.

A second principal area of investigation deals with the larger issues of western life. No person, individualist or not, is immune to the tensions inherent in the surrounding society. What, then, are these tensions? What are their sources, be they social, economic, political, ethnic, or intellectual? What are the mechanisms (for example, the media, social practices, and so forth) through which the tensions are expressed? How do persons of stature in the West, whether fictional or actual, respond to the expressions? How, moreover, does their ethnic origin affect their perception of the tensions *and* the nature of their response? And how do the tensions *and the responses* change with the passage of time and the evolution of the society? Indeed, the entire issue of the western hero *as a social figure* has not been given sustained, extended attention, yet it is one crucial to a fully developed portrayal of the West.

Some of these questions derive from the more specific issue of individualism. As the society comes to require of its members a greater acceptance of collaboration, whether social, technical, or intellectual, how does the hero react? If he or she accedes to societal necessity, what adjustments and compromises are necessary? And if he or she resists the demands, what are the consequences, to the person and to society? These questions might be dealt with as single-figure studies, examining the reputations of notable westerners, male or female; they might be addressed through studies of changes in the economic structure of the workplace or the region and the rationale given for the changes; or they might be full-fledged investigations of the patterns of authority and influence within a community as it goes through the stages inherent in any community's development.[15] Whatever the technique employed, the new insights into the workings of western society cannot help but be significant.

A third and final area of investigation specifically addresses issues of age, gender, and ethnicity as they pertain to the western hero. Western society has been diverse from the outset, yet the conventional view of it is dominated by the young, white, Anglo-Saxon, male hero. Many have striven to modify this stereotype, but an enormous amount of work remains to be done. What, for example, have been the characteristics of *female* culture in the West, and what changes have occurred? Is there evidence of "heroic" traits appearing in accounts of women, actual or fictional, in the West? What, in addition, have been the roles open to women, the roles appropriated by women, and the social implications of these roles? What, moreover, do we know of the various fully developed ethnic cultures in the West as they have accommodated to change? Even now, the conventional portrayal of Hispanic culture in the West still draws heavily upon guitars, siestas , and tequila, just as that of Native American culture, despite the best efforts of ethnologists, historians, and novelists, insists upon buckskins, feathers, and warpaint. *Can* non-Anglo figures operate in a heroic, non-stereotypical fashion? The question needs to be asked.[16]

These elements become even more provocative when viewed within the context of the evolving western city. The private eye is an instance of how one heroic type can be transmuted into another through the agency of the city, but what of other types? How has the nature of city life affected gender roles? How, if at all, have ethnic groups with integrated cultures adjusted to the requirements of the city? How, moreover, do the values embraced by those cultures force (or at least stimulate) a reevaluation of prevailing conventional values? Tony Hillerman's use of Navajo cultural values to pose questions about American urban values in his mystery novels has stimulated a growing body of scholarship, but these studies constitute only the skimpiest beginning; the need to understand the West cries out for an integrated investigation of the ethnic groups present in the region.[17]

It is, not surprisingly, American popular culture in general that offers some of the most provocative and intriguing expressions of the interweaving of these themes. Three of Clint Eastwood's films (two directed by him and all featuring him in a starring role) constitute a case in point. In *Unforgiven* (1992), Eastwood retells the mythic story of Shane, the retired gunman who takes up his weapons one last time in support of a cause. But the cause here is money, and the hero far less romantic than Schaefer's mythic figure. The film's resolution, unlike *Shane*'s poignantly affirmative climax, is disturbingly ambivalent, letting *Unforgiven* in many ways express the dark side of the western myth. He follows this film with *In the Line of Fire* (1993), a contemporary urban thriller involving a Secret-Service agent's efforts to protect the president from a deranged assassin. Urban and modern though it is, the film places resonant elements of "the Western" alongside modern concerns as its middle-aged hero strives to deal with feelings of guilt and his own sense of masculine individuality in the face of urbanization, gender issues, and politics; the finished work suggests the pervasiveness of the myth in every level of American culture.

The third film, *A Perfect World* (1993), is perhaps the most evocative of all, linking Eastwood with Kevin Costner in a game of wits as an aging Texas Ranger (Eastwood) pursues an escaped murderer (Costner) through the Texas landscape in the fall of 1963. Beneath its gritty realism and the irony imposed by the audience's nagging awareness of the impending assassination of John F. Kennedy, the film continues Eastwood's examination of the myth. His character must balance the realities of politics with his own sense of right and wrong, and must cope with an aggravating but

competent female associate as he struggles to resolve a hostage situation
that, in a long-ago effort to do good, he helped to bring about. Thus,
these three films, like other areas of investigation generally, provide reflections on the western hero and what his manifestations may say about
Americans' evolving vision of themselves and their society.[18]

Like the hero figure, the western landscape also plays an essential
part in the development of the myth. Simultaneously uplifting and threatening in its wildness, barren and rich in its prospects, and, throughout
most of the nineteenth century, limitless in its expanse, the land, stretching westward, offered for many an answer to the disappointments and
frustrations of the developing American society. For these persons, the
land offered an opportunity to "regain a lost imaginative contact with
some secret source of virtue and power in the universe," so that, whether
viewed as wild and invigorating or cultivated and sustaining, the American landscape "became one of the dominant symbols of nineteenth-century American society—a collective representation, a poetic idea . . . that
defined the promise of American life." It is a symbolic West that comprises regeneration through wildness and, perhaps more significantly, regeneration through escape.[19]

It is this symbolic West to which Leo Marx alludes when he speaks of
the varied ways in which the American individual encounters and responds to the land. One such encounter creates "a sense of ecstatic fulfill-
ment, a feeling of calm selfhood and integration with his or her
surroundings"; a second involves a "thrilling, tonic, but often traumatic
and finally chastening encounter with wildness"; while a third, the "interrupted idyll," offers "another interlude of serenity, peace, and joy" that
"is abruptly transformed by the intrusion of a machine or some other
manifest token of the dynamism of modern industrial society."[20] And it is
this symbolic West that occurs so tellingly in American literature of the
twentieth century, for, as Marx's analysis implies, the American relationship with the mythic land has been ambivalent, even contradictory.

The ambivalence of which Marx speaks is dramatized handily in three
notable American novels, each of which speaks to the tensions between
the West of the myth and the West of reality. For Robert Penn Warren's
Jack Burden, in *All the King's Men* (1946), the West offers escape, fulfill-
ment, and integration, for "when you don't like it where you are you
always go west . . . to lie in the comforting, subliminal ooze on the sea
floor of History." For Bernard Malamud's Seymour Levin, in the wryly
named *A New Life* (1961), the West is a place to start over, and the
West he finds in the forest of "Cascadia" (that is, Oregon) is integrat-
ing and thrilling:

> The mystery of the wood, the presence of unseen life in natural
> time, and the feeling that few men had been where he presently

was (Levin, woodsman, explorer; he now understood the soul of
Natty Bumppo, formerly paper; 'Here, D. Boone CILLED A.
BAR') caused him to nudge aside anxiety and continue to
venture among the trees in shade and sunlight.

And for Edward Abbey's George Washington Hayduke, the most individualistic member of *The Monkey Wrench Gang* (1975), "the country he was
headed for, the heartland of his heart, spread out before and beyond him
exactly as he'd dreamed it all, for three years, lost in the jungle war,"
offers a serene peace powerful enough to exorcise the horrors of his service in Vietnam.[21]

Burden, Levin, and Hayduke, each in his own way, are responding to
the myth. Burden has lost an ideal (his romanticized conception of his
beloved Anne Stanton), and wants somehow to escape the pain of accepting reality. He goes west. Levin is escaping a drunkard's existence in New
York. He seeks the "new life" available only in the vital West of virgin
land, pioneering, and progress. Hayduke is fleeing the trauma of Vietnam, yearning to purge himself of the terrible memories that his service
and imprisonment there created. For him, the answer is a literal return to
nature in the West. All three see in the West some form of the release they
believe it can offer, ignorant of the reality that will confront them in their
pursuit of the myth.

When at last the reality comes home to them, they respond in a variety of ways. Burden, a white southern male forced to acknowledge that
the West is "just like any place else, or wanted to think the same things
about itself," rationalizes his distancing himself from all feeling and responsibility and concludes that "nothing was your fault or anybody's
fault." Levin, a northern, urban Jew, clings to what he wants to believe,
even though he is in a wholly populated area in which the forest he found
so thrilling is no more than the domesticated trees of a forestry school
experimental station. Looking at the placid university town where he has
settled, he "imagine[s] the pioneers in covered wagons entering this valley for the first time . . . and the sense of having done the right thing in
leaving New York was renewed in him."[22] The reactions of these two, both
civilized, socialized persons, hint at their futures. Burden, slowly and pain-
fully, comes to accept the realization that involvement and responsibility
are inseparable from life, while Levin at last turns his back upon the whole
pernicious myth that he has unquestioningly accepted.

Only Hayduke, a native westerner, works to preserve the land of the
myth, as befits his role as the quintessential western hero. When his
longed-for idyll is decisively interrupted by the attributes of "progress,"
from strip mining and missile sites to jerry-built housing developments
and dammed-up rivers, he determines to keep the land as it *should* be—in
short, "like it was."[23] Joining forces with Doc Sarvis, an Albuquerque sur-

geon, Bonnie Abbzug, Doc's assistant/mistress, and Seldom Seen Smith, a jack-Mormon wilderness outfitter with three wives, Hayduke embarks on a campaign of sabotage (the "monkey wrenching" of the book's title), doing all he can to thwart the faceless minions of Progress and Big Business. But here, too, irony alters the situation: the only way Hayduke can preserve the land he loves is to introduce into it the techniques of the war he is striving to escape. Thus, for all the legendary power of the myth, none of the characters is able to escape the consequences of civilization or the past. In their failure is one of the major ironies of the myth of the western land.

That irony is that the act of escaping to the land brings civilization to the land. From the very outset, the image of the westward movement has been just that—"movement," as masses of people move across the continent, leaving one life, entering into another, and creating anew the society they have striven to flee. "To occupy the natural landscape," William Cronon writes, "meant, simultaneously, to occupy a human community." That community, in its turn, did not spring spontaneously from its people and its site. It was, instead, a community generated from their values, their customs, and their memories—a "new" society in the sense that its exact form had never before existed, but one that nevertheless incorporated countless recognizable elements from the past and therefore worked to destroy the very qualities the component people sought.[24]

The result of this process is that the virgin land and unfettered existence of the settler's dream has, for all practical purposes, never existed. Settling the West required governmental intervention and technological assistance; developing the West required the sacrifice of the very elements that made the West desirable; and the outcome has been a circumstance in which, in Mary Young's words, the exploitation of the region "created its own antithesis." And finally, from that antithesis comes the ultimate lesson of all western history: the admission, as Richard Astro says of Sy Levin's failed dream, "that a clear break with history is impossible, and that a belief in freedom cradled in nature—in the Garden as a source of redemption—disregards the obvious continuity of culture and experience as it is carried over the mountains to the West."[25]

Efforts to reconcile the tension between independence and history in the American West take a variety of forms. One serves primarily to institutionalize the myth in the American mind, making of the West what we *expect* it to be. The technology that opened the region to permanent settlement also opened it to casual visitors, and from the nineteenth-century urge to savor the wilderness quickly came the modern American tourist. Stimulated by magazines such as *Forest and Stream* and *Outing* or simply responding to a pervasive national mood, tourists began to work their way westward, seeking the region's unique sights and experiences. As they came, though, they demanded the comforts they knew in conjunction with the experiences they expected, so that the "selling" of the West as an awe-inspiring, mythic region in actuality created a western experience as managed in its way as any mining development or national park. Indeed, as Earl Pomeroy points out, "Those who made it their business to sell the West sometimes tried to preserve it, when they did not have to create it; inevitably they transformed it."[26] For the tourist, the natural West was what one made of it.

The continued development of western tourism, combined with the ambivalent and contradictory ways in which Americans look upon the western landscape in the present, attests to the durability of the myth, for virtually every observable fact of western life mitigates against the mythic vision. The region is a largely developed one. It is a region fraught with environmental problems, from air pollution to traffic congestion to dwindling water and power resources. It is one in which perceived "reality" is manipulated if not actually false (witness the popularity of the "Ponderosa Ranch" purported to be the site of television's *Bonanza*, a created piece of outright fiction that nevertheless draws hordes of admiring tourists annually).[27] Yet it is also a region to which Americans look for their recreation and, implicitly, their restoration—a paradoxical testament to the myth's power to overcome even perceived reality.

In this first effort of reconciliation, as with the western hero, are rich opportunities for further research. Perceptions of landscape and the land in western life urgently require careful investigation, exploring the ways in which they have affected the historical and social development of the region. Too often we consider "the West" a monolithic and uniform region; we need to examine carefully the many ways in which the varied western subregions are perceived and expressed, looking to their particular contributions to our larger sense of "western" land. What is more, Frederick Jackson Turner's insistence that "there is not *tabula rasa*" rings truer than ever, for studies of how individuals and groups adapt ethnic or extra-regional ways to the needs of life within the subregions of the West cannot help but shed light on the relationship of land and life.[28]

Also needing investigation is the later history of western tourism, and how extra-regional expectations of the West have shaped the region's later history; Earl Pomeroy's *In Search of the Golden West* appeared in 1957 and, for all its merits, requires updating. What are the tourist attractions of the "new West"? What are their origins, how have they been popularized, and what has been their influence on our attitudes toward the western land? How has institutionalized tourism worked to establish new—or reinforce existing—ethnic stereotypes? What changes has a tourist-oriented economy worked upon western society, whether urban or rural? And finally, how long can the myth of the western land endure in the face of increasing contradiction and paradox? The lengths to which society will go to perpetuate an institutionalized myth despite the imperatives of compelling realities offer a social commentary of notable importance.

A second form of reconciliation, the primitivistic urge to make (or keep) the West as it was, reaches from Cooper's Natty Bumppo to Abbey's George Hayduke and offers further opportunity for research. The frustrations are as great for Hayduke as they were for Natty, as Abbey makes clear in the posthumously published *Hayduke Lives!* (1990). Here he returns once more to the theme of environmental activism, reincarnating the Monkey Wrench Gang of the earlier work in a dark, disillusioned book notably lacking in the effervescent high spirits of its predecessor. All the characters are older, and with the exception of Hayduke, all find themselves with legitimate obligations and divided allegiances reflecting the extent to which they are socialized, acculturated persons.

Those obligations are undeniable. Doc and Bonnie are married, with a toddler son and another child on the way; sympathetic though they are to Hayduke's zeal, they cannot ignore their compelling responsibilities. Seldom, in financial straits, for the first third of the book cannot tolerate jeopardizing his river-running business for the sake of environmental principle; he initially refuses to have anything to do with Hayduke. Only Hayduke, like the western hero of old, remains independent, unfettered, and unrepentant, his manic obsession with the land as passionate as ever, and his determined commitment to environmental reform highlights much of the novel's ambivalence.[29]

That ambivalence Abbey stresses in two central chapters, "The Code of the Eco-Warrior" and "Earth First! Rendezvous." In the first, Doc Sarvis, reunited with Hayduke after several years, spells out what environmentalism *should* entail and *should* mean, an idealized manifesto as movingly eloquent as any of Abbey's earlier pronouncements. Hayduke swallows Doc's pronouncements whole, cheering him on at each new point. Readers, though, see a dramatic irony in Doc's statements that is lost on Hayduke: while Doc knows what he and Hayduke *ought* to do, he also knows that as a person with genuine obligations to family, profession, and society, there is much of the principle he *cannot* live up to, and even, realistically, *will not* do. And therein lies the irony, as the reader (like Doc, a real-world person having to weigh alternatives) has to weigh Doc's sadder-but-wiser perspective against Hayduke's "let's-get-with-it" attitude.[30]

Just as illustrative of Abbey's troubled vision is the second episode, a description of an Earth First! rendezvous. His sympathy with Earth First! goals ("We stand *for* what we stand *on!*") is understandable, since the real-life organization takes *The Monkey Wrench Gang* as its guide, actively engaging in spiking trees, blocking logging roads, and, possibly, sabotaging equipment. Yet the organization as he presents it is self-conscious, fragmented, and self-serving, and his portrayal of its various factions' posturing is as wickedly satiric as any of his caricatures of money-hungry

Mormons or faceless industrial bureaucrats. Adding to the irony is Abbey's presence in his own book. A nameless reporter who never becomes involved, he stands on the fringes, limits himself to taking notes, and, choruslike, reflects on the folly of everyone who's involved.[31] Thus, he suggests, however much we may admire the intent, reality inhibits resolution. Virgin land cannot be restored, and the West no longer holds a place for the detached, wholly independent hero.

Here, too, in Americans' perceptions of the land, their conventionalized expressions of that view, and their efforts to preserve the mythic qualities attributed to the land, is a fruitful area for research. At the heart of Abbey's two novels is a resonant echo of 1960s-counterculture mysticism, an idealistic sense that the land—*any* land—is somehow magical. The whole sweep of western counterculture movements and their links to visions of the land has yet to be examined definitively, yet it can reveal a great deal about actions and reactions in national attitudes toward the land in the decades following the 1960s. Has counterculture mysticism become accepted by the larger public? What exactly does "the land" (however one defines the term) now offer? And what exactly are the threats posed by development and "progress"? All need examining.

Other environmental studies might examine the profound social implications of land *and* water use; as Donald Worster suggests, the "hydraulic West" is at least as significant as the "pastoral West" in shaping the subregions and American perceptions of them, but has not received its due share of attention. The origins and progress of the "conservation vs. preservation" controversy (particularly as it impinges upon the cultural traditions of the West's ethnic groups) must continue to be examined, as national demands for oil, timber, and ore clash with demands for park and recreation areas, the preservation of endangered species, or the retention of ancestral lands, while revealing comparisons might be made between nineteenth-century arguments for and against the railroad and industrial development and twentieth-century arguments for and against airports and military bases.[32]

The third mode of reconciliation is perhaps the most fraught with potential for further research, for it looks to the extent to which western society accepts the consequences of community, from the settlement to the city, and strives to balance that reality with the vanished dream as it looks to the future. The evolving settlement generates its own rhythms, rituals, and patterns, and becomes an integral, functioning part of the social region.[33] As it does, though, it reflects the aftermath of the closed frontier, suggesting for researchers the ways in which American society has (or has not) confronted the issues emanating from the termination of the movement and the victory of established society, and offering possible avenues to the future. This is, as we have seen, the vision that informs the writing of Dashiell Hammett and Raymond Chandler, as they set their private investigators to work within the confines of the western city, trapped between the pressures of society and the expanses of the Pacific Ocean.[34] It is the vision that permeates three of Clint Eastwood's films of the early 1990s. And it is also the vision echoed in the ways in which the popular genre of science fiction has incorporated the myth.

Formulaic science fiction has, to be sure, long been associated with formulaic western writing—so much so, in fact, that the expression "space opera" is more derogatory than "horse opera," and the British critic Brian Aldiss can dismiss one author's entire corpus with the label, "Injuns among the stars."[35] In the more advanced forms of the genre, however, the dismissal is not so easy. Science fiction, by its very nature, deals with issues of technological, ethnic, and social change, often in the context of a hostile and undeveloped environment. It explores the social consequences of technological advances, and its speculation about alien contact and the possibilities of the human mind raises fundamental questions about human ethnicity and what, exactly, being human means. It deals, in short, with the very stuff of the western myth, and deals with it in ways that attest to the myth's inherent vitality.

The myth, in its original and evolving form, as David Ketterer points out, is a significant part of speculative fiction, for "the American experience has provided science fiction with its major analogical model." In developing that analogy, then, the genre has of necessity utilized and adapted familiar elements of American mythology. One element, obviously, is that of the frontier generally, with all it entails, for "our conceptions of the American frontier experience are deeply identified with problems of cultural self-definition, the American preoccupation with defining 'Americanness.'" It comes as no surprise to discover that the attributes of the frontiersman, as April Selley demonstrates, sharpen the point of television's enduring cult classic *Star Trek*, while the frontier myth itself provides a vocabulary for dealing with the future and its America as assuredly as it gave Lindbergh's flight its larger meaning. Indeed, the opening words of *Star Trek*, as well as of its successor on television, *Star Trek: The Next Generation*, are "Space: the final frontier," while *Star Trek: The Next Generation* faces the Western head-on in "A Fistful of Datas," directed by the Britisher Patrick Stewart and shown during the show's sixth (1992–93) season. The episode offers an affectionately tongue-in-cheek version of "the Ancient [*sic*] West," invokes a host of Western cliches in straightforwardly dead-pan fashion, and ends with the starship *Enterprise* flying off into an improbable sunset.[36]

Science fiction, then, offers a convenient way to explore the evolution of the mythic West as it confronts the future, and constitutes a valuable area for further research. If, as Gary Wolfe remarks, "humanity seems to have a way of producing the individuals it needs for the new frontiers it encounters," American society brings its myths along to help itself add resonance and meaning to life.[37] We need to investigate, therefore, how those myths are developing and adapting, for in their nature lie glimpses of the "rules of the game" for the United States of the future. On the individual level, for example, there is the matter of technical proficiency as it relates to new heroes. The traditional hero required only the skills of an agrarian craft society and could dispense with significant formal education, yet in a time that looks to the stars, technical and intellectual competence, to say nothing of a more-than-global awareness, are imperative. Can the hero type embrace these qualities and remain a credible hero? The issue needs to be examined in the full context of the western hero *and* society.

The issues, though, extend far beyond individual concerns. On a regional level, there is the ironic juxtaposition of the American West and future technology: from aerospace industry to technological education, Los Alamos to Silicon Valley, the West has become a principal site for the attainment of the future. Is a new kind of region in the process of emerging? If so, what are its implications for the future? The Old West was a territory of hunting, ranching, and mining; what are the traits of the New? Research investigating the "New" West in light of the "Old" seems essential, for the focus, tempo, and values of daily life exert powerful influences upon the area and its mythic sense of itself.

Finally, at the national level, what is likely to be the conceptual relationship between the closed frontier that has colored American history for a century and the endlessly open frontier of space? The latter is far less accessible than the former, yet fiction writers have little difficulty in applying elements of the traditional frontier to that of the future. Will historical reality follow suit? Will the stubborn environment of space and its imperious summons to accept the rigors of survival and the conditions of alien worlds exert the same degree of influence that those of the American West exerted? Answers will be speculative for decades to come, but the questions need to be asked, and researchers need to begin now to articulate and focus them.

Wolfe's optimism about humanity's propensity for creating the myths it needs may be justified, for the mythology of the frontier scene so central to *My Darling Clementine* blends provocatively with the conventions of science fiction in a more recent film, the comedy *Back to the Future III* (1990). The final installment of a trilogy of teen-oriented time-travel films, *Back to the Future III* takes its youthful hero, Marty McFly (Michael J. Fox), to the American West of 1885. There, as events unfold, he finds himself in the midst of a community festival that incorporates an overt allusion to the dance of Ford's 1946 film. This dance, to be sure, celebrates not a church but a courthouse, and the scene is dominated not by a cross and American flags but by hucksters' booths and an enormous clock. Nor is it Marty who is drawn into the dance, but Emmett ("Doc") Brown (Christopher Lloyd), the scientist-inventor from 1985 who is now, in 1885, the local blacksmith, and Clara Clayton (Mary Steenburgen), an assertive schoolmarm with a passion for astronomy and the works of Jules Verne. Nevertheless, the episode pointedly invokes Ford's mythopoeic sequence, reinforcing the allusion with a compelling auditory cue when the off-screen musicians quietly swing into "My Darling Clementine."[38]

The episode is a consciously self-referential moment, like so much else in the film. For full effect it requires viewers to be aware of Ford's film, and it asks them to supply a number of other associations to augment the references and resonances. (Several exteriors are shot in Monument Valley, and the film's other allusions gently poke fun at almost every cliché of the cinematic West.) Yet, in a larger sense, its modifying of Ford's evocative symbolism says much about the changing elements of the western myth. Ford's dance takes place in the full light of day, linking landscape and society in a single striking image; Zemeckis's takes place at night, with the surrounding darkness shutting out the land and focusing attention upon the community, complete within itself. Whereas Ford offers a marshal hero (Law and Order), Zemeckis advances an inventor-blacksmith (Technology and Commerce). Whereas Ford's community revolves about a church and a cross (Established Religion and Eternity), Zemeckis's centers upon a courthouse and a clock (Statutory Law, Secular Community, and Finite, Measured Time). Whereas Clementine Carter is a nurse before she's a schoolmarm (Convention plus Education), Clara Clayton is a free-spirited science teacher (Education, Science, and Female Individualism). And whereas Ford reflects upon the development of conventional American culture within a surrounding wilderness, Zemeckis offers a commentary upon a century and more of community, technology, and the evolving West.

Two incidents attest to this commentary. The first presents a traditional western gunman, here emblematic of Selfishness and Social Irresponsibility rather than Independence and Principle, in a classic main-street walkdown. Marty defeats him with wit rather than with weapons, then, Shanelike, leaves the settlement, never to return. Unlike Shane, though, Marty is going not into timeless myth but to his own era of 1985, helped along by Doc Brown's time machine. As he leaves town, he tosses his unused Colt's pistol (called a "Peacemaker" three times by its salesman) to Seamus McFly, his Irish immigrant great-grandfather, urging Seamus to use it not as a weapon, but as an investment to provide for his family. It is a minor episode, but in its social and cultural implications one as pertinent to the last decade of the century as Ford's dance on the church floor was to the middle years; Marty, the acculturated hero of the future, has learned a lesson lost on the larger society, whether past or present, and he tries to pass it on to his kin.

The other incident involves Doc Brown. He, even more than Marty, has acted in surprisingly heroic ways throughout much of the film, yet he chooses to stay behind, remaining with Clara in the West he has helped to shape. But his decision, too, is tempered by circumstances, for he reappears at film's end, returning to 1985 with Clara and their two sons, Jules and Vern, ready to explore past, present, and future in a steam-driven time machine built around a classically western locomotive. The resonances here are equally rich, for in Doc, Clara, and their family, Zemeckis supplies still further evidence of his melding of community, knowledge, technology, and progress, all bound together by the mythic symbol of western conquest, the locomotive.[39] Metaphor and myth work together to present a version of western myth that looks beyond tradition, quite literally, to its continuation in the future.

Can, then, the myth maintain its vitality, not to say its credibility, into a still more complex and demanding era? One critic, Jack Turner, offers a seeming denial: "The old western myth—the loner in a wild land, his ordeal, his victory, and his ride into the sunset—is dead, killed by history, its memory reduced to an absurd nostalgia by the surrealism of modern life." And, indeed, the traditional forms of the myth may well have outlived their time, as Edward Abbey suggests at greater length in *Hayduke Lives!* Here, cowboy Jack Burns, dressed like the Lone Ranger of radio and comic-strip fame, is for Abbey heroic in his intent but pathetic in his reality: "The shootist. The Masked Rider. Shane and Shinola, Tom Mix and Hopalong Cassidy, Sir Lancelot and El Cid, Gilgamesh, Jason, Siegfried and Luke Skywalker wrapped in one grubby Jungian package."[40] Yet behind Abbey's sardonic tone is a second voice, almost plaintive, that speaks to the enduring reality of the myth.

Sustaining that reality are two elements. One is the human need for myths in general. Empirical reality must be accepted, to be sure, but it is myth that reminds a diverse people of their common vision; rightly embraced and properly utilized, myths give a society the human and humane elements that it needs to balance the pressures that will inevitably develop. The other is the demonstrated adaptability of the western myth. As times change, popular art changes, adapting itself to the times and carrying the essential nature of the hero along with it. One generation created the airman and the private detective from the fragments of the western hero; the Cold War generation produced the spy; the *glasnost* era produced the older Doc Sarvis and Doc Brown—unheroic types on the surface, but persons whose willingness to temper the ideal with reality augurs well for the future.[41] Rather than debase a worthy ideal or struggle to preserve in isolation an outdated model, they accept themselves, the world, and the West as they are, drawing upon past *and* present to prepare the way for the future. As they do, they speak to the people, as mythic heroes have always spoken, of a society open to all, for a society worthy of its vision. No one could ask more of any hero or any myth.

Notes

1. A portion of this essay, in substantially altered form, has been published as "The Night Christopher Lloyd Danced with Mary Steenburgen," *Journal of Popular Film and Television* 20, no. 1 (Spring 1992): 29–33. Reprinted with permission of the Helen Dwight Reid Educational Foundation. Published by Heldref Publications, 1319 18th Street, N.W., Washington, D.C. 20036-1802. Copyright 1992.

2. *My Darling Clementine*. Directed by John Ford. With Henry Fonda, Cathy Downs, Victor Mature, and Linda Darnell. Twentieth-Century Fox, 1946.

3. A. Carl Bredahl, Jr., *New Ground: Western American Narrative and the Literary Canon* (Chapel Hill: University of North Carolina Press, 1989), 151. The criticism dealing with Ford's westerns is extensive, but of particular use are J. A. Place, *The Western Films of John Ford* (Secaucus, N.J.: Citadel Press, 1974); and John H. Lenihan, *Showdown: Confronting Modern America in the Western Film* (Urbana: University of Illinois Press, 1980).

4. Richard Slotkin, *The Fatal Environment: The Myth of the Frontier in the Age of Industrialization, 1800–1890* (New York: Atheneum, 1985), 16, 20.

5. In identifying these characteristics, Henry Nash Smith, *Virgin Land: The American West as Symbol and Myth* (1950; Cambridge: Harvard University Press, 1970), labels them, respectively, "The Sons of Leatherstocking," "The Garden of the World," and "Passage to India," and investigates them at length, although in different order. Critiques of Smith's argument appear in Cecil F. Tate, *The Search for a Method in American Studies* (Minneapolis: University of Minnesota Press, 1973); and Alan Trachtenberg, "Myth, History, and Literature in *Virgin Land*," *Perspectives* 3 (1977): 125–33. Smith responds to these and other criticisms in "Symbol and Idea in *Virgin Land*," in *Ideology and Classic American Literature*, ed. Sacvan Bercovitch and Myra Jehlen (Cambridge: Cambridge University Press, 1986), 21–35.

6. The early stages of the Western hero are examined in Book II ("The Sons of Leatherstocking") of Smith, *Virgin Land*, 51–120. Later and more comprehensive studies include Kent Ladd Steckmesser, *The Western Hero in History and Legend* (Norman: University of Oklahoma Press, 1965); John G. Cawelti, *The Six-Gun Mystique* (Bowling Green, Ohio: Bowling Green University Popular Press, 1971); and William W. Savage, Jr., *The Cowboy Hero: His Image in American History and Culture* (Norman: University of Oklahoma Press, 1979).

7. Slotkin, *Fatal Environment*, 20.

8. Lenihan, *Showdown*, 11.

9. *Outlook* magazine, quoted in John William Ward, "The Meaning of Lindbergh's Flight," *Red, White, and Blue: Men, Books, and Ideas in American Culture* (New York: Oxford University Press, 1969), 29.

10. James Oliver Robertson, *American Myth, American Reality* (New York: Hill and Wang, 1980), 201–2. See also Ward, *Red, White, and Blue*, 34–37. For the development of the aircraft industry in the West, see Wayne Biddle, *Barons of the Sky* (New York: Simon and Schuster, 1991); for Americans' response to aviation generally, see Joseph J. Corn, *The Winged Gospel: America's Romance with Aviation, 1900–1950* (New York: Oxford University Press, 1983).

11. A convenient overview of Western urbanization is Gerald D. Nash, "The West as Urban Civilization, 1890–1990," *Creating the West: Historical Interpretations 1890–1990* (Albuquerque: University of New Mexico Press, 1991), 159–95.

12. A good starting point for examining the origins and development of the private detective as mythic hero is Cawelti, *Adventure, Mystery, and Romance* (Chicago: University of Chicago Press, 1976). Of particular value for Hammett is Peter Wolfe, *Beams Falling: The Art of Dashiell Hammett* (Bowling Green, Ohio: Bowling Green University Popular Press, 1980). The western tradition in Raymond Chandler's works is discussed in Philip Durham, *Down These Mean Streets a Man Must Go: Raymond Chandler's Knight* (Chapel Hill: University of North Carolina Press, 1963). Joseph C. Porter, "The End of the Trail: The American West of Dashiell Hammett and Raymond Chandler," *Western Historical Quarterly* 6 (October 1975): 411–24, examines both writers in a broadly western context, as does Paul Skenazy, *The New Wild West: The Urban Mysteries of Dashiell Hammett and Raymond Chandler* (Boise: Western Writers Series no. 54, 1982).

13. Raymond Chandler, "The Simple Art of Murder" (1944), in *The Art of the Mystery Story*, ed. Howard Haycraft (New York: Grosset and Dunlap, 1946), 237.

14. Ray Oldenburg, *The Great Good Place* (New York: Paragon House, 1989), 292.

15. Robert Dallek, *Lone Star Rising: Lyndon Johnson and His Times, 1908–1960* (New York: Oxford University Press, 1991), typifies one form a single-figure study might take.

16. A useful starting point for investigation of gender and ethnic issues is Judy Alter and A. T. Row, eds., *Unbridled Spirits: Short Fiction about Women in the Old West* (Fort Worth: Texas Christian University Press, 1994).

17. The fullest study of Hillerman's works to date is Fred Erisman, *Tony Hillerman* (Boise: Western Writers Series no. 87, 1989). Cawelti, in *Adventure, Mystery, and Romance*, 252–59, addresses other aspects of the evolving ethnic hero in "The Jewish Cowboy, the Black Avenger, and the Return of the Vanishing American: Current Trends in the Formula." A fuller discussion of one kind of ethnic hero is John Ball, "The Ethnic Detective," in *The Mystery Story*, ed. John Ball (New York: Penguin Books, 1978), 143–60. Developments in popular literature and critical awareness since the 1970s, when Cawelti's and Ball's books appeared, make clear the need for further investigation; some useful texts are cited below, but much remains to be done.

18. *Unforgiven*. Directed by Clint Eastwood. With Clint Eastwood, Gene Hackman, Morgan Freeman, and Richard Harris. Warner Brothers, 1992; *In the Line of Fire*. Directed by Wolfgang Petersen. With Clint Eastwood, John Malkovich, and Rene Russo. Columbia Pictures, 1993; *A Perfect World*. Directed by Clint Eastwood. With Clint Eastwood, Kevin Costner, and Laura Dern. Warner Brothers, 1993. Although not dealing with Eastwood's films as such, Robert Murray Davis, *Playing Cowboys: Low Culture and High Art in the Western* (Norman: University of Oklahoma Press, 1992), offers readings of several other forms of Western film and opens the door to future studies of the genre. Film also figures prominently in Jane Tompkins, *West of Everything* (New York: Oxford University Press, 1992); the-

sis-ridden to a fault, idiosyncratic, and at times woefully uninformed, Tompkins's book rarely fails to stimulate ideas for further investigation—if only to challenge its glib assertions.

19. Smith, *Virgin Land*, 77, 123. See also Richard Slotkin, *Regeneration through Violence: The Mythology of the American Frontier, 1600–1860* (Middletown, Conn.: Wesleyan University Press, 1973).

20. Leo Marx, "Pastoralism in America," in Bercovitch and Jehlen, *Ideology and Classic American Literature*, 56–57.

21. Robert Penn Warren, *All the King's Men* (1946; New York: Modern Library, 1953), 327, 287. Bernard Malamud, *A New Life* (1961; New York: Avon, 1980), 172. Edward Abbey, *The Monkey Wrench Gang* (Philadelphia: J. B. Lippincott, 1975), 32. Useful discussions of Malamud's view of the western myth are John A. Barsness, "*A New Life*: The Frontier Myth in Perspective," *Western American Literature* 3 (Winter 1969): 297–302; and Richard Astro, "In the Heart of the Valley: Bernard Malamud's *A New Life*," in *Bernard Malamud: A Collection of Critical Essays*, ed. Leslie A. Field and Joyce W. Field (Englewood Cliffs, N.J.: Prentice-Hall, 1975), 143–55. The fullest account of Abbey's work to date is Ann Ronald, *The New West of Edward Abbey* (Albuquerque: University of New Mexico Press, 1982); also helpful is Paul T. Bryant, "Edward Abbey and Environmental Quixoticism," *Western American Literature* 24 (May 1989): 37–43.

22. Warren, *All the King's Men*, 287, 330; Malamud, *New Life*, 2, 66.

23. Abbey, *Monkey Wrench Gang*, 26.

24. William Cronon, "Revisiting the Vanishing Frontier: The Legacy of Frederick Jackson Turner," *Western Historical Quarterly* 18 (April 1987): 175. See also Jackson K. Putnam, "The Turner Thesis and the Westward Movement: A Reappraisal," *Western Historical Quarterly* 7 (October 1976): 403–4.

25. Mary Young, "The West and American Cultural Identity: Old Themes and New Variations," *Western Historical Quarterly* 1 (April 1970): 141; Astro, "In the Heart of the Valley," 147. The myth's ability to survive the contradictions of western development is a major theme in Patricia Nelson Limerick, *The Legacy of Conquest: The Unbroken Past of the American West* (New York: W. W. Norton, 1987).

26. Earl Pomeroy, *In Search of the Golden West: The Tourist in Western America* (New York: Alfred A. Knopf, 1957), 93–94, 152–53, 185. This pioneering account of western tourism is supplemented by Chapter 7, "The Dudes' West," of Robert G. Athearn, *The Mythic West in Twentieth-Century America* (Lawrence: University Press of Kansas, 1986).

27. Gerald D. Nash, *The American West in the Twentieth Century: A Short History of an Urban Oasis* (Englewood Cliffs, N.J.: Prentice-Hall, 1973), examines both western development and the resulting environmental problems; Kevin Starr, *Material Dreams: Southern California through the 1920s* (New York: Oxford University Press, 1990), 277–97, speaks of California's deliberate fictionalizing of its own reality.

28. Frederick Jackson Turner, "The Significance of the Frontier in American History," in *Prose and Poetry of the American West*, ed. James C. Work (Lincoln: University of Nebraska Press, 1990), 250.

29. Edward Abbey, *Hayduke Lives!* (Boston: Little, Brown, 1990), 104–5, 120–23.

30. Ibid., 107–16.

31. Ibid., 186–212; see also 206–7, 239–44.

32. Fred Erisman, "The Environmental Crisis and Present-Day Romanticism," *Rocky Mountain Social Science Journal* 10 (January 1973): 8–14, takes up one facet of environmental inquiry and implies others, while Donald Worster, "New West, True West: Interpreting the Region's History," *Western Historical Quarterly* 18 (April 1987): 141–56, looks at western land-use and water-use issues in a global context.

33. This is the process celebrated in so many of John Ford's films, and in *My Darling Clementine* in particular, as Bredahl, *New Ground*, 151, points out. Robert V. Hine, *Community on the American Frontier: Separate but Not Alone* (Norman: University of Oklahoma Press, 1980), offers a thoughtful examination of the process of social development in the West. How the city of Los Angeles evolved from small community to megalopolis, and what consequences resulted, occupies a good deal of Starr, *Material Dreams*.

34. See Porter, "End of the Trail," 414–19. Harold P. Simonson takes up the issue of the closed frontier in a broadly national sense in *Beyond the Frontier: Writers, Western Regionalism and a Sense of Place* (Fort Worth: Texas Christian University Press, 1989). A British novelist's reactions to the frontier myth and its implications are discussed in Fred Erisman, "Nevil Shute and the Closed Frontier," *Western American Literature* 21 (November 1986): 207–17.

35. David Mogen, *Wilderness Visions: Science Fiction Westerns* (San Bernardino: Borgo Press, 1982), 5–8; Brian W. Aldiss, *Trillion Year Spree: The History of Science Fiction* (New York: Atheneum, 1986), 209.

36. David Ketterer, *New Worlds for Old: The Apocalyptic Imagination, Science Fiction, and American Literature* (Garden City, N.Y.: Doubleday/Anchor, 1974), 26; Mogen, *Wilderness Visions*, 11; April Selley, " 'I Have Been, and Ever Shall Be, Your Friend': Star Trek, The Deerslayer and the American Romance," *Journal of Popular Culture* 20 (Summer 1986): 89–104. A useful comparison of the two incarnations of *Star Trek* is Clyde Wilcox, "To Boldly Return Where Others Have Gone Before: Cultural Change and the Old and New *Star Treks*," *Extrapolation* 33 (Spring 1992): 88–100. Chapter 4, "Playing With Cowboys: Science Fiction Westerns," of Davis, *Playing Cowboys*, 93–114, offers a selective but useful discussion of science fiction's affinity for the Western; although not treating science fiction in any fashion, David M. Wrobel, *The End of American Exceptionalism: Frontier Anxiety from the Old West to the New Deal* (Lawrence: University Press of Kansas, 1993), provides a helpful complement to some of the genre's concerns. One author's deliberate effort to combine science fiction with a particular vision of American society is examined in Fred Erisman, "Robert Heinlein, the Scribner Juveniles, and Cultural Literacy," *Extrapolation* 32 (Spring 1991): 45–53.

37. Gary K. Wolfe, "Frontiers in Space," in *The Frontier Experience and the American Dream: Essays on American Literature*, ed. David Mogen, Mark Busby, and Paul Bryant (College Station: Texas A & M University Press, 1989), 262.

38. *Back to the Future III*. Directed by Robert Zemeckis. With Michael J. Fox, Christopher Lloyd, and Mary Steenburgen. MCA Universal, 1990.

39. The locomotive as a metaphor for progress figures extensively in Leo Marx, *The Machine in the Garden: Technology and the Pastoral Ideal in America* (New York: Oxford University Press, 1964). American ambivalence toward the railroad (and, by extension, toward technology) is examined in Bernard Bowron, Leo Marx, and Arnold Rose, "Literature and Covert Culture," in *Studies in American Culture: Dominant Ideas and Images*, ed. Joseph J. Kwiat and Mary C. Turpie (Minneapolis: University of Minnesota Press, 1960), 84–95. Marx, "Pastoralism in America," in Bercovitch and Jehlen, *Ideology and Classic American Literature*, 36–69, offers a still broader view.

40. Jack Turner, review of Doug Peacock, *Grizzly Years: In Search of American Wilderness*, *Western American Literature* 26 (May 1991): 54; Abbey, *Hayduke Lives!*, 272. The full complexity of Abbey's vision is examined in Paul T. Bryant, "Echoes, Allusions, and 'Reality' in *Hayduke Lives!*," *Western American Literature* 25 (February 1991): 311–22.

41. Robertson, *American Myth*, 346. For examinations of two suggestive adaptations of the western myth, see Fred Erisman, "Western Motifs in the Thrillers of Donald Hamilton," *Western American Literature* 10 (February 1976): 283–92; and Fred Erisman, "Elmer Kelton's `Other' West," *Western American Literature* 28 (February 1994): 291–99.

8

Research in a Theatre
in the Round

Gene M. Gressley

As visitors approach "Centennial Village," a remarkably sophisticated restoration of a turn-of-the century Great Plains community in Greeley, Colorado, their attention is caught by a sign announcing, "Centennial Village—The Past in Progress." The preceding stimulating essays devoted to the research possibilities of the twentieth-century West assure us that the path to the past is indeed in progress.

Omnifarious as these essays are as to subject and interpretation, what will inevitably strike many readers is the commonality of themes, or methodologies if you will, that they advocate. Whether these authors are investigating the twentieth-century political scene of the West as does Robert Cherny in his masterful essay, or sketch the strata of urbanism with the insight of Roger Lotchin, or probe the management of our natural resources with the aplomb of Tom Cox, or introduce us to women's history sans the stridency of Betty Friedan, as does Glenda Riley, each essayist appeals to the value of a variety of approaches, which have common denominators, as they search for the alchemy of the twentieth-century past, in the land beyond the hundredth meridian.

One such thread that appears to have galvanized the attention of many of these historians is the potential of the comparative modus operandi for their specific field.[1] The frontiers of the American West as compared to other global frontiers have long proved attractive to Howard Lamar, Walter P. Webb, W. K. Hancock, Jerome Steffen, Robin Winks, Leonard Thompson, W. H. McNeill, and others. Perhaps in a subconscious effort to shed the skin of cultural "exceptionalism," the historians in the preceding pages have not been concerned with the frontier as the litmus test of their comparative beaker glasses, but have focused on the comparative routes that offer a map of understanding to the complexities of their research.

189

If we are to comprehend better our subregional West, we must remember the comparative tool. How else can we discern the traits, unique or otherwise, that hold significance for our regions? In sum, what is characteristic and what is not characteristic of our regional West?

The methodological dangers of the comparative approach are obvious. To try, as many tourists do, at least figuratively, to compare lands of dissimilar cultures, invites only the catalog of information about separate cultural and environmental habitats. To compare, for example, the pastoral economy of Siberia with the high, cold desert of Nevada is to produce fallacious conclusions. Some of the geographic and economic indices may be appropriate, but their equations lead only to distortions.

Another theme whose usefulness, like the comparative approach, has been realized by historians of the West is the West of fragmentation,[2] specifically, that *one* West is the West of imagination, and that indeed there are many Wests. Of course, realization does not always lead to conversion. Many historians of the West, with tuning-fork intensity, insist on a genre West, endowing their West with characteristics of many subregional Wests. It is not only the landscape of localism that we define; it is simply that we cannot discover the dynamism of the West in *one* West. For that *one* West simply does not exist, except as a fictional West.

The West, then, that does exist, although far from isolated or autonomous socially, economically, or politically, reflects a remarkable diversity, a variety, which sometimes seeks, but more frequently fails, to find a commonality of western identity—a failure except in the mythology of the West, a folklore of exceptionalism[3]—a mythology increasingly irrelevant in a society smashed by pickets of protest. Those Americans (and westerners) who march under the banners of feminism, civil rights, abortion rights, peace, or simply slogans of generational disenchantment find little solace in that imagined place—*the* West.

Although we recognize that the West's meaning can be perceived through decoding of the hieroglyphics of fragmentation, diversity, and particularism, we would just as quickly confess that there are inherent hazards in such methodological romps. The danger signs come quickest perhaps in cliometrics. Historians, as Gerald Nash in his essay in this volume notes, are continually mesmerized by and with historiographical fads. Cliometrics allowed its practitioners to find meaning in knowing "more and more about less and less." The result was a quantum swamp of static, stale, sterile, and often simply meaningless data, as historians frantically tried to decipher the code in the rows of binary dots.

In their search for an interpretive portal, it does not surprise us that these authors select as one of the keys (though non-skeleton) to be twentieth-century regionalism. Robert Cherny observes that the regionalism of the twentieth-century political West is a regional consciousness limited by subregionalism. Roger Lotchin, in his sprightly essay, uncovers his urbanism of today as issuing from the frontier. For Lotchin, that regional identity emanates from the frontier, as a slice of the heritage of the past. Fred Erisman circumscribes his regionalism to a specific place, which provides the frame for his literary metaphor.

Tom Cox, in a provocative examination of the interaction of natural resources and the environment, reminds us that even as volatile and vociferous western protest as the Sagebrush Rebellion does not sweep all regionalism along in its wake. The Robert Smylies and the Richard Lamms successfully muted the angry shibboleths flung about so randomly by the Sagebrushers. Gerald Nash, with his typical astuteness, insists that we remember the twentieth-century economic West as part of the international scene. Regional producers may chant the macroeconomic verse of jingoism, but they assiduously court the markets of the Orient and Europe. Richard Etulain creatively depicts the lack of uniformity among the belles lettres tradition of the regional West. With delightful illustrations, Glenda Riley shows us the bias that historians of the women of the West have faced in defining the descriptive "western" women, vis à vis the Northeast and the South.

Regionalism, then, is a powerful amalgamation, but a theme also fractured into many meters. Although western culture proscribes the limits on western regionalism, westerners allow localism to triumph in their thoughts. Westerners have a tenacious myopia in assessing regional issues via local perceptions. For many westerners, regional questions of environment, economics, or politics find more meaning in their verbal exchanges in the main-street barbershop than on the six o'clock news.

This is not to argue that the westerner is a mute when relating his local concerns to other regions. As the western animosity to the Washington bureaucracy attests, the westerner is not tongue-tied in spewing forth spleen. Nevertheless, most regional history looks inward, not outward.

Lest we forget the value and vitality of the regional conceptual thesis, all we have to do is finger the pages of Raymond Gastil, Merrill Jensen, Howard Odum, Joel Garreau, and Ira Sharkansky, among many. All voice their own views of what amounts to a personal regionalism.[4] What intrigues most is that regardless of the commentators, or the stance of those being commented about, the regional incantation comes with audible clarity, whether the speaker is a farmer in McCook, Nebraska, a suburbanite in Hillsborough, California, or a real estate entrepreneur in Phoenix, Arizona. Their individual convictions have a revivalistic fervor when questioned about subregional problems.

A third theme that preoccupies our essayists, as it has most Americans since 1789, is the innate tension between the states and the national government. Although federalism,[5] like the Constitution, is an evolving concept—westerners have been remarkably ambivalent, over time, to the federal presence.

The most arresting feature of federal/state relations during the 1930s, as James Patterson has adroitly noted, was the narrow ideological confines within which both the states and the national government had to maneuver.[6] Gerald Nash, in a series of essays and books, has brilliantly assessed the balance wheel of federalism in the West.[7] Of special concern to Nash has been how federalism and federal policies have affected the West's economic development. The recast West, for all its feints to the left, remains solidly in the pro-business, anti-central government (whether in the state house or national capital) camp, a stance reflected in its overall allegiance to the Republican party, or the conservative wing of the Democratic party.

Westerners may jealously retain a jaundiced ambivalence relating to the federal impact on their land, but in their more balanced moments they have to acknowledge that in the century from 1870 to 1970, the federal government invested in the West the fantastic (some easterners would argue "obscene") sum of circa three hundred billion dollars. That the West was hobbled by an uncomfortably small population and infiltrated by hordes of federal bureaucrats and an ineffective party system did not make their paranoia less, nor their perception of federalism more secure. Historically, the West has always felt that it was at the top of the teeter-totter of the federal system.

Westerners frequently translate this apprehension into litigious conduct, hoping against hope that the courts will redress the federal balance, or at least nod in their favor. In their proclivity of casting the courts as the last resort, westerners are reflecting the opinion of Americans generally. Unlike Europeans, who are comfortable with a strong state, Americans have opted for a federal system that is delineated by "relative statelessness."[8] In the United States, "only the law is sovereign,"[9] an understanding of the political state that, with its constitutionally instructed division of powers, leads only to increasing power of the legal establishment.

Of course, westerners realize, even if they do not admit it, that the judicial system can be remarkably fickle. Justice Brennan, in his vigorous dissent in the *National League of Cities* v. *Usery* (1970), proposed that in light of the tremendous increase in the grants-in-aid to the states, the national government should be asking for protection from the states, not vice versa! Had he been speaking historically, the good Justice would have provided only emphasis for his view.

Within a short time after Brennan's dissent appeared, the national government initiated a partial revenge on the states by readdressing the federal balance. A host of "nationalizing" statutes issued in the seventies was endorsed and promulgated by the Reagan presidency. This was an astonishing era, in which the former California governor, with his proclivity for lavish dispensing of the federal treasury, put some of the states into the peculiar position of advocating reductions in state aid.

Governor Bruce Babbitt, in his presidential campaign in 1988, addressed the question of the future of public land and states rights'/federal conflict. The governor of Arizona insisted that the answer was a balanced federalism—a specific question of share governance. Western audiences evidently were not in sympathy, if indeed they believed Babbitt.

Nowhere has federalism been so prominent in the West as in natural resources—especially those areas relating to water. As Donald Pisani, in numerous essays and pathbreaking books, has argued with so much ingenuity and intelligence,[10] westerners possessed a strong states' rights federalism with respect to water legislation in the nineteenth century, a posture westerners increasingly cherished as they moved into the twentieth century and discovered to their dismay, at least technically, that they had to surrender many of their states' rights to the national government.

True, westerners' capitulation came only with the comprehension that, in reality, they had no alternative, which became patently obvious in relation to unused water, but also if they hoped to attract federal underwriting. Ironically, as Pisani describes, the western water policy of the twentieth century was based on the seduction of the West by the federal government. For although westerners might be embarrassed to admit it, it was they who had implicitly argued for congressional legislative supremacy—especially relating to the problem of unused western water.

As has occurred so often in the history of the West, only when the federal government seemed to be taking away more than bestowing did western states "discover" states' rights. Westerners reacted with a slashing vengeance, fighting their neighbors for the federal largesse, screaming at the federal eagle for imagined or actual trespass of states' rights. Although the Reclamation Law of 1902 was designed to undermine western regionalism, instead it helped to codify the identity of the West.[11] Tocqueville, that incredible sage whose writing is so alluring as to invite perpetual quotation, stressed the merits of a constitutional covenant in a democratic philosophy. Tocqueville insisted that in a democratic society, power must be widely, if not evenly, shared. On this premise the federal government comes up short in the creation of federal water policy—which was neither farsighted in its allocation nor efficient in its implementation.

Just as the environment dominates and pervades the twentieth-century West, so environmental policy preoccupies the essayists in this volume. If western historians see the ghost of the federalist past hovering over them, the environmental issues appear more immediate, graphic, and challenging. One colleague recently commented, "Western history is no more; it is all environmental history!" To some that statement would be non sequitur; to others, that statement would be one born of the frustration with perceived historiographic overemphasis. And still to others, that statement is merely an accurate reflection of the capricious nature of historiographical fancy—as scholars are bewitched by first one and then another temptation. The primary issue is obviously not between the so-called new versus the so-called old historiography, but the understanding of western history per se, via practicing interpreters or would-be interpreters.

Say what we will, some of the most exciting, stimulating, and engrossing historiography of the West today relates to environmental topics. The New West historians, particularly, find their future and that of the West in environmental history. When did it all begin, this preoccupation with paradise lost? Americans, with their usual presentist blinders, attribute the environmental movement to a quiet lady from Maryland, Rachel Carson, whose book *Silent Spring*[12] captivated a public and entranced policymakers (primarily because Carson had seized the public's imagination).

Environmental thunder issued from a host of Jeremiahs. One who became a cult figure, and perhaps the most strident, was Edward Abbey. Abbey announced with cataclysmic fervor, "most of what I write about in this book [*Desert Solitaire*] is already gone, or going under fast. This is not a travel guide but an elegy. A memorial. You're holding a tombstone in your hands."[13] The message was stark, the West that was is gone!

In common with many religions, the environmental movement has had no clear-cut origins. Globally, there has been an interest for centuries in mankind's natural womb. Gilbert White, in 1877, published *The Natural History and Antiquities of Selborne*,[14] a book that sometimes receives the pedestal as formalizing the environmental mystique. Most certainly, the Victorian era gave the entire environmental debate a major push. In the United States the environment became a policy matter at the turn of the century, when the preservationist and the conservationist jousted for primacy in the vision of policymakers, a contest that featured victors and vanquished in a downtrodden/conquerors scenario over the next half-century. From the historian's perspective environmental history outcropped in the 1960s and 1970s with Roderick Nash, William Cronon, Donald Worster, and Richard White[15] publishing a flurry of tomes oriented toward attracting the professional and the populist alike to the environmental missionary movement. These were historians who based, or sometimes claimed a degree of lineal descendant of past masters, a roll call that included Frederick Jackson Turner, Walter Prescott Webb, James Malin, and Aldo Leopold—to name a few.

Although visitors traveling westward along Interstate 70 or 80 might be impressed, even inspired by the seeming homogeneity of the subregional environment that they encounter, such appearances are deceptive. Whether in the urban West, as Roger Lotchin in his perspicacious essay has recognized, or in the political West of Robert Cherny, major fissures rent the land of the twentieth-century West.

The West *fractured* is *the* West that is woven through these essays. Deep cultural divisions of class, race, gender, and ethnic lines, existing for years, were now reaching, on a daily basis, the front pages of the *Denver Post* and the *Los Angeles Times*. In the 1960s, Vietnam, although not as divisive an issue in much of the West as in the East, provided a fertile field in which to cultivate the political unrest of the seventies. In the West, as in the nation, this turmoil settled on such social issues as health care, education, and housing. The women's liberation movement, though receiving its impetus from the upper middle class, discovered class divisions as never before with the defeat of the Equal Rights Amendment.

The late 1970s saw class alliances increase with the variant patterns of ethnicity,[16] in part enhanced by the Immigration Reform Act of 1965. The changing character of ethnic culture was vividly illustrated by the influx and rooting of Asian and Latin American ethnics. Regional western historians, as Fred Luebke has perceptively observed,[17] failed to incorporate ethnicity into their work because of their methodological bent to think in spatial rather than cultural terms.

The society, perceived and lost, was a society in search of the therapeutic. Dismissed was the fact that America had seldom had a uniform creed, whether that overall creed concerned religion, language, or culture. Multiculturalism became a banner of emotion. Blissfully ignored was the fact that the national culture has always been multicultural. What disturbs so many is that this multiculturalism today means Balkanization and cultural separatism, a separatism that in reality is antithetical to diversity. Demonic tribalism does not create the atmosphere that nurtures mutual respect and a sense of collective national pride.

To the degree that Americans fail to recognize differences and accommodate to them, America loses its exceptionalism and mission. This is not to contend, of course, that the mission of America has always succeeded; just a glance at the history of race relations purges that thought, but if we sanctify victims (the WASP will soon be claiming the victim's role) we will only increase the number of worshipers in the temples of the demagogues—whose sermon is America divided.

Suddenly, or seemingly suddenly, in the 1980s flashing lights signaled a turn in the historiographical tradition of western historians. In part, this represented a reflection of the presentist milieu; the New West historians sent a warning closely followed by a call to arms for a reorientation of western history.[18] These New West historians stormed the battlements waving the guidons of conquest, victimization, and guilt. In other forms, as has frequently been commented on, the New West historians were only building on and adapting to the methodology of social historians of the past decade. Historians who were influenced by the Annales school argued for analysis of structure rather than the narration of events, for the cause of everyman—the great unwashed—rather than great men (the heroes now were the victims), for the "real" world of social and cultural organization, and, above all, for that prejudicial guilt embedded so deep within questions of race, class, and gender.

Especially attractive to this agenda was the methodology of history from below.[19] This "down-under" school of historians became increasingly popular during the late 1960s, with the activity of labor historians such as E. P. Thompson. Popular audiences of this era gave this underground history another push via the "Upstairs/Downstairs" syndrome. Now the gossip of the scullery maid seemed as important as the gossip in the drawing room. The age of humanity could only be revealed by giving each class equal weight in the history of our times.

This is not to trivialize the significance of history from below. Historians of the New West persuasion laudably insisted that they were restoring to history those groups—Chicanos, Native Americans, and Asians, among others—perceived as lost to history. In essence, the New West historians sought to provide, with identity, these ethnic groups, groups that had long been submerged by the glacial grinding of hierarchial social structure.

So some of the essays in this volume reflect, if at times subtly, the message of the New West historians. Roger Lotchin argues for increasing attention to the ethnic culture in twentieth-century urbanism. Glenda Riley calls attention to the need for more comparative research between gender and western ethnic women. Richard Etulain has imaginatively argued that the cultural history of the twentieth-century West will be disclosed only to the extent that ethnic culture is understood.

A final motif that has proven attractive to these essayists is the interdisciplinary procedure. Western historians, following their eastern peers, are increasingly reading and profiting from the many layers of scholarship of other disciplines. Anthropological speculations of Marshall Sahlins and Clifford Geertz find their readers in their specialized musings.[20] Sociologists, especially those involved in the problems of twentieth-century urbanism described by Nathan Glazer and Robert Nisbet, have attracted western urban historians. Journalists Neal Peirce, Marc Reisner, Joel Garreau, and Bill McKibben[21] interpret their America to readers. Political scientists whose names continually pop up in the footnotes of historians include Walter Dean Burnham and Nelson Polsby.[22] The fields could with ease be extended; but the point is self-evident: the western historian, in the tradition of his peers elsewhere, is liberating himself from static, disciplinary provincialism.

Howard Lamar, in a delightful address on the occasion of the Western History Association's twenty-fifth anniversary, noted how much there was to celebrate, and how much there was yet to be done.[23] Our essayists in this volume obviously agree with the distinguished Yale historian—opportunities lie ahead!

One of the major research areas that suggests satisfying rewards for the historian of the West centers on western legal history. As Willard Hurst showed us all years ago, law circumscribed and underpinned the economic and political foundations of the West.[24] Harry Scheiber, with seemingly felicitous ease, has moved beyond Hurst with his pathbreaking studies of federalism and the search for the cultural setting of the western legal system.

Yet the law of western development remains hidden and unexplored. John Phillip Reid, who is doing so much to retrieve the burial ground of western legal history, stated recently that "there is not available one instance of the legal history of a state, a province, or an Indian nation,"[25] a startling fact that blatantly illustrates how much remains to be accomplished.

Another immense area of western legal entanglement pertains to mining law.[26] Although nineteenth-century mining law promises an enormously rich province for investigation, twentieth-century mining law is a buried topic. The evolution of industrial mining liability and health care present an arresting subject for investigation. Here, comparative methodology would be especially pertinent in weighing the health-care systems in South African or Australian mining.

The evolution of the law of discovery has probably produced more mining litigation than any single aspect of mining law. If the nineteenth century is unknown, the twentieth-century concept of discovery is a historical black hole. In general, the problem of discovery for the historian of the twentieth-century mining industry may simply be attempting to unravel the reams of court decisions and commentaries.[27]

These two major topics of twentieth-century mining—discovery and mining policy—promise enormous rewards for those historians with tenacity. Specifically, the relationship between discovery and the federal lands and the condition favoring property rights and the perfection of titles deserve attention. What, historically, has been the role of the executive branch of government in administering mining law? The dissection of the enormous contemporary controversy surrounding the revision of the 1872 mining law presents nothing less than a history of the mining industry for the past century.

That the 1872 mining law has survived for more than a century is not only an anachronism—it is a phenomenon. Why was it, for instance, that up until 1950 the issue of mining-law revision was almost entirely an internal matter for the industry discussion?

Closely related to mining law in the early twentieth century was the enormous body of legal interpretation that enshrouded the petroleum industry.[28] From the Oil Placer Act of 1897 to the Mineral Leasing Act of

1920, the federal government attempted to treat petroleum and hard-rock mining as having the same parentage—legally speaking. It did not take long to discover the shortcomings of attempting to rationalize petroleum with hard-rock mining law. Extremely restrictive acreage limitations and artificial assessments were only two areas of puzzlement to those who drafted the Mineral Leasing Act of 1920.

One of the most auspicious topics of historical research lies in the evolution of the oil and gas lease. Such a study, as James Veasey realized, encompasses the interplay of corporate lobbies, federal legislation, and judicial decisions. The many layers of federalism would be exposed by a study of the mineral-leasing program of the federal domain.

The livestock industry of the nineteenth century has had innumerable studies of individual ranches, which basically prove that they are not singular enterprises.[29] However, the literature on the livestock industry of the twentieth century is as vacant as much of the South Dakota Badlands. For instance, the history of the enclosure movement (which would inevitably be intertwined with the economic development of the end of the open range) awaits its historian. With the Ellwood Barbed Wire collection and computerization many of the answers trapped in a couple of tons of manuscripts can now be obtained. This problem pervaded the nineteenth-century West, which not only overlapped into the twentieth century, but has an enormous impact and import for western land policy. The jurisdictional conflict among commission agents, feedlots, and livestock producers is a rich subject replete with political maneuvering and federal–state interplay. The role of livestock associations and grazing policy has received attention; but much more investigation of the eastern impact on the legislative agenda offers a rich field. Indeed, the legislation, which has evolved relating to livestock regulation, is uncharted. Nowhere is this point more vividly illustrated than in the marketing and regulations of the livestock industry.

Any time settlers followed their western star they soon became enmeshed in the quicksand of the public domain and federalism. As we all know, virgin land, lying open for the taking, has been the foundation of the American empire. Manifest Destiny may have been the rapacious ideology of a national crusade of violent conquest, but the motivating impulse was the public domain.[30] The land determined the social, political, and economic colonization system of the West.

If there was any doubt, in 1990, about the taut string of western emotion surrounding the issue of public land, it evaporated with the "Buffalo Commons" proposal of two eastern urban planners and geographers, Frank and Deborah Popper.[31] Out of New Jersey, the two scholars from Rutgers University rode into the Great Plains. Their idea was simplistic in its essence; the reaction was even more elemental.

The Poppers proposed converting much of the Great Plains, circa

139,000 square miles, into a vast zone of open land where buffalo and other wildlife could cavort, half-hidden by shoulder-high savannah. The Poppers' research (a plethora of statistics, graphs, and indices poured out of their computers) told the Rutgers planners that some 110 counties of the Great Plains were in trouble—losing population and their economic base. The only sounds in many of these rural towns were flapping doors on empty filling stations. The Buffalo Commons envisioned by the Poppers would be a huge national park, a veritable ecological monument to mankind's foolishness, followed by redemption. Not that their Buffalo Commons would be entombed, far from it; the Poppers foresaw an economic renewal of the domain beyond the ninety-eighth meridian: retirement communities, tourism, and recreation galore.

Whether the residents of the Great Plains wanted to admit it or not, their land-use patterns had produced an ecological disaster. In essence, the Poppers reiterated what many generations from John Wesley Powell to James Malin had observed, that the residents of the Great Plains had forced a humid ecological system on an arid land. The result was "the largest, longest-running agriculture and environmental mistake in United States history."[32]

In spite of the admonition of Frank Popper that they were not suggesting turning out the lights on the Great Plains "by Tuesday," the reaction from the Plains population was as predictable as it was violent. The Poppers made several speaking forays into the Plains communities. On occasion, they were accompanied by armed guards. The audiences were frequently hostile but seldom violent. Sometimes their audience was silent, sometimes vocal, but inevitably they were antagonistic. The Poppers labeled the outrage under four headings: pioneer gumption ("don't underestimate our determination and hard work"); dollar potential ("Plains production can feed the world"); eastern ignorance; and, finally, prairie zen ("our landscape is a powerful source of spiritual renewal").

The Poppers' missionary zeal may have been searing to many of their audiences, but converts were few except among "them." ("Them" are ecologists, environmentalists, and, above all, easterners—recently removed.)

Regardless of the merits or demerits of the Poppers' "utopian" vision for the Great Plains (in all the din, Deborah Popper had noted quietly, "You get very few second chances . . . when playing with continents"), the Poppers did provoke a national debate on land-use planning. The Poppers took a yellow marking pen to the major issues of land policy—issues that had been fermenting for the past century.

Land tenure has fascinated a parade of commentators about the West, but the relation between legislation, national and state federalism, and settlement remains a vast unknown, ripe for research. For instance, the entire issue of "desertification" has produced increasing interest, especially in view of the exhaustion of massive aquifers underlying much of the West. Although there have been few, if any, actual documented cases of "spreading deserts," there have been many examples of soil blowouts and the loss of plant cover.

Yet another subject of increasing interest to interpreters of the West will be the history of the poisoning of the land—be that poison selenium or salinity.[33] So far journalists have been alone (and often lonely) in their impassioned articles about the dangers of selenium poisoning as evidenced by malformed birds or aborted fetuses. In the 1930s, O. A. Beath and Irene Rosenfeld[34] were working in lonely splendor on the selenium problem, but few seemed to care about their research until the 1980s.

Historians of the land might well consider, with immeasurable profit, the institutional forces that have forged land policy for the last century. How valid, for instance, is the "Worster effect" dramatized by Donald Worster,[35] who proposed that federal subsidies for welfare relief and conservation have encouraged overexploitation of marginal, yea fragile, land? Over the decades, westerners have promoted (and endured) a history of cyclical rebellion against federal regulation. The residue after each of these "sagebrush" revolts has commonly been increasing centralization and regulation.

The philosophical underpinning of commodity developers of the land vs. the "preservationists" who seek the silence of the wilderness presents the opportunity for several arresting studies. Historically, each group has reached for its personalized Eden, an Eden that has eluded their political grasp. Developers pronounce a practical overview of land utilization, whereas their opponents remind everyone that the "big picture," commonly with a personalized filter, must not be forgotten. By tracing the roots of these opposing ethics, historians have the challenge of bringing enlightenment to a seemingly permanent, rigid debate on land-use policy, a debate that threatens to be frozen in time.

The ruptures between the metropolitan and rural Wests now permeate every debate about the West of the past, present, and future. The myth of the West as a land of the golden horn has resulted in eastern immigrants chanting the dream sequences that brought them west from Hartford; these were dreams that seem elusive, if nonexistent, to immigrants moving into the urban West from Mexico and Japan. Regardless of their roots, these expectations have resulted in a revolution in the contemporary policy issues of the West.

What drives this western myth? Michael McGerr, in a very provocative essay, declares that "why individualism persisted and outlasted democracy should be a central question of American historical writing."[36] McGerr and others have suggested that if historians of the West are to find the answers they so eagerly seek, they will first have to throw off the shackles of inferiority. McGerr has offered, in one sentence, one of the most important pieces of advice that he, or anyone else, could give western historians. "Insecure about their subject," writes McGerr, "western historians have rushed to follow historiographical fashion."[37] Years ago, Earl Pomeroy expressed a similar view of the writing and teaching of western history. Unfortunately, the McGerrs, the Pomeroys, and the Nashes have been voices crying in the western wilderness.

Nowhere is the historical straitjacket of western historians more in evidence than in divining the mythology of individualism and communitarianism of the twentieth-century West. Until we understand the complexity of the interrelationship between individualism and community awareness, we will not be able to penetrate the fog of the western myth.

As crucial as myth, land policy, and federalism are to fathoming the history of the twentieth-century West, even more vital to the West's salvation is water policy. Everywhere the westerner turns he encounters his wheel of fortune written in water law.[38] The western water scene is rife with contested and contestable issues swirling around water scarcity, actual or potential.[39] Exhaustion of water resources and groundwater supply are becoming synonymous terms in the West. Less realized is that the energy cost necessary for pumping water may halt the exploitation before exhaustion occurs.[40] All across the West, urban dwellers are pressing agriculturalists to reduce their water consumption. Yet the question is far more intricate than who becomes the beneficiary of water diversion. A radical and rapid reduction of rural irrigated acreage may lead to wind erosion, unless massive conservation measures are put in place. Salinity continues to advance, but salinity and sanity may be more compatible if genetics and soil technology manage to resolve the salinity problem.

These then represent some of the research opportunities and/or preoccupations of the historians of the West of the present. What of the twenty-first century? What will excite the future state? What will historians ponder as they stand at the arroyos of the unknown? Have the historians of past eras been as blind to the truth as the New West compatriots would have us believe? If one can consider verities, it certainly appears that much of the New West's roll call of causes—multiculturalism, environment, gender, class, and race—will continue to capture the imagination of historians who probe the past for that imperfect understanding.

For the West is at once defined and divided by multiculturalism, federalism, localism, regionalism, and environmentalism.[41] We risk little and forecast less by observing that these topics will occupy historical enterprise in the years two thousand plus.[42]

Twenty-first-century historians will obviously be charged with separating reality from the theme-park mentality of western legend—challenge enough for several generations of historians. Theme parks that are invented for any taste—be it fantasy marine, thrill, or adventure—are all devoted to escapism and contrived with artifice.

The westerner and the easterner lust after the natural resources of the West and have swallowed personal and genre myth upon myth. Both westerners and easterners have found it much more comfortable, yea delightful, to chase after folklore and resist reality. T. S. Eliot said it eloquently, "Human kind cannot bear very much reality."

Moving from myth to a regional focus, the complexity of western regionalism flows beyond federalism as the West increasingly becomes entwined in the economic and cultural net of the global arena. Westerners for years have been acutely aware that their economic policy rests on decisions in Washington and New York—and in even more recent decades on markets in Europe and Asia. As the West races toward the century's end, the rumblings in the Tokyo financial pits seem increasingly relevant, if frequently ominous.

This is not to contend that national history is obsolete (or, even worse, to indulge the metaphysical game "The End of History"), or to imply that regionalism and localism are passé. It is to say that global compression will be a major part of our comprehension as we clash with the twenty-first-century West.

Questions and research then abound for the future West, questions that have seemingly thwarted the counterpoint of intelligible answers. This should not be surprising considering tomorrow's generational assignments. What will be the conundrums that will entice? Questions as: What motivated the West's modernization? Was the engine of the West's redesign—transportation, the public–private mix of entrepreneurial spirit, or a half-dozen other factors? What of the social-cultural milieu fostering this economic climate? If the American West, after regional comparison, proves not to be exceptional, to what do we ascribe its presumed uniqueness? Above all, where do we place that mystic individualism that has so many idolaters at its altar?

Notes

1. We find Marc Bloch's use of the comparative method as valid as any, and more effective than most, to test hypotheses of contrasting historical problems. Marc Bloch, "Toward a Comparative History of European Societies," in *Enterprise and Secular Change*, ed. F. C. Lane and J. C. Riemersma (Homewood, Ill.: Dorsey, 1953), 494–522; Walter P. Webb, *The Great Frontier* (Boston: Houghton Mifflin, 1952); Howard Lamar and Leonard Thompson, eds., *The Frontier in History* (New Haven: Yale University Press, 1981); Jerome Steffen, *Comparative Frontiers: A Proposal for Studying the American West* (Norman: University of Oklahoma Press, 1980); W. K. Hancock, *Survey of British Commonwealth Affairs*, 2 vols. (London: Oxford University Press, 1937–1942); Robin W. Winks, *The Myth of the American Frontier* (Leicester: Leicester University Press, 1971); Monica Wilson and Leonard Thompson, *The Oxford History of South Africa*, 2 vols. (Oxford: Oxford University Press, 1969–1971); W. H. McNeill, *The Great Frontier: Freedom and Hierarchy in Modern*

Times (Princeton, N.J.: Princeton University Press, 1983); George Wolfskill and Stanley Palmer, eds., *Essays on Frontiers in World History* (College Station: Texas A & M University Press, 1983); C. Vann Woodward, ed., *The Comparative Approach to American History* (New York: Basic Books, 1968); George M. Fredrickson, "Comparative History," in *Past Before Us: Contemporary Historical Writing in the United States*, ed. Michael Kammen (Ithaca, N.Y.: Cornell University Press, 1980), 457–73; and a recent as well as one of the ablest overviews of the comparative approach, Walter Nugent, "Comparative Wests," in *The Oxford History of the American West*, ed. Clyde A. Milner, II, Carol A. O'Connor, and Martha A. Sandweiss, (New York: Oxford University Press, 1994), 803–34.

2. The theme of fragmentation is adroitly handled in Alan Brinkley, "Prosperity, Depression and War," in *The New American History*, ed. Eric Foner (Philadelphia: Temple University Press, 1990), 119–42; and in the same volume the following fragmentation has attracted Alice Kessler-Harris, "Social History," 163–84.

3. The literature of exceptionalism is not exceptional, but it is diffuse. Among the most helpful pages are Byron E. Shafer, ed., *Is America Different* (Oxford: Clarendon Press, 1991); David P. Calleo, *Beyond American Hegemony: The Future of the Western Alliance* (New York: Basic Books, 1987); Paul Kennedy, *The Rise and Fall of the Great Powers: Economic Change and Military Conflict from 1500 to 2000* (New York: Random House, 1987); Mancur Olson, *The Rise and Decline of Nations: Economic Growth, Stagflation, and Social Rigidities* (New Haven: Yale University Press, 1982); Walter Russell Mead, *Mortal Splendor: The American Empire in Transition* (Boston: Houghton Mifflin, 1987); Sanford M. Jacoby, "American Exceptionalism Revisited: The Importance of Management," in *Masters to Managers*, ed. S. M. Jacoby (New York: Columbia University Press, 1991); Daniel Bell, "The End of American Exceptionalism," *The Public Interest* 41 (Fall 1975): 193–224; and Samuel P. Huntington, "The U.S.—Decline or Renewal?" *Foreign Affairs* 67 (Winter 1988/89): 76–96.

4. Regionalism has faded in and out in twentieth-century America. The literature is vast, if not indiscriminate. Those items that seem the most helpful include William G. Robbins, Robert Frank, Richard E. Ross, eds., *Regionalism and the Pacific Northwest* (Corvallis: Oregon State University Press, 1983); Raymond Gastil, *Cultural Regions of the United States* (Seattle: University of Washington Press, 1975); Merrill Jensen, ed., *Regionalism in America* (Madison: University of Wisconsin Press, 1951); Howard Odum and Harry E. Moore, *American Regionalism: A Cultural Historical Approach to National Integration* (New York: Henry Holt, 1938); Kirkpatrick Sale, *Power Shift: The Rise of the Southern Rim and Its Challenge to the Eastern Establishment* (New York: Random House, 1975); Joel Garreau, *The Nine Nations of North America* (Boston: Houghton Mifflin, 1981); Joan Didion, *The White Album* (New York: Simon and Schuster, 1979); Ann Markusen, *Regions: The Economics and Politics of Territory* (Towata, N.J.: Rowan and Littlefield, 1987); R. Gold, *A Comparative Study of the Impact of Coal Development* (Missoula: University of Montana Press, 1974); Robert Gottlieb and Peter Wiley, *Empires in the Sun: The Rise of the New West* (New York: Putnam, 1982); Walter Isard, *Methods of Regional Analysis* (New York: John Wiley and Sons, 1960). A model for twentieth-century regional history is Hal K. Rothman's *On Rims and Ridge: The Los Alamos Area since 1880* (Lincoln:

University of Nebraska Press, 1992); Donald Worster, *An Unsettled Country* (Albuquerque: University of New Mexico Press, 1994); and the magisterial *Oxford History of the American West*.

5. As many have observed, the study of federalism began with the work of Harry Scheiber; his erudition and sophistication are evident on every page of the following: "Some Realism about Federalism: Historical Complexities and Current Challenges," in *Emerging Issues in American Federalism* (Washington, D.C.: Advisory Committee on Intergovernmental Relations, 1985); "Federalism and the American Economic Order, 1789–1910," *Land and Society Review* 10 (Fall 1975): 57–118; "American Federalism and Diffusion of Power: Historical and Contemporary Perspectives," *University of Toledo Law Review* 9 (Summer 1978): 619–80; and ed., *Perspectives on Federalism* (Berkeley: Institute of Governmental Studies, 1987). See also Aaron Wildavsky, "A Bias toward Federalism: Confronting the Conventional Wisdom on the Delivery of Government Service," *Publius* 6 (Spring 1966): 95–120; Daniel J. Elazar and John Kincaid, "Covenant, Polity, and Constitutionalism," *Publius* 10 (Fall 1980): 3–42; Vincent Ostrom, *Water and Politics* (Los Angeles: Haynes Foundation, 1953); Mancur Olson, "The Principle of Fiscal Equivalence, the Division of Responsibility among Different Levels of Government," *American Economic Review* 59 (May 1969): 479–87; Donald Pisani, "The Irrigation District and the Federal Relationship," in *The Twentieth-Century West: Historical Interpretations*, ed. Gerald D. Nash and Richard W. Etulain (Albuquerque: University of New Mexico Press, 1989), 257–92; Pisani, "State vs. Nation: Federal Reclamation and Water Rights in the Progressive Era," *Pacific Historical Review* 51 (August 1982): 265–82; Pisani, *To Reclaim a Divided West* (Albuquerque: University of New Mexico Press, 1992); Margaret Levi, *Of Rule and Revenue* (Berkeley: University of California Press, 1988); R. Scott Foster, *The New Economic Role of American States* (Washington, D.C.: Brookings Institution, 1988); Dan Tyler, *The Last Water Hole in the West* (Niwot: University Press of Colorado, 1992); Michael Lawson, *Dammed Indians* (Norman: University of Oklahoma Press, 1982); and Robert Souder, *The Last Frontier: Water, Diversion and the Destruction of Owens Valley Agriculture* (Tucson: University of Arizona Press, 1994).

6. James T. Patterson, *The New Deal and the States* (Princeton, N.J.: Princeton University Press, 1969).

7. See the following by Gerald Nash: "Where's the West?" *Historian* 49 (November 1986): 1–9; "The Twentieth-Century West," *Western Historical Quarterly* 13 (April 1982): 179–81; "Mirror for the Future: The Historical Past of the Twentieth-Century West," in *The Twentieth Century American West*, ed. Thomas G. Alexander and John F. Bluth (Provo: Charles Redd Center for Western Studies, 1983), 1–27; *The American West in the Twentieth Century: A Short History of An Urban Oasis* (Englewood Cliffs, N.J.: Prentice-Hall, 1973); *The American West Transformed: The Impact of the Second World War* (Bloomington: Indiana University Press, 1985); Nash and Etulain, *Twentieth-Century West*; Nash, *Creating the West: Historical Interpretations, 1890–1990* (Albuquerque: University of New Mexico Press, 1991); and a monumental bibliography of the twentieth-century West, which reminds us of how much has been done, rather than "ear trumpeting" our lamentations of how much more there is to do, is Richard W. Etulain et al, eds., *The American West in*

the Twentieth Century: A Bibliography (Norman: University of Oklahoma Press, 1994).

8. For a fascinating anatomy of the concept of the state, see J. P. Nettl, "The State as a Conceptual Variable," *World Politics* 20, no. 4 (1968): 561–86.

9. Seymour Martin Lipset, "American Exceptionalism Reaffirmed," in *Is America Different? A New Look at American Exceptionalism*, ed. Byron E. Shafer (Oxford: Oxford University Press, 1991), 1–45; and David M. Wrobel, *The End of American Exceptionalism: Frontier Anxiety From the Old West to the New Deal* (Lawrence: University Press of Kansas, 1993).

10. Donald Pisani, *From the Family Farm to Agribusiness: The Irrigation Crusade in California and the West, 1850–1931* (Berkeley: University of California Press, 1984); "Water Law Reform in California, 1900–1913," *Agricultural History* 54 (April 1980): 295–317; "The Origins of Western Water Law, Case Studies from the California Mining Districts," *California History* 70 (Fall 1991): 242–57, 324–25; "Conflict over Conservation: The Reclamation Service and the Tahoe Contract," *Western Historical Quarterly* 10 (April 1979): 167–90; "Deep and Troubled Waters: A New Field of Western History?" *New Mexico Historical Review* 63 (October 1988): 311–31; "Enterprise and Equity: A Critique of Western Water Law in the Nineteenth Century," *Western Historical Quarterly* 18 (January 1987): 15–37; "Federal Reclamation and Water Rights in Nevada," *Agricultural History* 51 (July 1977): 540–88; "Forest and Conservation, 1865–1990," *Journal of American History* 72 (September 1985): 340–59; "Reclamation and Social Engineering in the Progressive Era," *Agricultural History* 57 (January 1983): 46–63; "Water Reform in California, 1900–1913," *Agricultural History* 54 (April 1980): 295–317; *To Reclaim A Divided West*; and see also n. 5.

11. Pisani, *To Reclaim A Divided West*, xiv.

12. Rachel Carson, *Silent Spring* (Boston: Houghton Mifflin, 1962).

13. Edward Abbey, *Desert Solitaire: A Season in the Wilderness* (New York: McGraw-Hill, 1968), xiv.

14. Gilbert White, *Natural History and Antiquities of Selborne* (London: Macmillan, 1877).

15. Roderick Nash, *The Rights of Nature: A History of Environmental Ethics* (Madison: University of Wisconsin Press, 1989), *Wilderness and the American Mind* (New Haven: Yale University Press, 1967); William Cronon, *Changes in the Land: Indians, Colonists and the Ecology of New England* (New York: Hill and Wang, 1983), *Nature's Metropolis: Chicago and the Great West* (New York: W. W. Norton, 1991); William Cronon, George Miles, and Jay Gitlin, eds., *Under an Open Sky: Rethinking America's Western Past* (New York: W. W. Norton, 1992); Richard White, *Land Use, Environment, and Social Change: The Shaping of Island County, Washington* (Seattle: University of Washington Press, 1980), *"It's Your Misfortune and None of My Own": A New History of the American West* (Norman: University of Oklahoma Press, 1991); Donald Worster, *Dust Bowl: The Southern Plains in the 1930s* (New York: Oxford University Press, 1979), "History as Natural History: An Essay on Theory and Method," *Pacific Historical Review* 53 (February 1984): 1–9, *Nature's Economy: The Roots of Ecology* (San Francisco: Sierra Club Books, 1977), *Rivers of Empire: Water, Aridity, and the Growth of the American West* (New York: Pantheon, 1986), *The Wealth of Nature* (New York: Oxford University Press, 1993), "Rediscovering the West:

The Legacy of John Wesley Powell," in *Old West / New West: Quo Vadis*, ed. Gene M. Gressley (Worland, Wyo.: High Plains Publishing Co., 1994), 101–22; and Worster, ed., *Under Western Skies: Nature and History in the American West* (New York: Oxford University Press, 1992).

16. Ethnicity, race, class, and multiculturalism have become flash-point words in an incendiary culture. The literature on the "cultural wars" is acrimonious, biased, and politicized. Any researcher who tiptoes through the bog of cultural populism and cultural relativism may lament the trip. A flavorful, if frequently unbalanced assessment, of this circus ring may be located in the following—though the reader should have fair warning that many of the disputants exercise oxymoronic philosophy: Arthur M. Schlesinger, Jr., *The Disuniting of America* (New York: W. W. Norton, 1992); Henry Louis Gates, Jr., *Loose Canons: Notes of the Cultural Wars* (New York: Oxford University Press, 1992); Paul Berman, *Debating P.C.* (New York: Dell Publishing Co., 1992); Lawrence W. Levine, *Highbrow, Lowbrow* (Cambridge: Harvard University Press, 1988); Darryl J. Gless and Barbara H. Smith, *The Politics of Liberal Education* (Durham, N.C.: Duke University Press, 1992); Arthur Schlesinger, Jr., "What Should We Teach Our Children about History?" *American Heritage* 43 (February/March 1992): 45–52; Lynn Hunt, ed., *The New Cultural History* (Berkeley: University of California Press, 1989); Daniel Bell, "America's Cultural Wars," *Wilson Quarterly* 16 (Summer 1992): 74–107; Robert Hughes, "The Fraying of America," *Time* 139 (February 3, 1992): 42–49; Richard Polenberg, *One Nation Divisible* (New York: Penguin, 1980); George M. Fredrickson, *The Arrogance of Race* (Middletown, Conn.: Wesleyan University Press, 1988); Mario T. García, *Mexican Americans: Leadership, Ideology and Identity, 1930–1960* (New Haven: Yale University Press, 1989); and for those readers with an insatiable appetite, much more can be found in the works of Roger Kimball, Diane Ravitch, Bill Graves, William Raspberry, Dinesh D'Souza, ad infinitum.

17. Frederick C. Luebke, ed., *Ethnicity on the Great Plains* (Lincoln: University of Nebraska Press, 1980).

18. The New West literature, although not always as emotional as the "cultural wars," encompasses many of the same battlement slogans underscoring class, gender, and race. An introduction to the New West viewpoint can be quickly and readily achieved by following the arguments of Patricia Nelson Limerick, *The Legacy of Conquest: The Unbroken Past of the American West* (New York: W. W. Norton, 1987); Worster, *Under Western Skies*; Limerick, Clyde A. Milner, II, and Charles Rankin, eds., *Trails: Toward a New History* (Lawrence: University Press of Kansas, 1991); Gary Holthaus, Patricia Nelson Limerick, Charles F. Wilkinson, and Eric Stryker Munsam, eds., *A Society to Match the Scenery* (Boulder: University Press of Colorado, 1991); Cronon, Miles, and Gitlin, *Under An Open Sky*; Stewart L. Udall, Patricia Nelson Limerick, Charles F. Wilkinson, John M. Volkman, and William Kittredge, *Beyond the Mythic West* (Salt Lake City: Peregrine Smith Books, 1990); White, *"It's Your Misfortune and None of My Own"*; Richard White and Patricia Nelson Limerick, *The Frontier in American Culture* (Berkeley: University of California Press, 1994); and Gressley, *Old West / New West*.

19. Frederick Krantz, ed., *History from Below: Studies in Popular Protest* (Oxford: Oxford University Press, 1988); E. P. Thompson, "History from Below," *The Times*

Literary Supplement 7 (April 1966): 279–80.

20. Marshall Sahlins, *Culture and Practical Reason* (Chicago: University of Chicago Press, 1976), *Historical Metaphors and Mythical Realities: Structure in the Early History of the Sandwich Islands Kingdom* (Ann Arbor: University of Michigan Press, 1981), *Islands of History* (Chicago: University of Chicago Press, 1985); Clifford Geertz, *The Interpretation of Cultures: Selected Essays* (New York: Basic Books, 1973), and *Local Knowledge: Further Essays in Interpretative Anthropology* (New York: Basic Books, 1983).

21. Marc Reisner, *Game Wars: The Undercover Pursuit of Wildlife Poachers* (New York: Viking, 1991); Sarah Bates and Reisner, *Overtapped Oasis: Reform or Revolution of Western Water* (Washington, D.C.: Island Press, 1990); Reisner, *Cadillac Desert: The American West and Its Disappearing Water* (New York: Viking, 1986); Garreau, *Nine Nations of North America*; Joel Garreau, *Edge City: Life on the New Frontier* (New York: Doubleday, 1991); and Bill McKibben, *The End of Nature* (New York: Random House, 1989).

22. Walter Dean Burnham, *The Current Crisis in American Politics* (New York: Oxford University Press, 1982), *Critical Elections and the Mainsprings of American Politics* (New York: W. W. Norton, 1970); Nelson Polsby, *Community Power and Political Theory: A Further Look at Problems of Evidence and Interference* (New Haven: Yale University Press, 1980), *Congress and the Presidency* (Englewood Cliffs, N.J.: Prentice-Hall, 1986), and *Consequences of Party Reform* (New York: Oxford University Press, 1983).

23. Howard Lamar's upbeat and perspicacious address is found in "Much to Celebrate: The Western History Association's Twenty-Fifth Birthday," *Western Historical Quarterly* 17 (October 1986): 398–416.

24. The best interpreter of J. Willard Hurst is Harry Scheiber; see especially Scheiber, "At the Borderland of Law and Economic History: The Contributions of Willard Hurst," *American Historical Review* 75 (February 1970): 744–75. Another excellent examination of Hurst and Hurstian paradigms is in *Wisconsin Law Review* 6 (1980). Hurst is, and has been, prolific. Those volumes of favorite citation include *Law and Conditions of Freedom in the Nineteenth Century United States* (Madison: University of Wisconsin Press, 1956); *Law and Social Process in United States History* (Ann Arbor: University of Michigan Law School, 1960); *Law and Economic Growth: The Legal History of the Wisconsin Lumber Industry* (Cambridge: Harvard University Press, 1964); *The Legitimacy of the Business Corporation in the Law of the United States* (Charlottesville: University Press of Virginia, 1970); and *Law and Social Order in the United States* (Ithaca, N.Y.: Cornell University Press, 1977).

25. John Phillip Reid, "The Layers of Western Legal History" (unpublished manuscript, 1992), 2. Author's personal collection.

26. Again, much has been accomplished, much is to be done. For the beginnings, one should consult William E. Nelson and John Phillip Reid, *The Literature of American Legal History* (New York: Oceana Publications, 1985). One should not miss the pleasure and opportunity of perusing the refreshing work of Charles Wilkinson, "Law and the American West: The Search for an Ethic of Place," *University of Colorado Law Review* 59 (1988): 401–25; and "The Law of the American West: A Critical Bibliography of the Nonlegal Sources," *Michigan Law Review* 85

(1987): 953–1011. Water and natural-resource law has captivated twentieth-century legal commentary. A magnificent work is John D. Lesky, *The Mining Law: A Study in Perpetual Motion* (Washington, D.C.: Resources for the Future, 1987); also, see Arthur C. Veatch, *Mining Laws of Australia and New Zealand* (Washington, D.C.: U. S. Geological Survey Bulletin, no. 505, 1911). Veatch was an amazing character, who was "onto" the prolific overthrust oil belt in the Rockies sixty years before it was discovered. He deserves a biography for this perception and so much more! Curtis H. Lindley, *American Law Relating to Mines and Mineral Lands* (San Francisco: Bancroft-Whitney, 1914), and subsequent revisions; Lawrence M. Friedman, *History of American Law* (New York: Simon and Schuster, 1973); Michael J. Bean, *The Evolution of National Wildlife Law* (New York: Praeger, 1968); Paul W. Gates, *History of Public Law Land Development* (Washington: U.S. Government Printing Office, 1968); Frank Berry, "Discovery under the Mining Laws," *Arizona Law Review* 8, no. 1 (1966): 84–101; William H. Rodgers, Jr., *Environmental Law* (St. Paul, Minn.: West Publishing Company, 1977); one of the most imaginative treatments of the interstices of diplomacy, legal conflicts and rights, conservation and development is in Arthur F. McEvoy, *The Fisherman's Problem: Ecology and Law in the California Fisheries, 1850–1980* (New York: Cambridge University Press, 1986); and David C. Frederick, *Rugged Justice* (Berkeley: University of California Press, 1994).

27. See n. 26.

28. J. Leonard Bates, "The Midwest Decision, 1915: A Landmark in the Conservation Movement, 1907–1921," *Pacific Northwest Quarterly* 51 (January 1960): 26–34; Senate Subcommittee on Antitrust and Monopoly, *Petroleum, the Antitrust Law and Government Policies*, 85th Cong., 1st sess. (Washington, D.C.: U.S. Government Printing Office, 1957); American Bar Association, Section on Mineral Law, *Legal History of Conservation of Oil and Gas: A Symposium* (Chicago: American Bar Association, 1939); Gerald Nash, *United States Oil Policy* (Pittsburgh: University of Pittsburgh Press, 1968); Robert E. Hardwicke, *Antitrust Laws, et al. v. Unit Operation of Oil or Gas Pools* (New York: American Institute of Mining and Metallurgical Engineers, 1948); B. I. Kaufman, *The Oil Cartel Case: A Documentary Study of Antitrust Activity in the Cold War* (Westport, Conn.: Greenwood Press, 1978); Joseph A. Pratt, "The Petroleum Industry, Anti-Trust and the Decline of Monopoly Control in Oil," *Journal of Economic History* 40 (December 1980): 815–37; J. I. Weaver, *Unitization of Oil and Gas Fields in Texas: A Study of Legislative, Administrative and Judicial Politics* (Washington, D.C.: Resources for the Future, 1986); and Peter A. Coates, *The Trans-Alaska Pipeline Controversy: Technology, Conservation, and the Frontier* (Bethlehem, Pa.: Lehigh University Press, 1991).

29. The twentieth-century literature of the livestock industry is specialized, nonhistorical, and often distinguished by prose that guarantees nonreadership. A few items of moderate utilization include N. H. Engle, "Competitive Forces in Wholesale Marketing of Prepared Food Products" (Ph.D. diss., University of Michigan, 1929); Rudolph Clemen, *The American Livestock and Meat Industry* (New York: Ronald Press, 1923); Dale E. Butz and George L. Baker, Jr., *The Changing Structure of the Meat Economy* (Boston: Harvard University Press, 1960); Herrell De Graff, *Beef Production and Distribution* (Norman: University of Oklahoma Press, 1960); Robert

Adudell, "The Meat Packing Industry and the Consent Decree" (Ph.D. diss., North-western University, 1960); Louise C. Wade, *Chicago's Pride: The Stockyards, Packingtown, and Environs in the Nineteenth Century* (Urbana: University of Illinois, 1986); Willard F. Williams and T. T. Stout, *Economics of the Livestock Meat Industry* (New York: Macmillan, 1964); Terry G. Jordan, *North American Cattle Ranching Frontiers: Origins, Diffusion and Differentiation* (Albuquerque: University of New Mexico Press, 1993); and W. D. Rowley, *U.S. Forest Service: Grazing and Rangelands: A History* (College Station: Texas A & M University Press, 1985).

30. It has been said that the history of the public domain is the history of the West; if so, the historian of the West who has dominated the literature of the public domain is Paul Wallace Gates. Irrespective of the plaudits, to ignore the historiography of Paul Gates is to be uninformed on public-land policy. His classic, of course, is *The History of Public Land Law Development* (Washington, D.C.: U.S. Government Printing Office, 1968). In general, the public domain and land policy have attracted substantial attention, so much so that no attempt will be made except to provide a scatter of suggestions: John Opie, *The Law of the Land* (Lincoln: University of Nebraska Press, 1987); Roy M. Robbins, *Our Landed Heritage: The Public Domain* (Lincoln: University of Nebraska Press, 1976); Rowley, *U.S. Forest Service*; Wesley Calef, *Private Grazing and Public Lands: Studies of the Local Management of the Taylor Act* (Chicago: University of Chicago Press, 1960); William Voigt, Jr., *Public Grazing Lands: Use and Misuse by Industry and Government* (New Brunswick, N.J.: Rutgers University Press, 1976); E. L. Peffer, ed., *The Closing of the Public Domain: Disposal and Reservation Policies, 1900–1950* (Stanford, Calif.: Stanford University Press, 1951); Vernon Carstensen, *The Public Lands: Studies in the History of the Public Domain* (Madison: University of Wisconsin, 1962); J. G. Francis and R. Ganzel, ed., *Western Public Lands* (Totawa, N.J.: Rowman and Allenheld, 1984); F. O. Foss, *The Politics of Grass: The Administration of Grazing on the Public Domain* (Seattle: University of Washington Press, 1960); G. D. Libecap, *Locking Up the Range: Federal Land Controls and Grazing* (Cambridge, Mass.: Ballinger Publishing Co., 1981); and Mary W. M. Hargreaves, *Dry Farming in the Northern Great Plains: Years of Readjustment, 1920–1990* (Lawrence: University Press of Kansas, 1993).

31. Journalists, officials of chambers of commerce, sociologists, urban planners, historians, and politicians analyzed, emoted, and computerized the Poppers and "Popperism." Until the Poppers' book appears, the one easy guide to their concepts is Anne Mathews, *Where the Buffalo Roam* (New York: Grove Weidenfeld, 1992). The storm out of the West can be assessed from the flurry of newspaper comment. Some of the more interesting, if not always germane, comment can be found in Brueme Wilson, "Are We Being Buffaloed," Laramie County (Wyo.) College *Wingspan*, October 9, 1991; "State Lawmaker Criticizes Visit by 'Buffalo Commons authors,'" *The Wyoming Eagle*, August 13, 1991; James M. Flinchum, "Where the Buffalo Roam," *Wyoming Tribune-Eagle*, August 11, 1991; Max Maxfield, "Poppers' Idea Worthy Topic Discussion," *The Wyoming Eagle*, August 22, 1991; Bob Budd, "Buffalo Breath," *Cow Country* 32 (September 1991): 6; Charles Pelkey, "Buffalo Backers Want to Restore Past Landscapes," *Casper Star-Tribune*, August 15, 1991; "Buffalo Commons Draw Ire," *Torrington Telegram*, August 16, 1991; "Buf-

falo Range Called Bad Idea," *Denver Post*, August 18, 1991; "Farm Bureau Officials Tour Goshen County Farm," *Torrington Telegram*, August 23, 1991; "'Buffalo Commons' Plan Challenges Plains Residents," *Scottsbluff Star-Herald*, August 17, 1991; "Locals Oppose 'Buffalo Commons,'" *Torrington Telegram*, August 21, 1991; "Pair Explains Controversial 'Buffalo Commons,'" *Scottsbluff Star-Herald*, August 17, 1991; "Senator Wallop Does Not Picture Wyoming as Buffalo Pasture," *Douglas Budget*, September 4, 1991; "A Small Western Town Rides into the Sunrise," *New York Times*, August 16, 1992; "Profs Skeptical of Commons Plan," *Rocky Mountain News*, May 5, 1991; "Proponents of Vast Plains Park to Speak," *Greeley Tribune*, April 25, 1991; "Buffalo Commons, Romantic Fantasy from the East," *Rocky Mountain News*, April 18, 1991; "Cycles Gave Poppers Radical Idea for the Plains," *Colorado Daily*, May 2, 1991; and "Return of the American Frontier," *Columbia* 3 (Summer 1991): 3–4.

32. Anne Mathews, "The Poppers and the Plains," *The New York Times Magazine*, June 24, 1990, 24–26, 41, 48–49, 53.

33. "David Love, His Warnings about Selenium in Wyoming and the West Aren't New, but the Trouble Is Few Want to Hear that Thousands of Acres Are Poisonous to Plants, Cows, and People," *High Country News* 24 (February 10, 1992): 1, 8–10, 12.

34. Irene Rosenfeld, *Selenium: Geobotany, Biochemistry, Toxicity and Nutrition* (New York: Academic Press, 1964); O. A. Beath, *The Story of Selenium In Wyoming* (Laramie: University of Wyoming Publications, 1963).

35. Donald Worster, *Dust Bowl: The Southern Plains in the 1930s* (New York: Oxford University Press, 1979).

36. Michael McGerr, "Is There a Twentieth-Century West?" in Cronon, Miles, and Gitlin, *Under an Open Sky*, 254.

37. Ibid., 255.

38. See n. 10.

39. Donald Pisani to Gene M. Gressley, April 26, 1992.

40. Louis C. Hunter, *A History of Industrial Power in the United States* (Charlottesville: University of Virginia Press, 1979), vol. 1.

41. Nash, *American West Transformed*; Nash, *World War II and the West* (Lincoln: University of Nebraska Press, 1990).

42. Richard Lowitt, *New Deal and the West* (Bloomington: Indiana University Press, 1984).

Contributors

Robert W. Cherny is professor of history at San Francisco State University, where he teaches courses on the history of the United States during the Gilded Age and Progressive Era, U.S. political history, and labor history. His most recent books are *San Francisco, 1865–1932: Power, Politics, and Urban Development,* with coauthor William Issel (1986), and *A Righteous Cause: The Life of William Jennings Bryan* (1985; repr., 1994). He has been an NEH Fellow and has served as president of the Society for Historians of the Gilded Age and Progressive Era.

Thomas R. Cox is professor emeritus of history at San Diego State University, where he teaches courses in environmental history and the rise of modern America. He is author of *Mills and Markets: A History of the Pacific Coast Lumber Industry to 1900* (1974) and of *The Park Builders: A History of State Parks in the Pacific Northwest* (1988). He is coauthor of *This Well-Wooded Land: Americans and Their Forests from Colonial Times to the Present* (1985). He is a past president of the Forest History Society, was a Fulbright professor in Japan, and is currently completing a history of the lumberman's frontier and a study of the trans-Pacific timber trade and its impact.

Fred Erisman, Lorraine Sherley Professor of Literature at Texas Christian University, has published extensively in the areas of children's literature, regional and western literature, detective/suspense fiction, and science fiction. He is coeditor (with Richard W. Etulain) of *Fifty Western Writers*, a contributor to *A Literary History of the American West* and *The Twentieth-Century West: Historical Interpretations,* and author of the Western Writers Series pamphlets on Tony Hillerman and Laura Ingalls

Wilder, in addition to numerous shorter studies of literature and popular culture.

Richard W. Etulain is professor of history and director of the Center for the American West at the University of New Mexico, where he teaches courses in western cultural history and historiography. Recent books include *The Twentieth-Century West: Historical Interpretations,* coedited with Gerald D. Nash (1989); *The American West: A Twentieth Century History*; coauthored with Michael P. Malone (1989); and editor of *Writing Western History: Essays on Major Western Historians* (1991). Published in 1994 were *Contemporary New Mexico 1940–1990,* which he edited, and *The American West in the Twentieth Century: A Bibliography.* He has just completed *Re-imagining the Modern American West: A Century of Fiction, History, and Art* (1996).

Gene M. Gressley is retired All-University Professor at the University of Wyoming. He is the founding director of the American Heritage Center, which he directed for thirty-two years. Author of *Bankers and Cattlemen* (1966) and *The Twentieth Century West: A Potpourri* (1977), he is also editor of *Voltaire and the Cowboy* (1977) as well as of the recently published *Old West / New West: Quo Vadis?* He is preparing a history of the petroleum industry in the Rocky Mountain region.

Roger W. Lotchin is professor of history at the University of North Carolina at Chapel Hill, where he teaches courses on urban history and western history. He is the author of *San Francisco, 1846–1856: From Hamlet to City* (1974) and of *Fortress California, 1910-1961: From Warfare to Welfare* (1992), and the editor of *Martial Metropolis: U. S. Cities in Peace and War* (1984). He is currently working on a study of the impact of World War II on southern cities, and is completing a manuscript on the impact of World War II on western cities.

Gerald D. Nash is Distinguished Professor Emeritus of History at the University of New Mexico, where he taught courses in U.S. and twentieth-century western history. Among his publications in these fields are *The American West in the Twentieth Century* (1973), *The American West Transformed: The Impact of World War II* (1985), *World War II and the West: Reshaping the Economy* (1990), *Creating the West: Historical Interpretations, 1890–1990* (1991), and *A. P. Giannini and the Bank of America* (1992). He is completing a book on the military-industrial complex in the American West.

Earl Pomeroy is professor emeritus of the University of Oregon and the

University of California, San Diego. Among his books and essays are *The Territories of the United States, 1861–1890* (1947), *In Search of the Golden West: The Tourist in Western America* (1957), and *The Pacific Slope* (1965), as well as "Toward a Reorientation of Western History: Continuity and Environment" (1955). He is completing a volume on the twentieth-century West for the New American Nation series.

Glenda Riley is the Alexander M. Bracken Professor of History at Ball State University and the recipient of many awards, including a Distinguished Fulbright, several NEH fellowships, the Palladin Writing Award, and the *Journal of the West* Best Article Award. Her most recent books are *The Life and Legacy of Annie Oakley* (1994) and *Inventing the American Woman: An Inclusive History* (1995). She recently presented the Calvin Horn Lectures at the University of New Mexico, which have been published as *Building and Breaking Families in the American West* (1996).

Index

Note: Boldface numerals indicate an extended treatment of a subject.

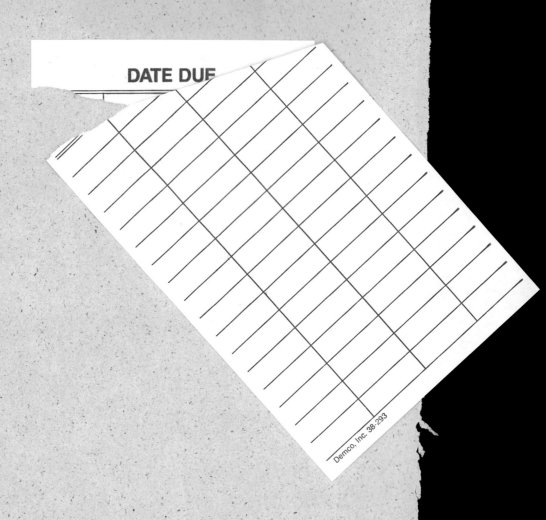

DATE DUE

Demco, Inc. 38-293